A Decade of British Housing

1963-1973

EDITED BY **David Crawford**

The Architectural Press Ltd, London
Halsted Press Division
John Wiley & Sons, New York

The Editor wishes to thank John Noble and Roger Thompson
for help with the selection of schemes and guidance on the
general slope of the book; the Housing Centre Trust for
giving him the free run of their library and research facilities;
and above all, his wife for patiently deciphering and typing
his manuscript. The original appraisers of housing schemes
featured in this book are acknowledged at the end of this
book.

First published in book form 1975
© The Architectural Press Ltd, 1975
ISBN 0 85139 135 4

Distributed in the U.S.A. by
Halsted Press, a Division of
John Wiley & Sons, Inc. New York.
Library of Congress Cataloging in Publication Data
Main entry under title:
A Decade of British housing, 1963-1973.
    1. Housing—Great Britain.   2.   Public housing—
Great Britain.   I. Crawford, David.
HD7333.A3D43   301.5′4′0941   75-17185
ISBN 0-470-18520-1

Printed and bound in Great Britain by
R. J. Acford Ltd, Industrial Estate, Chichester Sussex

Contents

Introduction: A Fast-changing Decade   *page* 7

Statistical Information   19

1 Courtyard Housing at Dundee   21

2 Point Royal Flats, Bracknell   32

3 Housing at Ravenscroft Road, West Ham   41

4 Houses at Frome   51

5 5M Housing at Gloucester Street, Sheffield   57

6 5M Housing at Woodhouse, Sheffield   68

7 Canada Estate, Neptune Street, Bermondsey   79

8 Housing at Winstanley Road, Battersea   88

9 Housing at St. Mary's Redevelopment Area, Oldham   100

10 Housing at Laindon, Basildon   114

11 Housing at Reporton Road, London sw 6   128

12 Co-ownership Housing at Barnton, Edinburgh   137

13 Co-ownership Housing at Baron's Down, Lewes   149

14 Housing at Windsor   158

15 Welsh Village Housing at Cefn-coed-y-cymmer   170

16 Housing Estate at The Lanes, Rotherham   182

17 Housing at Linden Grove, London se 15   192

18 Housing Estate at The Brow, Runcorn   206

19 Housing and Old People's Home at Burghley Road, London nw 5   216

20 Housing at Lillington Street, Westminster   229

21 Housing at The Barbican, City of London   236

Notes   249

Acknowledgements   251

*The London suburbs' flirtation with the Modern Movement:
Howard houses built in West Molesey in 1934—for
£395 a time.*

A Span development at Blackheath designed by Eric Lyons.

*St. Bernards, Croydon (architects: Atelier, 5), another of the
all too rare post-war examples of imaginative design
commissioned by speculative developers. The section (below)
shows the interesting use of different levels.*

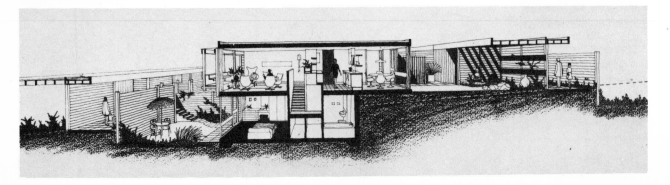

Introduction: A Fast-changing Decade

BY David Crawford

The 1960s and early 1970s have proved to be a period of greater change in the face of British housing than any other time since the large-scale provision of homes for people to buy for themselves or to rent from local authorities (as opposed to private landlords) first began to develop in the years after the First World War.

Public housing—that provided by local authorities or voluntary housing organisations—is naturally more subject to change than the private sector. This is because the pace setters among the public clients tend to be few, large,* well equipped with technical skills and able to experiment and innovate without the responsibility to a profit motive. The private builder, on the other hand, is selling ultimately to an individual.

Again, the public sector's traditional role has been to respond to need rather than demand (though since 1949 its statutory duties have no longer been extended only to the working class) and people in need can be offered more radical solutions than those who feel they are exercising their own choice of a way of life.

Not that the speculative private sector, in post-war years at least, has offered much of a real choice to would-be owner occupiers; for even if the purchasers weren't tempted to be conservative, the builders, developers and building societies combined would represent a trinity of conservative forces more than strong enough to discourage all but the hardiest (or wealthiest).

This was not always the case, however. In the years when the great owner-occupancy revolution was quietly getting under way, when "most new property was still built for letting, but there was a growing tendency to erect speculatively for sale . . . it was in the houses built for sale that the new designs were most apparent. No doubt investors were conservative, preferring solid looking property, whilst potential owner occupiers were vulnerable to icing on a lighter cake."[1] Nor was this the only time when boldness was favoured in the private sector. Around 1932, for example, London's speculative builders enjoyed a mild and short-lived flirtation with the Modern Movement in architecture; and in the 1960s the Span estates designed by Eric Lyons came to represent a whole new way of living for the design-conscious middle classes. Imaginative efforts have also come from some of the larger developers, eg Wates at St. Bernards, Croydon (designed by Atelier 5) and Bovis at Studland Park, Newmarket (architect Ralph Erskine). But such phenomena have unfortunately been rare.

For this reason, few private developments have been treated in the *AJ* Building Studies from which those published in this volume are selected. Even so, there have been detectable changes in fashions and standards in the private sector and

*Small authorities can however produce very successful housing—see, for example, the Cefn-Coed scheme on pp. 170-181

the indications are that, from the mid-1970s onwards, economic forces if nothing else may impose some radical rethinking on the new house types that the owner occupier of the future will find available.

But in recent years the history of change and innovation in housing has largely been that of change and innovation in the public sector; and to set this in context it is helpful to make a brief comparison of the overall housing situation in the early 1960s with that of the present day.

In those days, almost as many people still rented privately as from local authorities; but the percentage of private tenancies has now shrunk to less than half that of council tenancies (see Table 1, p 19) and a new 'third arm' of housing—the voluntary movement of housing associations and societies—is growing up slowly, but steadily, to replace the privately rented sector.

At the same time, owner occupiers have risen from two-fifths to over a half of all households. Mortgage interest rates in the early 1960s stayed below seven per cent, and this was the time when tens of thousands of new owner occupiers were able to take the chance of establishing themselves in a life style which their parents had never dreamt of. Housebuilders and developers, too, were happy, with a future of apparently unlimited demand to look forward to, although the shortage of land available for residential development, particularly in the South East, was already making itself felt. The output of the private sector in this period is shown in Table 4, p 19.

Local authorities then had as their main aim the building of as many council homes as possible for the lowly paid; latterly, they have been encouraged to sell council houses and to release their own land for subsidised private development, in a bid to keep the owner occupier market buoyant at the lower end which controls entry into the whole sector. The watchword during the 1960s was the sheer quantity of houses that could be built, by private and local authority developers, to meet the election promises of political parties and maintain the reputation of housing ministers—300 000, 400 000, 500 000 a year. Nowadays the emphasis is much more on environmental quality, and the identification of areas of particular stress in place of mass clearance programmes.

Obsolescence in housing is no longer interpreted as strictly as it used to be, although the problem of the slums remains with us—between 1967 and 1971, 550 000 dwellings were made fit, but a further 400 000 became unfit. Wholesale demolition, however, need no longer be the answer—and while official statistics for the early 1970s showed demolitions and closures of dwellings in the English conurbations still running ahead of completions,[2] a whole battery of alternatives less massive in scale had come into their own by the end of the 1960s—among them conversion and rehabilitation (in the Oldham redevelopment for example (see pp 100–113) the consultants recommended retaining 15 per cent of the houses). Another is infill, represented by three schemes in this volume, Reporton Road (see pp 128–136), Burghley Road (see pp 216–228) and Linden Grove (see pp 192–205).

Over two million homes have been improved since the introduction of grants for the purpose in 1949, and their extension during the 1960s has greatly speeded up the process (see Table 9, p 20). More improvement still would undoubtedly be undertaken if the building industry were better geared to cope with it; but even so, whole areas have blossomed again out of decay, with undeniable environmental gains—although the sociological consequences have sometimes proved worrying.

For what can happen under unfettered market conditions, as shabby old streets full of private working class tenants become attractive and expensive hunting grounds for owner occupiers, is a straight shift from one class to another with the less well off moving out of areas close to city centres (repeating the exodus of a century earlier when the railways smashed through inner London at a loss of 100 000 low-cost homes). One of the results has been a drain in the pool of workers available for London's service industries. David Eversley, the Greater London Council's former Chief Strategic Planner, describes vividly what happened in Barnsbury where, in spite of good intentions and local authority involvement, "most of the houses went to the highest income groups, the housing association conversions did not qualify for subsidy and failed to become available for people in acute need, the houses which were rebuilt were

Alton East, on the LCC's Roehampton Estate. Mixed development with low rise blocks as here, kept the tower blocks from getting out of hand.

Barnsbury rescued from decay—but only after the higher-income groups moved in.

cleared, by one means or another, of the poor, the old, those without secure tenure".[3]

Again, a decade ago, local authority housing in major conurbations tended towards the monumental. In London, Birmingham, Glasgow and dozens of other cities (but principally in London), the tower block hit the sky and the familiar street was stood on end to become a liftshaft. The percentage of flats in the total public sector output rose steadily from less than a third towards the end of the 1950s to over half by the mid 1960s (see Table 2, p 19). By this time also, flats in high rise blocks of ten or more storeys were accounting for a sixth of all public sector dwellings approved (see Table 3, p 19), although the concept of mixed development, pioneered by the former London County Council at Ackroydon (1952) and Alton East (1955), continued to enable a proportion of families in inner urban schemes to live in terraced houses or maisonettes, and so have the use of a garden.

Since then, however, the tower block has declined dramatically in popularity (although there will always be special cases where it is needed; an intensive central area scheme such as the Barbican (page 236 onwards) is a good example and so is Bracknell's Point Royal (see pp 32–40), where a particular kind of user not often catered for in new towns was in mind). By 1971, only 2·5 per cent of the local authority housing stock of England and Wales was in blocks of ten or more storeys (6·4 per cent in Greater London).[4]

Local authorities have instead begun to build low rise and high density developments in inner urban areas; the street may have become a deck (as at Reporton Road (see pp 128–136) and other derivations of Sheffield's seminal Park Hill of the late 1950s) but at least it is horizontal again, and the provision of ground or level access to as many homes as possible has again become a desirable aim in planning (see, for example, The Lanes, Rotherham, pp 182–191). Council homes are also becoming less immediately distinguishable from those of the owner occupier and are beginning, in some cases, to represent better value. During the 1950s there was a tendency to trim council dwellings down in size to save money, but the trend during the 1960s was in the reverse direction. This culminated in the coming into force as mandatory requirements on January 1 1969 of the Parker Morris standards first recommended in 1961[5] which laid down minimum living space, heating and amenity standards for council homes, dependent on the type of design and number of occupants intended. (One of the earliest (pre-mandatory) examples of Parker Morris in practice is the Ravenscroft Road development in West Ham (see pp 41–50)). Private houses and flats, on the other hand, are not subject to such standards (those of the National House-Builders' Registration Council[6] are much less stringent as their prime function is to provide a constructional guarantee) and the whole sector is more vulnerable to economic pressures; sub-Parker Morris homes for sale are no rarity.

In many ways, therefore, the mid 1970s have reversed the position as it stood at the beginning of the 1960s. But none of these changes has yet proved adequate to remove finally from housing the status of a national problem which it has officially held for fifty years.

The continuing problem

We may at last, after years of post-war effort (over seven million new dwellings have been built since 1951) have a crude surplus of dwellings over households: in 1951, 14·6 million households were accommodated in 13·9 million dwellings; in 1971 there were 18·5 million households in 18·7 million dwellings. But the areas of surplus and demand have yet to coincide in the right places. We still have local and even regional shortages; we still have one and a quarter million unfit homes out of nineteen million (seven per cent of the total) and about three million lacking at least one basic amenity; we still have a million people living in overcrowded conditions; we still have families that cannot find a house to suit them—to rent or to buy—however hard they work and save. Their problems could get more rather than less difficult, for during 1973, starts on both public and private sector homes began to fall sharply after the years of relatively high output on which confident forecasts of a healthy housing surplus in the 1970s were being based (see Table 4, p 19).

These forecasts have foundered on harsh economic facts and we are just entering an era in which, for the developed and industrialised nations of the world, the economic facts look as if they are going to get harder. Perhaps we have left our housing problem too late ever to solve, if indeed it is capable of ultimate solution. "There will never be a time at which housing problems will be 'solved': housing is simply not capable of that kind of simplistic treatment."[7]

In a real crisis of course, as in war time, radical new solutions can emerge and be generally accepted. Administrative difficulties are short-circuited; personal tastes and preferences severely circumscribed; what needs to be done is done and everything else has to wait—if necessary, indefinitely. In the past, it has always proved difficult to create in peace time the sense of emergency that exists in war time, but

perhaps the energy crisis and the curtailment of indefinite economic growth will prove the catalyst. At the end of the Second World War, for example, we had the means to solve our housing problem at least quantitatively, though quality for many people would have had to take second place. Both Winston Churchill and Aneurin Bevan then looked forward to the contribution that prefabrication and mass production, both exploited to the full for the war effort, could make to the reparation of the ravages of the Blitz.[8]

In the event, of course, the chance was lost once the military crisis was passed largely because, as Anthony Jackson puts it,[9] of "an unconvinced private industry reflecting public preferences". Nor were the architectural writers and critics of the day any more disposed to consider mass housing as primarily an economic or production problem. They had a point. The 125 000 prefabricated houses that did get built as a temporary solution perpetuated uneconomic densities and looked unattractive *en masse*. Worse was to come when they continued in use well after the end of their planned ten-year life span (40 000 were still in occupation at the end of the 1960s.)

Even had the full range of available methods (there were over 100 of them) been exploited by an enthusiastic construction industry, what is the guarantee that we would not, by now, have been drawing up crash programmes to remove the lot of them as inferior housing which had become as great an embarrassment as other good ideas of their time, such as the 19th century "model dwellings for the industrious classes" which, as Nicholas Taylor has pointed out[10] had become some of the worst slums of London by the 1960s?

After all, we are still building slums even now—or, at least, housing which seems set fair to become the slums of another generation. Among them are the architecturally brutal and regularly vandalised tower blocks of the typical 1960s mass housing scheme ('. . . in regard to council house vandalism, more takes place on flatted, rather than cottage estates and in larger rather than smaller estates')[11] of which the Canada Estate 'the most obviously vandalised of any housing estate in London'[12] is a good example (see pp 79–87). Other slums in the making could well include some of the cheaper and poorer quality homes now being built on speculative estates, structurally sound perhaps, but poor in amenity.

So perhaps we did well to rein our enthusiasm for the 'prefabs'; but in another decade and a half, prefabrication and mass production had become respectable again as a vital

Early prefabs—a solution from the start, or doomed to be slums in the making?

Later industrialised—CLASP in action, originally for schools (as here) but later for a variety of building types.

component of the housebuilding industry. They arrived in the guise of industrialised, or system building, with the support of the government of the day and backed by investment from most of the larger construction firms. The government was concerned because it foresaw the impact in an expanding economy of a saturated industry, and a consequent progressive shortage of building labour, on the annual targets of house completions which had become a political touchstone. As Lord Greenwood, who was Housing Minister in the 1966–1970 Labour Government said in an interview three years later:[13] 'I smile a little wryly at the thought that Harold Macmillan was a great success when 300 000 [houses] were built, and I was severely criticised when 414 000 houses were built, not because it was 414 000 but simply because it wasn't 500,000. It was, in fact, a record figure.' In the heyday of industrialised housebuilding, the then Ministry of Housing and Local Government (later merged with others in the super ministry of the Department of the Environment, created by the 1970 Conservative Government) itself became deeply engaged in systems. In 1962, it began a programme of development work which saw the light of day a few years later in the shape of the (admittedly short-lived) 5M lightweight modular component system.

5M (M stands for the building module of 4in (approximately 100mm) introduced in the 1920s by A F Bemis) was itself derived from the CLASP industrialised building system developed originally for schoolbuilding and subsequently commercially marketed world wide.

By that time, there was already plenty of interest among local authorities in using systems for their housing programmes; in the same year, for example, a group of towns in Yorkshire set up the Yorkshire Development Group (YDG) specifically to try and make system building more efficient in their housebuilding programmes. So, when in 1963 the MoHLG wanted to develop a 5M-based system which would not only help to solve the housing shortage, but also allow a variety of house types and encourage the flexibility in interior planning recommended by the Parker Morris Report of 1961, Yorkshire was a logical place to carry out some experimental schemes and Sheffield, Leeds and Hull, the progenitors of the YDG, each provided a site. The results in Sheffield, where the city council simultaneously used 5M in a scheme of its own, are described on pp 57–78.

Several other housing schemes included in this book are examples of industrialised building: Winstanley Road (Wates), pp 88–99, St Mary's Redevelopment Area, Oldham (Laing Construction's 12M Jespersen) pp 100–113, Laindon 1, in Basildon New Town (Siporex), pp 114–127, Barons Down (Quikbild), pp 149–157, Ward Royal, Windsor (Wates), pp 158–169.

By 1965, there were 224 industrialised building systems available in Britain from 163 developers; 138 of them specifically recommended for housing.[14] (Percentages of local authority housing built by industrialised methods between 1960 and 1962 are given in Table 5, p 20). Many industria-

Industrialised housing on the monumental scale—Yorkshire Development Group (YDG) development in Leeds.

lised systems, particularly the factory-based pre-cast concrete systems, were mainly geared to the crude quantitative approach to mass housing represented by the early 1960s advance of the tower block. Systems were competitively evolved (or imported from abroad) by the larger contractors eager to secure their stake in the huge housing programmes of the early 1960s. They represented in many cases a major capital investment and the achievement of the required return and satisfactory profit figures demanded that the component producing factories be kept in full swing. In too many cases, it proved to be not so much a beaver as a dinosaur.

Sociologists had begun to question the desirability of high block living even before the introduction in 1967 of the housing cost yardstick gave local authorities and their architects the incentive to explore the possibilities of low rise development. The yardstick, introduced as a condition of government subsidies for public sector housing, identified the growing need for higher density development in cities, which had been recognised five years earlier,[15] with high rise (and therefore relatively more expensive) forms of construction, and subsidies for high density housing were calculated accordingly.

For urban local authorities it was therefore sound economics to apply the high density subsidy to low rise (but still high density) methods which their architects could demonstrate were perfectly feasible and had only been neglected because of the absurdly low norms of housing density carried over from pre-war practice.* (Lillington Street (see pp 229–235) with a density of 630 bedspaces per hectare (255 per acre) is a good example of what could be achieved). A much stronger reaction followed the collapse in May 1968 of Ronan Point, a 23 storey system-built block in the London Borough of Newham which suffered progressive collapse after a gas explosion. Apart from the bad publicity, there was the effect on the yardstick of the new safety standards required as a result of Ronan Point, which made high-rise a much less economic proposition than previously. Industrialised building is, however, as Table 5, p 20 shows, by no means dead and the early 1970s have witnessed the growth of research into some even more radical solutions than flourished in the 1960s, though these will be geared to much more flexible and small-scale uses than previously.

Housing in the mid-1970s

Britain's housing problems of the mid-1970s have certain similarities with those which heralded the 1960s, eg the continued inability of the public sector to ensure the completion of its programmes, which led to the original drive for industrialised building. More recently, however, and in spite of the busy years of the early 1970s when the building industry was working to capacity and seemed on the verge of justifying optimistic government forecasts of a housing surplus just round the corner, the problem has become more complex than that of competing for labour in the construction industry.

The fall in public sector housebuilding starts can be explained partly by the shift of emphasis towards improvement; but council housing was, in any case, threatening to become financially unrewarding for the larger private contractors. The restrictions of the yardstick had begun to

*'Before the [Second World] War there was little or no recognition of the need to be economical in the use of land and maximum net densities of 8 houses per acre [20 houses per hectare] or less were frequently imposed on new developments.'[15]

Ronan Point after the May 1968 gas explosion which triggered off progressive collapse—but high rise was, in any case, already coming into disfavour.

bite heavily on profit margins as inflation became more serious, and a market allowance had to be built in. At the same time, there was no shortage of alternative work for the building industry.

Financial problems, too, in the form of soaring interest rates and land values, were beginning to bear heavily on all kinds of housing by the early 1970s. Interest rates rose from 4 per cent in early 1960 to 13 per cent in late 1973 (see Table 10, p 20) with effects on the borrowing of builders, developers, local authorities and voluntary housing organisations alike, and also on their ability to earmark and acquire land in advance of development.

Land prices have also risen alarmingly. A comparison with *The Financial Times* share index shows that, between 1959 and 1972, shares rose 192 per cent while the average price of an acre of agricultural land rose 662 per cent. Over a similar period, housebuilding costs excluding land (ie wages and material costs) only doubled.

Land is most expensive where it is in most demand and this

naturally tends to be the case in the crowded south eastern corner of England. Figures published by the Nationwide Building Society[16] which accounts for seven per cent of all mortgage advances made by building societies in Great Britain, show that, during 1973, site values as a proportion of prices of new houses on which the society approved loans rose as high as 38·6 per cent in London and the South East and 40·1 per cent in the south of England. Overall, the Nationwide's figures show an increase in the share of house prices represented by land values of 41 per cent between 1966 and 1973, even though in individual areas (such as Scotland) it barely changed (see Table 7, p 20).

Social housing is to some extent immune from increases of this scale since if housing, as a social service, is really needed, it can ultimately be provided at an appropriate cost to the taxpayer or the ratepayer.* In normal circumstances, there are practical limits to what local authorities can afford to pay for housing land. But in the long run, if housing needs to be provided socially, it will be; although yardsticks may have to be abolished or modified drastically to attract builders, or councils' own building departments strengthened to do the job themselves.

Private housebuilding is a different matter, and is intimately linked to the question of what prospective housebuyers can and will afford; if there is any doubt about houses being sold, they are not built. As Table 6, p 20 shows, average prices of homes for sale have risen more than threefold between 1962 and 1973, with new, modern existing and older houses all showing very much the same kind of increase in value. Up till 1970, new house prices and housebuilding costs moved at roughly the same rate, but after then house prices shot ahead.

Mortgage interest rates increased from 5½ per cent to 11 per cent between 1960 and 1973 (see Table 10, p 20) and by late 1973 there was a considerable crisis of confidence about the prospects of the continued availability of owner occupancy for every other household in the country, a situation arrived at after a steady build-up over the years, as shown in Table 1, p 19. Some developers were even offering potential housebuyers a subsidy on their mortgage for a period of years, in a bid to get their houses sold.

In a White Paper published earlier that year,[17] the government stated publicly, for the first time, its belief that the private sector alone could no longer be relied on either to provide the volume of homes to buy that people wanted, or to prevent price rises such as those which had been experienced in the early 1970s. Local authorities were now, therefore, to be officially encouraged to do what only a few had attempted previously on their own account—to build for sale on their own land. The cost of land in the homes produced could be subsidised to the tune of 20 per cent of its market value—the same percentage as that allowed off the prices of council homes sold to tenants after 1970. The aim was to induce off the local authority waiting lists those households whose ability to buy a home in the commercial market had been diminished by the widening gap between earnings and their ability to undertake mortgage repayments.

A 1962 Rowntree survey based on a national sample found more working class than non-working class owner occupiers;[18] and in 1970, 50 per cent of people buying their homes through the Nationwide Building Society earned £30 per week or less. Two years later, only 24 per cent did. An earlier attempt to keep the lower income potential housebuyer in the field was the Option Mortgage Scheme. Introduced in 1968, this gave the benefit of a government

subsidy to people whose incomes were too low for them to gain the income tax relief enjoyed by ordinary mortgage holders, and was backed up by an Option Indemnity Scheme designed, by means of a small premium, to take care of the deposit housebuyers have to provide which again was often beyond the means of lower income earners. On the introduction of the scheme, four per cent of existing mortgage holders switched and the interest recoverable under the scheme rose fivefold between 1968 and 1972 (see Table 11, p 20).

It is still too early to say how far the new experiment may go towards alleviating the shortage of homes to buy (and so automatically taking some of the pressure off the local authorities' own housing lists and reducing the number of council dwellings that will need to be built). Already, local authorities, many of whom are looking to developers as natural partners in the exercise (as in a joint scheme by Wates and the London Borough of Bromley) have had to face a crucial dilemma.

Were they to follow their natural instincts as builders of council homes and try to incorporate Parker Morris minima in the homes they build for sale, even though this was likely to put the cost up and so militate against the whole purpose of the exercise (and the subsiding of the land)—namely to make homes to buy available as cheaply as possible? Or were they to abandon Parker Morris in their homes for sale and so promote a difference in standards between modern local authority dwellings and the lower end of the private market?

The likeliest answer can be gained from what has been happening to the private sector itself. A survey by the Building Research Establishment in 1968[19] showed that

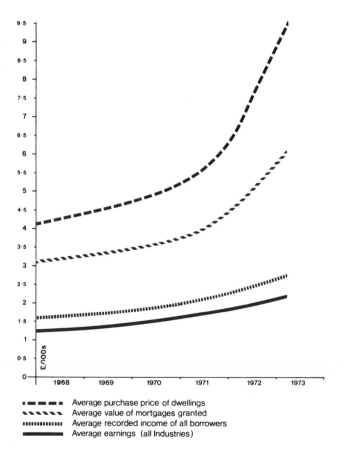

- ▪ ▪ ▪ ▪ Average purchase price of dwellings
- ⌐⌐⌐⌐⌐ Average value of mortgages granted
- ▪▪▪▪▪▪▪ Average recorded income of all borrowers
- ▬▬▬ Average earnings (all industries)

In 1971 and 1972, house prices went through the roof, as shown above—and even though prices subsequently levelled off, the market has yet to settle.

*Rates = local taxes in the United Kingdom.

Upper floor

Building down to the purchasing power of the market—out goes the third bedroom in the Greaves "Prelude House".

Building smaller homes for those who need them—a 22-storey block of flats for single working people built at Leicester following DOE research.

Parker Morris space standards were being adopted by developers in 62 per cent of bungalows and 73 per cent of houses, and a contributor to Housing Review two years later could write that: "public housing is less generous in the floor and site area allowed to each housing unit".[20] The industry was, of course, building for an expanding private market and for a rising expectation in standards, the popularity peak of the single, open-plan through living room had waned, and by 1970 more than twice as many new houses with four or more bedrooms were being bought than in 1962 (see Table 8, p 20).

By 1973, however, the huge price rises and the uncertainty of mortgage finance caused by soaring interest rates generally had taken their toll, and the private sector was preparing to cut standards to keep prices down. A substantial proportion of new homes built for sale, particularly those to terrace or bungalow layouts, were now falling below the Parker Morris standards and a continued decline was being forecast. ('. . . we are, in the private sector, rapidly settling for internal space standards over 30 per cent less than those evolved in the twelfth century').[21]

One way in which developers were proposing to cut space (and so cut costs) was to scrap the third bedroom (an accepted feature of speculatively built homes from their beginning), retain the all-in-one living room which had started to fall out of favour again, and so produce 'starter homes' which, it was reckoned in one case, could be sold at prices at least twenty five per cent below that of a traditional three-bedroomed semi-detached.

Short of some radical rethinking about the way land is used in the private sector, many would argue that this represents a genuine attempt to solve a real problem; but, as with the prefabs of the immediately post-war era, what happens when the starter homes outgrow their welcome? Will there be larger houses, at reasonable prices, for their owners to move to? If not, will they get used to housing conditions which provide nowhere to relax away from the rest of the family, or to study, or to pursue a hobby?

Is the life impoverishment which could follow from restricting the sizes of people's homes the best way to approach the dawn of the long-promised leisure revolution (whether this is produced by economic growth or by the lack of it)?

One of the ironies of the situation is that there is no shortage in Britain of people who could comfortably be accommodated in smaller homes—among them seven million single workers, one third of the country's total work forces. Of all households in England and Wales in 1966, 61 per cent contained no dependent children;[22] and the Central Housing Advisory Committee's ninth report on council housing found that while 46 per cent of all households in the country in 1966 consisted of one or two persons, only 3.5 per cent of all dwellings contained two rooms or less.[23]

Not enough is being done to redress this imbalance. The public sector is still largely concerned with families, and a survey by the Department of the Environment of 110 local authority projects approved between July 1968 and June 1969 showed that 70 per cent were for households of three or more people. Among the few authorities which have catered for economically active one and two person households are Bracknell[24] (see pp 32–40) and Leicester.[25]

The private sector as a whole is not interested in providing specifically for small households, even though starter homes and the like would in ideal circumstances be designated as one-person dwellings. For the typical purchasers of new homes, however small, will be young couples with the earning power to sustain the mortgage and the presumption in the majority of cases of having a family in the not too distant future.

When satisfactory housing becomes difficult to obtain, a number of consequences follow, all of them contributing to increased pressure on the stock of available housing. First, more people tend to live longer in undesirable conditions. Second, young couples or single people are thrown into competition with families for the shrinking amount of privately rented accommodation available. Third, more people will turn to the possibility of improving older housing, thus increasing pressure on the stock of it and on the private tenants who inhabit much of it. Fourth, there will be greater demand for council housing which already commands long waiting lists in virtually every built up area in Britain. As Table 4, p 19 shows, starts and completions alike in the public sector began to decline in 1968.

Some Avenues of Progress

One answer to the problem, of course, is the so-called 'third arm' of housing—the voluntary housing associations, co-operatives, societies and trusts which provide housing of various kinds on a non-profit basis. This movement received its first major boost in modern times in 1961, when the Housing Act of that year allocated £25 million for such organisations as part of a determined Government bid to fill the widening middle ground between owner occupancy on one hand and private tenancy on the other. In 1965, this move was consolidated by the inauguration of the government-backed Housing Corporation, with £100 million to spend on voluntary schemes which were also to be part-financed by building societies, local authorities or insurance companies.

The third arm is in a good position, apart from filling the gap between owner occupancy and council tenancy, to cater for the needs of special interests inadequately recognised by the other sectors—for example young single

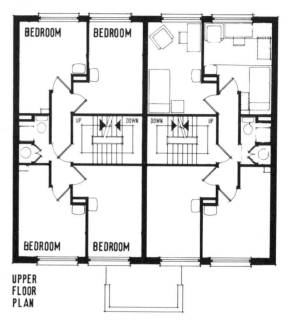

UPPER
FLOOR
PLAN

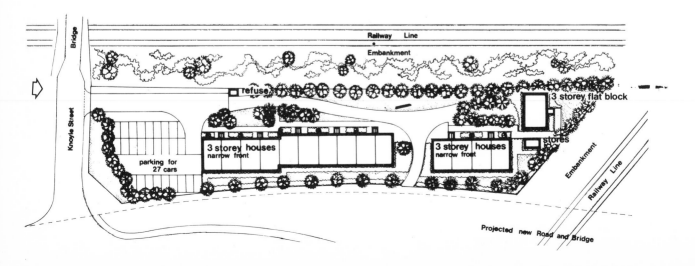

workers. Fifty seven per cent of all Housing Corporation-backed schemes in 1973 included studio- or one-bedroom flats or bedsitting rooms.[26] There is also scope for voluntary housing groups to cater for the needs of the young and single. By 1973 for example a society called Student Co-operative Dwellings had amassed impressive backing from commercial organisations and public authorities for its plans to build low-cost co-operatives for students and young people in their early working years.

Between 1965 and 1973, the Housing Corporation approved plans for 54 625 dwellings in fair-rent and co-ownership schemes (mainly the latter, which could qualify for the option mortgage subsidy), of which some 30,000 had been completed by the end of 1973. (Two examples are described in this volume: Southfield (pp 137–148) which is pre-Housing Corporation and Barons Down, Lewes (pp 149–157)).

During that same period, while the total stock of dwellings in the country rose to about 19 million, the stock of privately rented accommodation was falling by around a quarter of a million units a year—almost a hundred times the output of the voluntary housing movement. The third arm, then, still has a long way to go.

Some six per cent of the total housing stock is made up of the output of the new voluntary housing groups; the old established trusts (eg Guinness, Peabody and Sutton), some of which are extending their operations; mobile homes (eg caravans and houseboats); and various forms of accommodation tied to employment.

The latter has become increasingly rare in the 20th century outside the agricultural field—one industrial example, at Frome, is discussed on pp 51–56. However, the increasing shortage of housing for service workers in city centres is leading to its revival in the form of plans for housing over bus garages and new schools in London.

But a much more fundamental approach to the whole range of problems related to housing concerns what has become the single most important element in housing for virtually any organisation which provides it, whether a commercial developer, a local authority or a voluntary housing organisation—the land. Some interesting new approaches to land use and its relation to built form were evolved during the 1960s. The courtyard houses of the Ardler scheme at Dundee (see pp 21–31) are good examples of the variety of low-rise solutions found to be available to local authorities. Not that such answers were necessarily original; the closely interlocking houses at Dundee can be traced back to Le Corbusier's L-shaped villas of 1922 which 'contained all essential elements of the modern courtyard house'.[27]

Courtyards were also one of the land-saving alternatives to rectilinear streets put forward in their Cambridge research by Sir Leslie Martin and Lionel March. Richard MacCormac describes a hypothetical application of continuous courtyards in his appraisal of the Burghley Road scheme (see pp 216–228); a scheme which embodies them is Pollards Hill, in the London Borough of Merton.

A radical rethink of land use was long overdue, for housing land in Britain has for years been squandered for the sake of

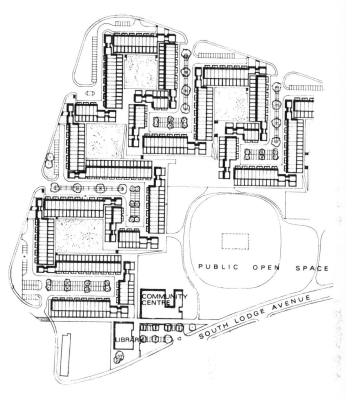

Pollards Hill, Merton—putting the Cambridge courtyard thinking to work in the interests of saving land. Plan is 1:1788.

two shibboleths. One is low densities, still the norm in the private sector* (where flats form no more than ten per cent of total new construction in a typical year) and in much of the public sector outside the major conurbations. (The new towns up to and including Milton Keynes have continued to foster the assumption that low densities are a hallmark of good planning). The other shibboleth is free vehicular access.

To see how little our overall approach to land use has changed this century it is instructive to recall the Tudor Walters Committee of 1918 which enshrined in its recommendations for local authority housing many features later common to both public and private housing developments.[28]

---

*A survey of twelve typical private developments in various price brackets, completed between 1955 and 1968 and chosen by the Royal Institute of British Architects to encourage Span-type community layouts, showed densities ranging from 12 to 57 dwellings per hectare (5 to 23 per acre); the 8 schemes in the (overcrowded) south east averaged 33 dwellings per hectare (13·5 per acre).[29]

Facing page top: Another imaginative solution for the young and transient—Student Co-operative Dwellings' pilot scheme at Lewisham built by Wates and financed by Commercial Union and the Government (through option mortgages).

Facing page, lower two: The site (see second picture and bottom plan) which Lewisham offered was too restricted for ordinary council houses, but ideal for young people living in e.g. bedsitter clusters (see upper plan).

It recommended sites on the outskirts of towns rather than in their centres; low densities ("in ordinary circumstances no more than twelve houses . . . should be placed on any acre [0·4 hectares] of land"); lavish road provision (inherited from the by-law street); and a 21m (70ft) separation between house frontages.

The intentions were of course of the best but the effect over the years has been to turn the one-time standards of progress into a universal straitjacket of regulations that has frozen thinking about land use in housing. This has especially become true with the car assuming more importance in the urban landscape. In modern housing developments, careless planning which unthinkingly works within all the highway and other regulations has been able to consign up to 50 per cent of the total area developed to the various elements of access. This has become less true of the public than of the private sector but not always; for while the DoE survey referred to earlier[30] found that "Roads and footpaths occupied an average 20 per cent of the site" it also discovered that "in extreme cases this reached 35 or 40 per cent" and again that "on average the proportion of the site occupied by buildings is less than 20 per cent at all densities. Roads in modern housing areas, whether public or private, have been laid out according to two criteria, neither of which has anything to do with housing. To quote the basic handbook of the 1960s on the subject: 'Urban roads should be designed to be safe and to permit the free flow of traffic at reasonable speed.'[31] The first objective is obviously crucial, but it is when safety is linked to the requirement of convenience for vehicles that the trouble starts.

Roads in Urban Areas laid down recommended lane widths for estate roads which have been treated as minima and often increased in practice by local highway authorities. These have exercised a powerful sanction—their ability to refuse to adopt for maintenance purposes any roads whose layout they disapproved of. In addition, generous passing and turning space has been allowed for large vehicles (dustcarts, fire engines and furniture removal vans) on the assumption that their drivers could never be expected to back out of an estate they had once entered.

To this there has had to be added the width of footpaths (and sometimes verges) and the length of the standard 6m (20ft) open plan (and therefore useless) front garden designed to afford driveway space and maximum visibility for the average car. All told these dimensions add up to at least 21m (70ft) between house frontages—a distance first laid down for nineteenth century bye-law streets and subsequently hallowed because it suited the car.

Road junctions in new housing areas have also been equipped with wide radius curves designed, in the words of Roads in Urban Areas, "to permit the free flow of traffic at reasonable speeds" as well as to avoid accidents. Junctions of this kind however encourage a "glance and carry on" mentality rather than the safer "slow, be prepared to stop, check, move on again" approach. In spite of the ample visibility provided they can be a real hazard to cyclists and pedestrians, who can easily be missed when the driver's eye is briefly scanning the wide open space for another car. Safety therefore is in fact endangered instead of enhanced. The fallacy of Roads in Urban Areas has been exposed by research by the Department of the Environment[32] into road accidents in British towns in 1971. Their findings, which will influence future road design standards, suggest strongly that post-war estate roads have proved no safer—and possibly even more dangerous—than narrow Victorian or Edwardian streets for certain classes of road users, eg pedestrians and children on bicycles. These can best be protected by sharp corners forcing traffic virtually to halt.

Further research by the Department has shown that large vehicles need less manoeuvring space than was supposed. Economics and safety factors therefore combine to suggest that land can be more efficiently developed for housing than in the past by making only realistic allowance for access.

A bold step already taken in this direction was the publication by the Essex County Council of a new set of planning guidelines for residential development.[33] The Essex thinking involves a descending hierarchy of roads off through traffic routes culminating in new kinds of estate roads. One proposal is for residential culs-de-sac where motorists and pedestrians can safely share the same narrow space because cars will only be able to move at walking pace, first through a deliberately narrow entrance and then into a space closely confined by walls and buildings. House to house frontages can then be reduced from over 21m (70ft) to as low as 6·4m (21ft), with provision for cars to park and be garaged at the side of houses, instead of in front of them (see opposite).

The saving of space is considerable; and the loss to motorists a matter of a few minutes only per day. Amenity is not only safeguarded, but increased, since all the saving is at the expense of public access space and useless open plan front gardens, while the clustering of homes round a tight streetscape recalls the attractive qualities of villages and old towns. The Essex mews court is based on the individual houses and gardens which are still the staple of the private sector; developed for higher density local authority or voluntary housing schemes, the land savings would be proportionately all the greater.

But even at the relatively lower densities likely to be favoured for some time to come by private enterprise, the saving in site costs of an estate developed as land-sparing mews courts would provide a refreshing range of choices for the same (or a lower) ultimate cost to the purchaser. Many more homes could be built on the same part of a site and therefore more cheaply; or a few more homes provided to a much higher standard of living space, materials or finish; again, some gardens could be greatly increased in size. Examples of all these possibilities could be available in a single development, so providing a mix of accommodation at different standards and prices and enabling people to match their changing needs and circumstances to another dwelling in an area they have become used to, something which is impossible in the typical speculative estate of virtually identical houses.

The Essex guide took four years to bring to fruition, with discussions at every point involving highway engineers, public utilities, commercial developers and officials of the Department of the Environment. When published in 1973, it contained the accolade of a personally signed foreword from the Secretary of State for the Environment, a further indication of the alarm felt by the government over housing in general, and the fate of the private sector in particular. Its philosophy, however, represents the culmination of thinking which was becoming evident even before the publication of the design guide, or the emergence of the energy crisis for which it proved an appropriate planning scenario. During the 1960s, there was more than one instance of the concepts of unrestricted freedom and convenience for the motorist, and of the rigid separation of cars from pedestrians which this entails, being challenged in housing projects.

Anthony B Davies' Laindon housing scheme, for example, which was started in 1964, allowed play areas to spill over into parking areas (see pp 114–127). Apart from anything

space between buildings (old standards)

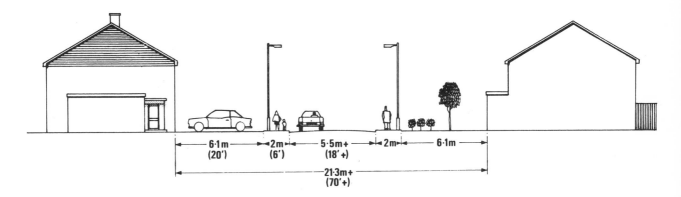

6·1m
(20') 2m
(6') 5·5m+
(18'+) 2m 6·1m

21·3m+
(70'+)

possible space between buildings (new standards)

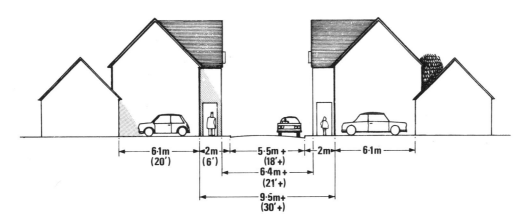

6·1m
(20') 2m
(6') 5·5m +
(18'+) 2m 6·1m

6·4m+
(21'+)

9·5m+
(30'+)

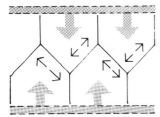

Considerable spatial variety is possible within this chevron shaped site, which, grouped as shown provides a compact layout avoiding back to back overlooking
N.B. The rigid grid is only diagrammatic, on actual sites the principle can be maintained but using a more informal layout.

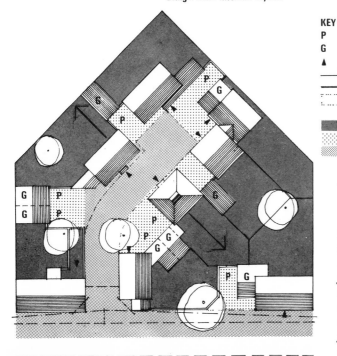

KEY
P Parking
G Garage
▲ Front door
→ Main prospect
─ 2 m. wall
...... Minimum highway area required in court
Private zone
Public zone
Adopted highway in public zone

The first major breakthrough in freeing housing layouts from the rigidity of road standards came with the Essex Design Guide for Residential Areas. These illustrations from the Guide show (top) the typical local authority road width; (second) the kind of alternative Essex wants to encourage; (bottom) a mews court winning space back from roads to provide a compact but attractive layout; and (second from bottom) the chevron pattern that could be formed with interlocking mews courts.

else, this was a common sense recognition of what happens in any case in the most rigid of Radburn schemes, where children often prefer the hard surfaces of carparking areas to play on.

Another example is Runcorn Development Corporation's Halton Brow Estate (see pp 206–215). Begun in 1969, this was the first housing scheme to be produced wholly within the development corporation's own architect's department and represents a deliberate reversal of Radburn principles which the development corporation architects felt, produced neither satisfactory segregation, nor a satisfactory housing environment.

The shared access roads at Halton Brow (courts and culs-de-sac), are as little as 3·05m (10ft) wide, two way, pave-mentless and winding, to deter dangerous car speeds (Runcorn is in any case a highly public-transport-oriented new town, with a purpose-built network of bus-only express-ways designed to reduce the need for private cars).

As Keith Ingham and Frank Williams say in their review of the scheme (see pp 209–215), 'On entering the culs-de-sac, the driver has a sense of being tolerated only, and not being present as of right. The closeness of the buildings and the curvilinear roads reduce speeds to a minimum, and he feels it would be a gross discourtesy to blow the horn at a pedestrian sharing the same route. The principle of sharing the circulation route is the basis behind the whole success of the scheme.'[34]

Whatever happens to world reserves of fossil fuels, there is now enough planning evidence for the confident assertion that the car need never again be the unchallenged master of the way we design our housing. (Significantly even in the United States, birthplace of the mass production car and the freeway, work began in 1972 on a car-free housing scheme—the New York State Urban Development Cor-poration's project for 2 100 homes on Welfare Island). This evidence, properly used and backed by public authorities in all sectors, offers an unparalleled opportunity to rethink the economically critical relationship between housing and land. Our past record is not encouraging: 'So fossilised has our thinking become that even when modern 'town house' type terraces are used, and garages siphoned off into courts of their own, the houses are still automatically set back from the road.'[35] This automatic and mindless wastefulness should not be allowed to recur.

Another urgent need is to re-assess the potential of sites not previously thought of as suitable for housing. Student Co-operative Dwellings' pilot Lewisham project for example occupies a site bordered on two sides by railway lines, which make it unattractive for family housing. Again, railways, roads and waterways can be built over to provide valuable new housing sites in the hearts of cities. London's under-ground has already been rafted over for a major office development at Moorgate, and feasibility studies for housing projects on the same lines were got under way in the early 1970s. Sites such as these would prove ideal for housing transport and other service workers close to their jobs.

At the same time as these new approaches to land use have been developing, new forms of construction have begun to emerge in the public sector. One of these starts from the division between the structures and interiors of housing schemes proposed by Professor N J Habraken of Holland[36] and developed in the UK by PSSHAK (primary system support housing and assembly kits).

In 1970 the GLC's housing division's research and develop-ment group became hosts to the Architectural Association-based innovators of PSSHAK and selected an experimental site in North London. By separating the interior divisions

Homes from metal containers—a GLC experiment in North London shows a new approach to industrialisation.

of a housing scheme from its structure, which can be built in any form of construction, PSSHAK offers both tenants and local housing authorities a new degree of flexibility. The tenants can choose for themselves the internal layout that suits them best and have partitions installed accordingly; when they leave, their home can be completely altered for the next comers. The council in turn can, by moving the lightweight party walls between units, redistribute the accommodation in any part of a PSSHAK scheme to meet changing patterns of need among those on its waiting list—large families at one time, at another, one- or two-person households.[37]

Another approach, also stemming from the GLC's need to tackle London's housing problems—12 000 homeless families and over 200 000 on council waiting lists in 1973[38]—involves new forms of industrialised building. One is based on the use of metal containers, similar to those used for modern freight transport, to provide two-person dwellings. The idea came from a company concerned with building multi-storey carparks. Each unit would consist of three 8·5m × 2·5m (just over 28ft × 8ft) containers, one consisting of balcony, kitchen and part of a bedroom, the second of the rest of the bedroom, the bathroom and part of a living room, and the third of the rest of the living room, hall and storage space. These containers could be stacked up to three or four storeys high and linked to external service and circulation towers.

Timber, as opposed to metal, boxes have also been examined. Britain's housing problems may be far from being solved but the evidence is that there is no shortage of ingenious solu-tions. The record of a decade which follows in this book is impressive, and is already being extended by the exploration of new forms of tenure, construction and layout. But the most fundamental question of all is that of priorities.

Britain spends some £1 500 million a year in building new homes and improving existing ones. About half of this is spent by the public sector and half by the private.[39] Government contributions alone come to over £170 million for construction and improvement (see Table 9, p 20) and the value of tax concessions to owner occupiers amounted to over £300 million annually by 1971. Yet in that year, only 2·9 per cent of Britain's gross national product was spent on housing, compared with 4.5 per cent in Ireland, 5·9 per cent in West Germany, 6·7 per cent in France and 5·9 per cent in Italy. Can we, in the light of these figures, claim that we are yet taking our housing problem seriously enough?

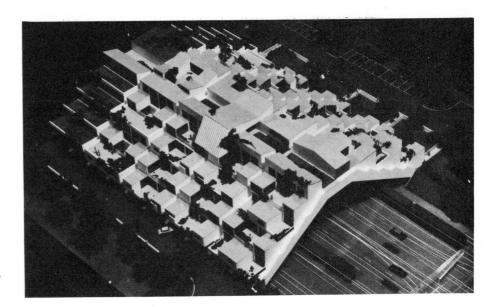

Another way to gain space for housing without raiding Britain's precious stock of land—a Siege Systems proposal to build homes on a massive concrete raft over railway lines and so on—a technique already used for office developments.

Statistical Information

Table 1: Housing stock by tenure, percentages for Great Britain, 1950–1972

Period	Owner occupied	Rented public sector	Privately rented	Other
1950	29·5	18·0	44·5	8·0
1951–1960*	42·0	26·6	25·7	5·7
1961–1965*	46·3	28·3	20·0	5·4
1966	47·1	28·7	18·8	5·4
1967	47·8	29·2	17·7	5·3
1968	48·5	29·6	16·6	5·3
1969	49·0	30·0	15·8	5·2
1970	49·5	30·5	14·9	5·1
1971	50·1	30·7	14·2	5·0
1972	51·0	30·6	13·4	5·0

*Percentages relate to end of period stated.

Source: Social Trends nos 1–3, HMSO, 1970, 1971 and 1972.

Table 2: Percentage of flats and houses in total public sector output, England and Wales, 1945–1972

Year	Flats %	Houses %
1945–1956 annual average	18·5	81·5
1957	30·8	69·2
1958	35·5	64·5
1959	40·6	59·4
1960	42·4	57·6
1961	42·2	57·8
1962	44·8	55·1
1963	47·9	52·1
1964	49·2	50·8
1965	52·3	47·7
1966	51·8	48·2
1967	48·7	51·3
1968	48·9	51·1
1969	51·1	48·9
1970	53·3	46·7
1971	52·7	47·3
1972	50·7	49·3

Source: MOHLG Housing Statistics and DOE Housing and Construction Statistics.

Table 3: Percentage of high rise dwellings in total public sector dwellings approved, England and Wales, 1960–1972

Year	Flats with storey height of:				Houses:
	2–4	5–9	10–14	15+	
1960	33·0	4·6	6·6	3·0	52·8
1961	32·2	5·6	7·1	3·8	51·3
1962	32·5	4·6	7·6	5·1	50·2
1963	31·2	4·3	8·6	9·1	46·8
1964	31·1	5·4	6·8	11·9	44·8
1965	30·2	4·6	6·3	10·6	48·3
1966	26·8	9·1	6·2	10·4	47·5
1967	27·0	9·4	3·9	9·7	50·0
1968	30·8	10·5	3·5	5·9	49·3
1969	35·9	8·0	1·8	3·8	50·5
1970	38·6	7·2	1·0	1·7	51·5
1971	41·4	5·2	1·5	1·9	50·0
1972	44·5	5·2	0·7	1·3	48·3

Source: MOHLG Housing Statistics and DOE Housing and Construction Statistics.

Table 4: Housing starts and completions, private and public sectors, Great Britain, 1960–1972, in thousands

	Starts				Completions		
Year	Public	Private	Total		Public	Private	Total
1945–1950	848·0	174·9	1 022·9		663·3	158·2	821·5
1960	126·3	182·8	309·1		129·2	168·6	297·8
1961	122·9	189·4	312·3		118·5	177·5	296·1
1962	137·7	186·0	323·7		130·6	174·8	305·4
1963	168·6	199·4	368·0		124·0	174·9	298·9
1964	178·6	247·5	426·1		155·6	218·1	373·7
1965	181·4	211·1	392·5		168·5	213·8	382·3
1966	185·9	193·4	379·3		180·1	205·4	385·5
1967	213·9*	233·6	447·6*		203·9	200·4	404·4
1968	194·3	200·1	394·4		191·7	222·0	413·7
1969	176·6	166·8	343·5		185·1	181·7	366·8
1970	154·1	165·1	319·1		180·1	170·3	350·4
1971	136·6	207·3	343·9		158·9	191·6	350·5
1972	123·0	227·4	350·4		122·8	196·3	319·1
1973	112·8	214·9	327·7		107·5	186·1	293·6

*In 1967, the Greater London Council changed its definition of a start, affecting 4,623 homes in that year.

Source: MOHLG Housing Statistics and DOE Housing and Construction Statistics.

Table 5: Industrialised dwellings as a percentage of total public sector output, England and Wales, 1964–1972

Year	Tenders approved (%)	Completions (%)
1964	21·0	14·4
1965	29·1	19·2
1966	38·6	26·3
1967	42·4*	30·8
1968	39·4	34·2
1969	30·1	38·0
1970	19·4	41·3
1971	18·8	32·7
1972	19·3	26·1

*In 1967, the Greater London Council changed its definition of a start, affecting 4,623 homes in that year.

Source: MOHLG Housing Statistics and DOE Housing and Construction Statistics.

Table 6: Index of private house prices compared with housebuilding costs, United Kingdom, 1962–1973 (1965 = 100)

End of last quarter of	New homes	Modern existing homes	Older homes	Housebuilding (wage and material costs)
1962	82	80	83	89
1963	86	88	89	93
1964	93	94	95	97
1965	100	100	100	100
1966	106	104	104	103
1967	112	111	113	109
1968	120	118	121	113
1969	125	125	129	117
1970	133	131	140	131
1971	161	160	166	142
1972	237	222	234	169
1973	264	254	268	200

Source: Nationwide Building Society, Occasional Bulletins.

Table 7: Site values as percentage of prices of homes bought through the Nationwide Building Society, in selected areas of Great Britain, 1966–1973

End of last quarter of	London & South East	East Anglia	North East	Scotland	Great Britain
1966	25·6	19·5	15·8	12·9	19·9
1967	28·3	21·0	16·2	14·7	21·3
1968	27·3	21·5	15·9	14·1	21·7
1969	28·4	22·5	15·6	13·1	22·1
1970	28·5	21·6	16·2	12·7	21·9
1971	31·9	23·9	17·0	11·7	23·6
1972	37·5	33·8	17·0	11·4	28·4
1973	36·7	30·5	19·2	13·3	28·1

Source: Nationwide Building Society, Occasional Bulletins.

Table 8: Number of rooms in new houses mortgaged by the Nationwide Building Society in 1962, 1966 and 1970

Year	Reception rooms, % with			Bedrooms, % with			
	1	2	3+	1	2	3	4+
1962	69·5	29·4	1·1	0·8	31·6	62·2	5·4
1966	70·9	28·1	1·0	0·2	21·3	70·7	7·8
1970	61·8	35·2	3·0	1·1	17·0	70·4	11·5

Source: Nationwide Building Society, Occasional Bulletins.

Table 9: The cost of housing: government contributions to permanent housing in England and Wales, 1960–1971

Year	Construction of permanent dwellings	Contributions to conversions and improvements (£ millions)		
		Public sector	Private owners	Total
1960/1	61·0	0·3	2·5	63·8
1961/2	63·6	0·5	3·3	67·4
1962/3	66·0	0·7	4·3	71·1
1963/4	68·0	1·1	6·1	75·2
1964/5	73·0	1·3	6·6	80·8
1965/6	77·7	1·4	7·2	86·3
1966/7	82·4	1·7	8·3	92·4
1967/8	94·1	2·0	9·3	105·4
1968/9	107·1	2·6	10·5	120·3
1969/70	125·5	3·1	11·5	140·1
1970/1	156·6	4·2	13·1	173·9

Source: MOHLG Housing Statistics and DOE Housing and Construction Statistics.

Table 10: Bank rate* and mortage interest rates, 1960–1973

Year†	Bank rate (%)	Mortgage interest rate (%)
1960	6	6
1961	7	$6\frac{1}{2}$
1962	$5\frac{1}{2}$	$6\frac{1}{2}$
1963	4	6
1964	7	6
1965	6	$6\frac{3}{4}$
1966	7	$7\frac{1}{8}$
1967	$6\frac{1}{2}$	$7\frac{1}{8}$
1968	$7\frac{1}{2}$	$7\frac{5}{8}$
1969	8	$8\frac{1}{2}$
1970	$7\frac{1}{2}$	$8\frac{1}{2}$
1971	6	8
1972	9	$8\frac{1}{2}$
1973	13	11

*Became known as the minimum lending rate in 1972.

†Rates given are the highest attained in the year in question. At the beginning of 1960, bank rate was 4 per cent and mortgage interest rate $5\frac{1}{2}$ per cent.

Source: Building Societies Year Books.

Table 11: Amount of interest recoverable from the government under the Option Mortgage Scheme, 1968–1972

Year	Interest recoverable (£000s)
1968	3 756
1969	7 003
1970	10 077
1971	12 647
1972	20 113

Source: Annual reports of the Chief Registrar of Friendly Societies, Part II, Building Societies.

1 Courtyard Housing at Dundee

designed by	Baxter, Clark & Paul
partner	R. R. Black
senior architect	A. Steele
staff	D. Hamilton
	G. A. T. Johnston
quantity surveyor	Dundee Corporation city quantity surveyor
heating consultants	North of Scotland Hydro Electric Board
main contractor	Dundee Corporation Building Department

These courtyard houses were chosen by Edinburgh University Architecture Research Unit as the subject of a sociological study to check and compare results of an investigation into the Unit's own first building programme.

Development from the neighbouring four-storey block with Law Hill in background. Roofscape is reasonably neat and informal layout apparent.

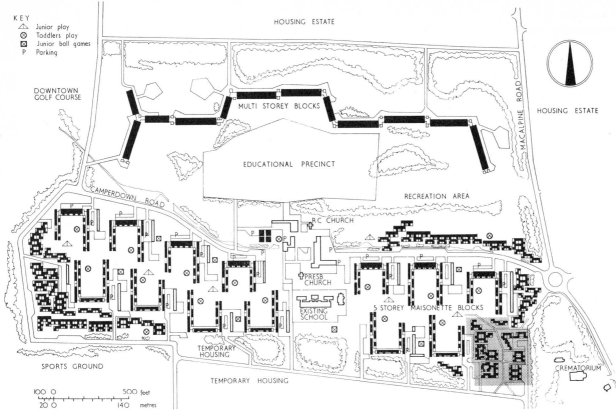

KEY
△ Junior play
⊗ Toddlers play
⊠ Junior ball games
P Parking

1 *Site plan of Ardler estate at Dundee showing original proposals by Baxter, Clark & Paul for Phase 1 (south-east area), phase 2 (south-west area) and phase 3 (north area). Phases 2 and 3 were subsequently developed by others. (1:7 500) The shaded area in the extreme south-eastern corner is the site of the courtyard housing, located here among other reasons to screen the crematorium from the rest of the development.*

CLIENT'S REQUIREMENTS AND SITE

An area of some 57·5 hectares (142 acres) has been developed by Dundee Corporation as a neighbourhood unit for an estimated population of 13 000. The site is in three distinct areas, the two major ones grouped together to form the main development. Of the latter, an area of 21·0 hectares (fifty-two acres) was developed with five-storey walk-up blocks and single-storey courtyard housing.

The remainder of the site was subsequently developed by a package dealer following a change of policy by Dundee Corporation, and the architect's original master plan has been varied considerably.

The site of the courtyard housing was formerly occupied by temporary prefabricated housing, most of whose tenants have been rehoused in the new development. On this side, 187 courtyard dwelling units have been provided, to accommodate 734 people. A sub-area containing forty-seven units, of which 34 per cent are five-person, 51 per cent four-person, 4 per cent three-person and 11 per cent two-person, has been the subject of an investigation by the Architecture Research Unit of Edinburgh University, which in 1962 completed an estate of 45 single-storey courtyard houses at Inchview, Prestonpans, for the East Lothian County Council.

PLANNING

Main traffic is carried on a perimeter road, with service culs-de-sac formed by the existing road pattern but terminated at the core. There is clear segregation of traffic from pedestrians, with pedestrian units between the housing units, the core and the schools complex.

Garaging is provided for 50 per cent of dwelling units, with hard standing for the other 50 per cent. An additional 25 per cent hard standing is provided for visitors' cars and service vehicles.

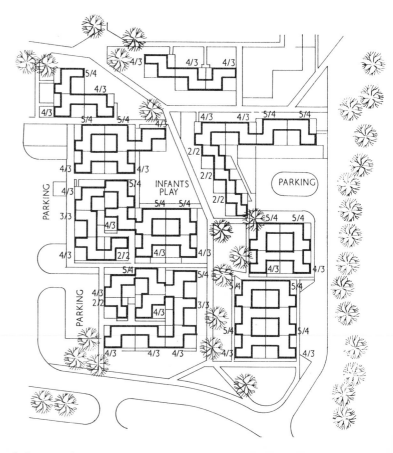

2 *Layout of courtyard housing at Dundee. Dwelling sizes are indicated, eg 4/3 means four-person three-room. (1:1 500)*

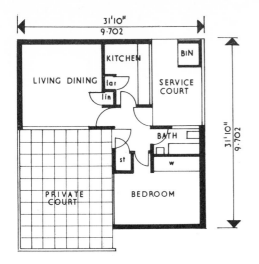

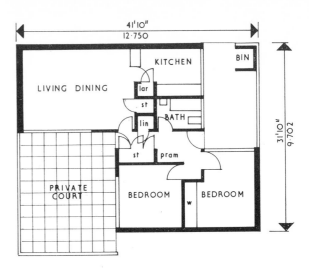

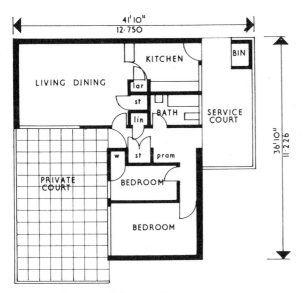

4 *Plans of courtyard houses. From top: two-person two-room, three-person three-room, (right) four-person three-room, five-person four-room.* (1:192)

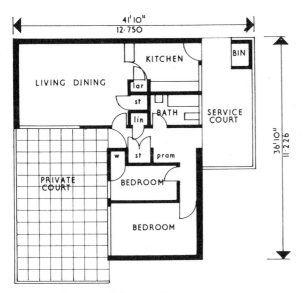

3 *Isometric diagram of five-person four-room courtyard house*

The detailed planning of dwelling units, the grouping of buildings and the organisation of spaces in between, was influenced by the social research study.

APPRAISAL

There is a continuing interest in courtyard housing as a means of providing medium-density accommodation for family living. Obvious advantages of this form are its higher density relative to terrace housing and therefore more economical use of building land; its low construction cost compared with high-rise developments; its notable privacy and avoidance of problems of overlooking into neighbouring gardens and dwellings; and its provision of direct access from dwelling to outdoor space, which is particularly important in a family dwelling.

Disadvantages are the restricted outlook from dwellings; limited outdoor space available if the dwelling is sufficiently compact to allow economical sharing of external walls; and the difficulty of handling, visually, large areas of roofing where the development is overlooked.

The architects, appointed in 1960, prepared a master plan for the whole development and acted as architects for the courtyard housing and for some of the five-storey walk-up housing in the first area. At the time of designing, the Prestonpans courtyard houses had been built but the follow-up report on them[1] had not been published.

1

2

3

1 *Entrance to scheme by way of spinal footpath. High-rise development in background was originally intended in the architects' master plan to be linear in form with the type of deck access characteristic of the Park Hill and Hyde Park schemes in* *Sheffield. This would have provided a visually more satisfactory back-drop to angular foreground*
2 *Further into scheme with entrance courtyards to houses, right, reached by branch footpaths providing additional privacy. Wet-dasl*

Density planned for the development as a whole was ninety bed spaces per acre; the courtyard housing alone covers 1·6 hectares (4 acres) at an effective density of forty-eight persons per acre.

Number and types of houses in the group studied are:

Type	No	Per cent
4-room, 5-person	16	34
3-room, 4-person	24	51
3-room, 3-person	2	4
2-room, 2-person	5	11
Total	47	100

Most of the housing was intended for families with two or three children. Rightly, but unfortunately from the point of view of any sociological appraisal of the scheme, all courtyard housing was offered to tenants of the prefabs originally on the site. This group of people had an age structure quite different from those for whom, in the long term, it can be assumed the houses were designed. The average age of the male heads of households was fifty, of the female heads forty-eight years; 58 per cent of the total population were over forty and only 4 per cent were under ten years—that is, there were only six children under ten years among the 157 residents.

This circumstance compromises the value of the Dundee study[2] which was undertaken by the Architecture Research Unit to check and compare results of the earlier investigation carried out by the unit on its own courtyard housing at Prestonpans. In particular it was intended to provide further information on courtyards and the privacy afforded by this form of housing. Conclusions of the study are described in the report as follows:

'For the most part the results of the Dundee study were largely in agreement with those of the Prestonpans study; consequently, while the overall conclusions do not differ substantially from those of the original study, they can be stated with greater confidence and authority.

'On the first of the topics studied it was found that the majority of housewives were well satisfied with the courtyard house type and with what it had to offer. The three or four tenants who were less enthusiastic complained of

rendering is generally well executed although some variations in texture—not apparent here—show the need for good craftsmanship with this type of finish

3 *View from branch footpath seen in* **2**. *The need for a plain back-drop is even more apparent. Landscaping and planting is very well executed by Corporation Parks Department*

4 *At a bend in the spine footpath four-storey blocks can be clearly seen. The two-room houses on right have cut-outs in their fences—giving additional view for couples expected to use these types. These reduce privacy only if one is nosy enough to cross the grass*

5 *Looking across a spine footpath up a branch path captures some of the intimacy of layout which, by and large, has been sacrificed to need for privacy. Low fences on right are to entrance courts*

4

5

lack of outlook, or too much privacy or of both but these complaints were not shown to be necessarily due to the form and nature of the courtyard house.

'On the second topic it was found that the courtyards were well liked particularly because of the privacy provided and their small size which allowed for ease of maintenance. The results confirmed that the idea of an enclosed outdoor space was acceptable to most people. Main uses of the courtyards had been for clothes drying, gardening, sitting out and storage; children's play was hardly mentioned as there were very few young children in the scheme.

'Findings on privacy indicated that this was an important element in many people's lives and that the meaning most often associated with it was freedom to live one's own life without unwanted interference or intrusion from others

6

7

9

10

11

6 *Entrances to two-room dwellings on east side of scheme showing blockwork dustbin recess which is perhaps a little too coarse. A garage is on right*

7 *Another view of entrance court from garage service road. The variety of textures provided is very pleasing although some difficulty has been experienced with the large expanses of stained wood*

8 *Infants' play area before being equipped. The ground moulding is not as positive as architects would have wished*

9 *Garage courts are neatly designed and unobtrusively planned around additional parking spaces*

10 *View from perimeter road of very interesting adjoining four-storey walk-up housing designed by same architects*

11 *Another view of walk-up housing from an access deck*

living round about. Measured by such standards the court-yard houses appeared to provide the kind of privacy that informants wanted.'

The practical value of confirming these findings on privacy is limited unless at the same time it can be ascertained that the courtyards cater adequately for other essential family functions such as children's play. It is arguable whether this scheme should have been retained as the subject of the study once the abnormal age structure of the population had been noted. While the *safety* of the courtyard for children's play was appreciated by tenants, the report admits that only one child used the courtyard a lot; the rest tended to play outside the house and courtyard 'probably for the sake of company' eg in the basic play areas provided in the scheme.

The implication might be that the courtyards were too small for the parents to allow a normal size of playgroup—say of three or four children—to operate without causing havoc. Pressure on the use of courtyards by children of large families was mentioned in the Prestonpans report but a 'normal' playgroup includes some of the children's friends, particularly when the family is small. If groups even of this size have to resort to the toddlers' communal playground then it could be argued that the private playground—that is, the garden or courtyard—is not adequate, and perhaps less adequate than the normal small garden. This is specu-lative, but if the study population had been chosen so as to allow investigation in this area—since the small garden size is implicit in the courtyard layout—then speculation would be unnecessary.

Perhaps the most important difference between the Dundee and Pestonpans houses is in the courtyard arrangement. At Prestonpans a single courtyard was provided, access to the house being directly off the footpath 'vennels', or through the courtyard. At Dundee a small entry and service court is provided in which a dustbin recess is placed and which is accessible directly from the kitchen; the garden courts are accordingly rather smaller than at Prestonpans. Surprisingly, the Dundee report does not discuss the comparative merits or otherwise of this double courtyard arrangement. It does, however, mention the service court as a likely place for an outside store which was felt necessary in view of the clutter found there. Judging, however, from photographs in the report of the kind of materials and equipment, mainly gardening, stored there, it seems that the garden court might be a better site.

Opinions expressed by tenants about detailed design features of these houses were not, by and large, ones which would be useful to designers since they, or equally satisfac-tory alternatives, tend to be standard features in modern houses. Exceptions among the best-liked features are privacy, which gets a high rating and is considered further below, and the single-storey plan. The latter response is difficult to evaluate since all tenants come from single-storey prefabs, but the single-storey arrangement was also popular at Prestonpans where few tenants had previously experienced single-storey living.

Among opinions on least-liked features, the only significant one—but this of some importance—related to the small size of the kitchen. Reasons included larger size of prefab kitchen to which tenants had been accustomed: 9·48 m² (102 sq ft) compared with 8·08 m² (87 sq ft) and a less satisfactory layout in the new kitchen, involving less economical use of space, separation of cooker and sink, inadequate space for equipment such as washing machines and less drawer space (which, admittedly, had been generous in the prefabs).

The main reason for this criticism, however, was the tenants' use of the kitchen for eating—in spite of a service

hatch to the adjacent dining-recess in the living-room. This was not, as the report rightly points out, merely a stubborn perpetuation of old habits: there has been widespread recognition of families' demand for kitchens of at least 9·29 m² (100 sq ft) in area. Blame here must be laid on the standards current at the time of the design.

The report deals at some length with the question of privacy. Three types of privacy were considered and these were defined by the tenants themselves in the course of questioning.

The first, described by most tenants, was 'to live their own life without unwanted interference or intrusion from those living round about'. In particular it was thought best to avoid 'running in and out of one another's houses' and to avoid borrowing household items. The second type was freedom from inlooking; that is, protection from neighbours and passers-by being able to see into the house or garden.

On both these counts these houses rate highly although

12

14

15

16

17

18

19

12, 13, 14, 15 *Restricted child's play is clearly appropriate in courtyard but what of more rumbustious groups? Again, pets can enliven the space but there seems to be a threat from gardening equipment: an outside store is essential*
16, 17, 18 *Dividing wall with hatch between kitchen and dining space can be taken for what it is, ignored or 'improved'*
19 *Restricted outlook onto a neighbouring blank wall about which some tenants complained*

20

21

20 *Cut-out in fence was generally appreciated; effect of release, particularly valuable with a small courtyard, can be seen here*
21 *Service courtyard, which prevents the kitchen window and front door directly overlooking the access paths*

there were some complaints of the converse effect—that is, a lack of outlook. Fences to courtyards, which were prefabricated in panels, were designed with 'cut-outs' to the two-room dwellings since these were expected to be inhabited by more elderly tenants. The response of the tenants generally however, made it clear that more cut-outs would have been preferred although it is not clear that these would have been satisfactory at all times of the day. A better solution, although slightly more expensive, might have been a panel that could be swung down for additional view when required. Some kitchen windows looked only onto a neighbouring blank wall and this was fairly consistently deprecated.

None of the housewives had been accustomed to noises normally associated with houses with party walls and most comments on noise relate to this type—neighbour's tv, doors banging and plumbing. Noises did not, however, seem to cause much disturbance, nor did tenants feel under much constraint to limit the amount of noise they made.

District heating was suggested but electrical underfloor heating was corporation policy at the time. Heating was restricted to the living-rooms and hall only, and owing to the type of floor finish combined with partial heating, condensation difficulties have been experienced, mainly in one bedroom of the bedroom wing. When bedroom doors are open in the evening warm air from the hall condenses out onto the cold bedroom floor. Additional storage heaters have therefore had to be installed.

External walls are either of ($\frac{3}{4}$ in) roughcast rendering on a ($4\frac{1}{2}$ in) brick outer leaf (2 in) cavity and (4 in) block inner skin; or of stud framing lined externally with horizontal weather-boarding and internally with modulation board and plasterboard. Rendering is well applied on the courtyard housing; however, importance of good craftsmanship with this type of finish can be seen in variability of work on the walk-up housing. Roofs are timber framed finished with

house types; the double courtyard plan which provides greater variety of outline than the single courtyard; and the informal layout based on a spinal footpath which changes direction as it moves through the group.

Generally, this courtyard scheme seems to have been successful in many ways. It provides a high degree of privacy combined, except in the case of a few houses in the denser parts of the scheme, with a reasonable outlook; it offers a double courtyard arrangement which, in its division of function between service and recreation, is a marked improvement on the single courtyard type; in external appearance it is crisp yet informal. Further investigation of these houses may be worthwhile when the population contains a greater number of young children and a clearer idea can be formed of the response to the courtyard arrangement from a mixed population.

Since the Dundee development, Baxter, Clark & Paul have built courtyard houses of similar design in Blairgowrie, Perthshire (1966-67), Peterhead, Aberdeenshire (1967), and Keith. Banffshire (1967–68). The Blairgowrie Development received a Saltire Commendation in 1967 and the Keith Development received a Saltire Award in 1968. Planning modifications are a larger dining/kitchen and provision of an external store indicated within the house shell and accessible from the garden or living court. Heating is from a centrally placed warm air unit.

SUMMARY

Contract for 187 houses and seventeen garages
Total floor area: 13 227 m² (142 380·sq ft)
Type of contract: Scottish Conditions (1954) (local authority amendments),
Tender date: September 1963.
Work begun: November 1963.
Work finished: February 1965.
Tender price of foundations, superstructure and finishes including drainage to last collecting manhole:
£338,500
Tender price of external works including drainage beyond collecting manhole: £57 357.
Total: £395 857

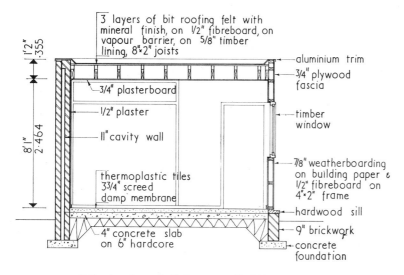

5 *Section through living-room.* (1:72)

2 Point Royal Flats, Bracknell

These flats are a
remarkable example of
integration with the site,
a simple planning solution
(including 100 per cent
car parking), and structural
expression in precast
concrete

designed by	Arup Associates
job team	
architect	Philip Dowson
engineer	Derek Sugden
job architect	Keith Barnes
job engineers	Peter Brett
	Alan Anderson
quantity surveyor	Denis Stone
main contractor	Rush and Tompkins

CLIENT'S REQUIREMENTS

Point Royal is a point block of flats to serve as a focal point for a neighbourhood, and to consist of small units of accommodation suitable for single persons or married couples without children. The block was to provide a substitute for the traditional boarding house accommodation and flatlets normally lacking in a new town development such as Bracknell. The units were to be in the proportion of four one-bedroom flats to one two-bedroom flat and one bed-sitting-room, based on the room areas laid down in the Ministry of Health *Housing manual* 1949. With the decentralisation of the Meteorological Office in mind, the flats were to be designed for probable occupation by 'technologists' in a then income bracket of between £900 and £1 250 a year. The whole block was to be electrical with underfloor heating. One garage per flat was to be provided.

SITE

The site, roughly a triangle of about 1·80 hectares (4½ acres) which includes the well treed grounds of a demolished rectory, lies on the side of a small hill and falls gently away towards the south. Boundaries on two sides are formed by roadways which serve to separate the site from the surrounding Easthampstead housing development, while the third side is bounded mainly by open land and garden fences.

Below ground, the site consists of stiff or very stiff grey silty clay containing layers of fine sand, with a top layer of more sandy soil of a variable nature.

PLANNING

The most natural position for the new building was on the site of the old rectory. The tall mature trees lining the rectory drive form an irregular v, the arms of which open out to frame the block which stands on the crest of a rise.

Right from the outset it was determined to segregate the pedestrian and vehicular and service access to the base of the tower. This was both to preserve green areas and to avoid providing the inhabitants of this high building with a view of 100 garage roofs and attendant asphalt surrounds. The solution was to place the tower in the centre of a circular concrete roof deck of a semi-underground garage, the bowl was formed on the 'cut and fill' principle. This deck, or terrace, is separated from the site by an open trench or ha-ha on its circumference thus providing visual continuity between the green and the foot of the building. Bridges provide access for pedestrians onto the deck.

All vehicular access, refuse collection, service and storage areas, etc, are planned below this deck with direct lift access to upper floors. Taking all relevant factors into consideration, this particular solution proved to be no more expensive than providing individual garages.

The split hexagon floor plan was chosen as providing the most economical arrangement compatible with the original brief of a point block, while achieving considerable savings in area of floors and external walls over a rectangular plan of similar accommodation, ie one bedsitting-room, four one-bedroom flats and one two-bedroom flat.

The external shape was derived from splitting a regular hexagon and opening the two halves to introduce the seventh element, the staircase, the door to which had to be within 6·09 m (20 ft) of the furthest flat. By maintaining the regular angles, and limiting the special conditions to the stair and lift area (which is in any case a special), it reduced the number of precast element types to a minimum.

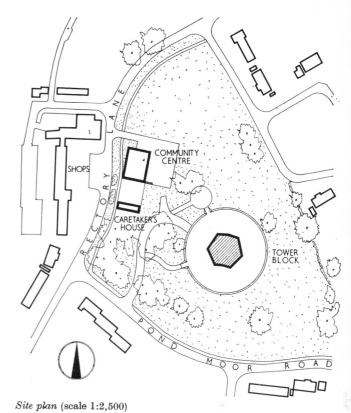

Site plan (scale 1:2,500)

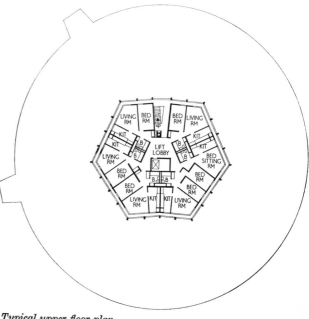

Typical upper floor plan

Within the typical floor plan three prefabricated service cores, each consisting of two bathrooms and two kitchens, are grouped to simplify service requirements. The internal bathrooms are artificially ventilated through the main service duct in each core. Each kitchen is fully equipped with ventilated larder, sink unit, worktop, high and low level storage units, the latter including a drying cabinet in addition to the linen cupboard in each bathroom. Also each flat, with the exception of the bedsitting-room type, has a large cupboard in the entrance hall for storage of outdoor clothes, travel cases, etc.

The plan of a typical flat has been arranged so that all rooms with standard equipment, ie bathroom, bedroom and kitchen, are rectangular. All living areas are separated from a possible noise source in the central lift hall by a buffer formed by the internal bathrooms and flat entrances.

The architect believes that the irregular shape of the living-rooms has certain advantages over a rectangular room of the same area. The two long walls radiating away from each other provide a more definite separation of the sitting and dining spaces, and the resultant double plane window commands a fine view of the surrounding countryside.

A single stair/two-lift access plan was adopted in preference to a double staircase solution. In the latter case an area of good aspect would inevitably have been lost to the second staircase and circulation areas would have been increased. The necessary secondary means of escape has been provided by an external gallery, linking all flats on each floor with the escape staircase.

The cladding of tall buildings has to solve a number of problems. The solution applied at Bracknell stems from a design for new buildings at Somerville College, Oxford, prepared in the late 1950s and subsequently used also for buildings at Corpus Christi College, Cambridge. The principles embodied in this solution are:

1 Precast concrete has to be detailed with a view to weathering. Thus it is important to prevent dirt laden water from glass surfaces discharging over precast units. (Long continuous surfaces are to be avoided on columns as well, from the point of view of tolerance and equally to ensure that an organised weathering develops—note column/beam details.)

2 The problems of maintaining and cleaning high buildings are considerable and it is a great advantage to have access to the whole of the exterior.

3 The extension of the floor and ceiling plane of the rooms into the galleries allows low glazing and thus a down-view of the ground. This at once reduces the feeling of isolation which living high with high sills can cause, while equally creating a sense of security and of 'place'. The gallery which was catered for within the original frame, also provides a secondary means of escape from every room. The ceiling extension reduces glare, improves the quality of light and helps to protect the large windows from the sun; it can also simplify the window and panel detailing which occurs behind the structural plane and is therefore independent of it and well protected from weather.

Undoubtedly the effect of this particular solution is to reduce the apparent mass of the building, and by virtue of the consequent strong modelling it helps to produce a unity, rather than an agglomeration of similar parts.

APPRAISAL

As a focal point for the neighbourhood the Point Royal block of flats is certainly impressive and satisfies this part of the brief very well. It is placed among trees at the top of a hill adjacent to a community centre and shops.

Landscaping is well detailed, cars are parked out of sight

2 *Ha ha separating pedestrian deck and car parking below from rest of site. Detailing of the bank and deck edge is particularly interesting*

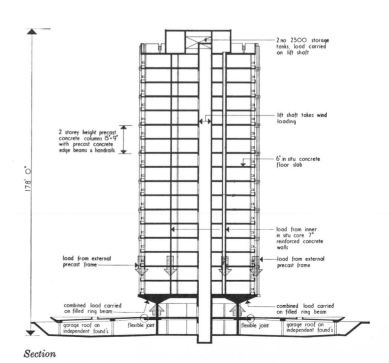

Section

below ground, and the appearance of the block changes with the weather in a most dramatic way. In other respects, however, it appears to have been an afterthought and is not very well related to the surrounding houses and shops. This lack of relationship is particularly obvious here in a new town, where sites need not be designed individually. The site is separated from adjoining shops and housing by a vehicular route, its pedestrian routes do not lead to other similar segregated routes (it is not even possible to walk right across the site), and near views from the block are mainly into the conventional back gardens of surrounding houses.

It should be emphasised that this unsatisfactory planning is not the fault of the architects who designed Point Royal. Regrettably, it is typical of the piecemeal way in which many smaller areas of British new towns are formed. As this is the only major disappointment in the scheme, it is important that the planning responsibility of those providing the site for a building such as Point Royal should be

fully realised. Their responsibility does not stop at visual effect; they must also design for *all* activities in the spaces around buildings and ensure that they are related to each other in a safe, imaginative and economical way over a large area.

The split hexagonal plan with six flats per floor provides the required proportions of different sized flats at each level, and 100 per cent car parking is provided at the base of the block under cover of a circular pedestrian terrace.

At first sight the plan shape, with its obviously economical external wall to floor ratio, seems to be asking for trouble in the detailed layout of each flat. This plan, however, is notable for the way in which all the awkward shapes associated with hexagonal plans are kept to places where they are not only inoffensive but also positively useful. All rooms that are tightly planned (kitchens, bathrooms and bedrooms) are rectangular, and spaces that are more varied in their use (landings, entrance lobbies and living-rooms) take up the awkward angles.

The decision to have six flats on each floor has meant that two of them get very little sun in their living-rooms. This would be a serious defect in flats for families but may not be so important for the intended occupants of this particular building, who are likely to be out for most of the day. One further problem has arisen from the decision to mix different sized flats on each floor. This has worked very well with the exception of the bedsitting-room type, in which the bedsitting-room (although to the specified *Housing manual* standards) itself appears to be rather too small to take all the furniture that even a single person would like to have. At this point, as well, the excellent planning arrangement of buffer rooms to avoid sound annoyance between dwellings is missed.

One other place where the shape of the block has pinched the plan is in the kitchen. It is just possible to get a row of kitchen fitments along each side of the central work space, but another 150 mm to 300 mm (6 in to 12 in) in overall width would have made all the difference between a cramped and a spacious layout. The geometry of this particular block seems to restrict the placing of internal partitions more than a rectangular plan would have done. The covered car parking space beneath the block is particularly economical because of its circular access route serving parking bays on each side. The terrace above separates pedestrians from vehicles and provides cover for the parked cars. It also provides covered access from cars to lifts serving the flats. The site is on the crown of a hill and very little excavation was needed. This appears to be an economical solution to the car parking problem, from the points of view both of cost and of land use. The only defect appears to be the client's decision to incorporate 100 per cent car ownership before the demand actually existed rather than allow space in siting for future growth in car ownership.

The detailing of both external cladding and internal finishes is imaginative and sensible. Of particular interest is the detailing of columns and beams to overcome problems of erection tolerances and weathering, the method of direct glazing behind the non-loadbearing concrete mullions, and the 'balustrade' at the edge of the circular terrace: this is formed by turning up the edge of the concrete slab at a low angle.

Internally, the architraves, skirting and doors are detailed in an unusual way for housing—all on the same plane. This must have placed a strain on the craftsmanship of a traditional house builder, but it has been remarkably successful. In certain other places the strain seems to have been too much, for instance externally—the high quality precast

roof drained by
3no internal rain
water pipes

rain from face of
columns collected
at every other
floor gallery, and
with water from
galleries drops via
drip holes to
floor below

water from all upper
galleries collected at
first floor level by
10no rain water outlets
connected by ring
pipe to drops from
3no internal rain water
pipes from roof

Diagrammatic illustration of the way rainwater is disposed of, being a system of controlled weathering (scale 1:48)

3

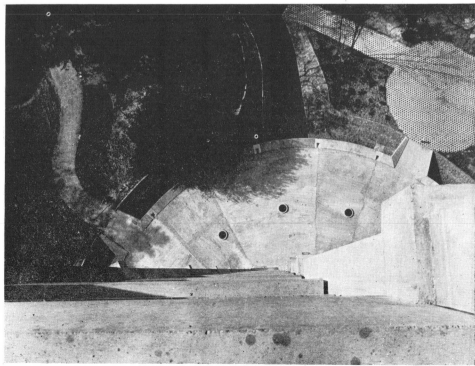

4

5

6

7

8

9

10

3 *Precast concrete cladding to escape galleries, detailed to prevent unsightly staining*
4 *Looking from an escape gallery down to pedestrian deck and landscaped lawns. The hexagonal hollow paving provides access for fire engines*
5 *Detail of precast concrete*

safety rail bolted to stanchion
6 *Living-room, showing floor to ceiling glazing fixed direct to precast concrete mullions*
7 *Partition between living-room and kitchen*
8 *High level fanlight, cooker against wall and shallow depth worktop in kitchen*

9 *Landing with bush hammered in-situ concrete lift shaft*
10 *Detailing of a typical bathroom door frame*
11 *Entrance hall with lifts*

11

12 *Junction between precast and
in-situ concrete above entrance
floor*

concrete cladding was badly chipped in many places during
handling. This was not noticeable from the outside but
it did give an unfinished look to the structure when viewed
at close quarters from inside the flats.

Down-to-floor glazing in each room is dramatic and an
advantage resulting from the decision to have an escape
gallery around each floor serving a single escape staircase.
The protection afforded by these galleries has simplified the
problem of window detailing and gives a sense of spaciousness and security despite the height of most of the flats
above the ground. The hexagonal shape of the block is seen
to advantage in the living-room, where the windows give a
changing quality of light that will be most exhilarating at
different times of day. However, the detailed design of the
opening lights has proved a source of trouble, with the
vertical sliding sashes are very draughty at sill junctions and
the lifting handles on each side of the living-room sash are
too far apart to be used comfortably by anyone of average
size and strength. Ventilation in the kitchen is provided by
one wide fanlight only and while this may be adequate, it is
difficult for a woman of below average height to operate it
without using steps.

The quality of fittings and finishes throughout is high. The
colours of floor finishes and bathroom fittings have been
changed at each floor to allow tenants who prefer a flat with a
particular aspect to have a choice. However, while the
quality of fittings in the kitchen and bathroom in particular
is good, it is a pity that the kitchen work top area is small
and that the cooker is placed in an awkward position against
the larder wall. The lack of width in the kitchen, mentioned
previously, has been overcome to a limited extent by
reducing the depth of one built-in unit but this produces an
irregular shape that is irritating in appearance and destroys
the usefulness of the work surface. One unfortunate
economy cut was the omission of extract ventilation from
the drying cabinet. It seems likely that the normal condensation problems of a kitchen will be aggravated when
this cabinet is used.

In the bathroom a spacious and well finished layout is
marred by the wc pan being placed too close to the adjacent
wall. Also, the linen cupboard in the bathroom has no
heater—a particularly questionable economy in a position
where condensation can be expected.

Another regrettable omission, in view of the type of tenant
for whom this block was built, is that of a delivery hatch
for each flat.

The communal landing at each floor level is generous in area
and attractive in appearance, but the position of the refuse
chute hopper opposite the lifts is unfortunate, requiring care
on the part of the users or good daily cleaning by the caretaker
to prevent the 'luxury' quality of the landing being spoiled
by spilt refuse.

These criticisms of the building may seem mainly to be of
minor details but they do cover many points that cause
everyday irritation to the occupants of housing. However,
they should not detract from the considerable achievements
in the appearance and general planning of this distinguished
and unusual building.

13

14

13 *Detail of precast concrete enclosure to tower, specially designed to accommodate the processes of weathering*
14 *Detail of in-situ concrete base to tower*

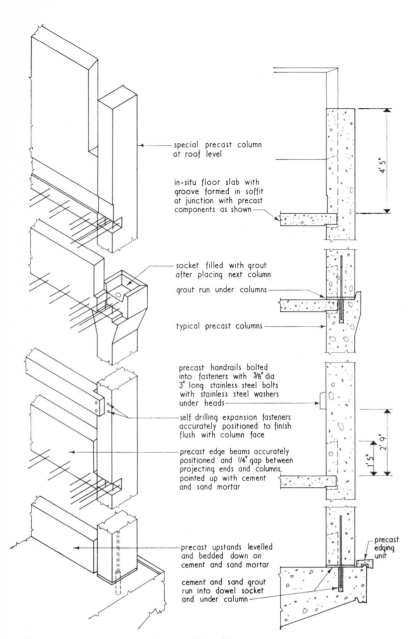

special precast column at roof level

in-situ floor slab with groove formed in soffit at junction with precast components as shown

socket filled with grout after placing next column

grout run under columns

typical precast columns

precast handrails bolted into fasteners with ⅜" dia 3" long stainless steel bolts with stainless steel washers under heads

self drilling expansion fasteners accurately positioned to finish flush with column face

precast edge beams accurately positioned and ¼" gap between projecting ends and columns, pointed up with cement and sand mortar

precast upstands levelled and bedded down on cement and sand mortar

cement and sand grout run into dowel socket and under column

precast edging unit

4' 5"

2' 9"

1' 5"

Detail of precast concrete units assembly (scale 1 : 48)

SUMMARY

Ground floor area: 60·29 m² (649 sq ft) (entrance hall only).
Total floor area: ·9007 m² (96,957 sq ft).
Type of contract: RIBA firm price and other modifications (private edition with quantities).
Tender date: January 1961.
Work began: April 1961.
Work finished: December 1963.
Net habitable floor area: 5007 m² (54 859 sq ft).
Gross floor area: 9007 m² (96 957 sq ft).
Tender price of foundation, superstructure, installation and finishes including drainage to collecting manhole: £264 846.
Tender price of external works and ancillary buildings including drainage beyond collecting manhole: £9 808.
Total: £274 654.

3 Housing at Ravenscroft Road, West Ham

These houses by the MOHLG Development Group were designed to demonstrate the use of the Parker Morris standards in practice for low cost housing and were based on a social survey of family life in the West Ham area of East London

designed by Ministry of Housing and Local Government Development Group
H. J. Whitfield Lewis, chief architect in succession to Cleeve Barr
Oliver Cox, assistant chief architect

staff John Bartlett
Ian Fraser
John Merry
John Noble
Peter Randall
In collaboration with the Borough of West Ham, T. E. North, borough architect

quantity surveyor J. A. Burrell
In collaboration with Ministry of Housing and Local Government
D. W. Nunn, principal quantity surveyor

main contractor John Laing Construction Ltd

CLIENT'S REQUIREMENTS

In this project it is particularly difficult to separate client's requirements from planning aims since both were evolved jointly by the team of ministry architects and sociologists working in collaboration with officers of the local authority. It was agreed to provide only four-, five- and six-person dwellings, larger dwellings being in such small percentages that they could be omitted in a scheme of this size. Smaller dwellings were omitted because they would have called for more complex forms of building, possibly requiring a caretaker. The proportions required were:

4 person: 30 per cent
5 person: 40 per cent
6 person: 30 per cent

This gives an average house size of five people. The net residential density agreed with the local planning authority was 198 persons per hectare (eight per acre), giving 40 houses per hectare (sixteen per acre), and for this site:

11 four-person houses
16 five-person houses
12 six-person houses
39 houses in all.

One car space was required for every house. Fifty per cent are in garages (13 per cent grouped) and 50 per cent in hardstanding (31 per cent grouped). Additional parking for visitors can be along the service roads.

SITE

This lies in the southern part of the London Borough of New Ham, with the docks one mile to the south. The site is flat and is approximately 1 hectare (2·5 acres) in area. It is surrounded by Victorian housing with a probable life of about thirty years. The site was cleared after the buildings were partly demolished by a bomb in the 1939–1945 war and until recently was occupied by temporary bungalows. The South boundary is New Ham Way (formerly Beckton Road), a main traffic route subsequently it was widened carrying heavy traffic day and night and hence a source of noise, fumes, dirt, vibration and possible danger. On the west are the gable walls and garden fences of existing terraces in Ravenscroft Road, on the north Kildare Road and on the east Douglas Road. There is a shortage of housing sites in the borough and it was necessary to develop this one for housing in spite of the nearness of Beckton Road. There is also a shortage of open space in the neighbourhood.

PLANNING

The primary aim of this project was to apply the recommendations in *Homes for today and tomorrow*[1]—particularly higher standards of space, heating and equipment—to produce flexible plans more suited to the needs of the occupants, and to make adequate provision for cars and children. There was no overall plan for the area so the site was considered on its merits.

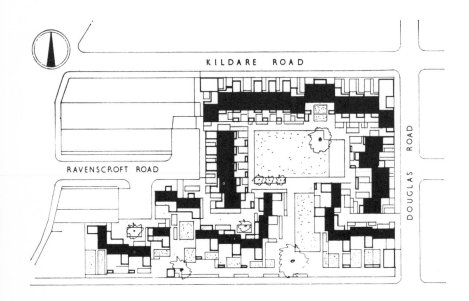

Site plan (scale 1:768)

The part of Ravenscroft Road which divided the site into two parts was closed, so that a central open space could be provided. This is for the particular use of the new tenants and is therefore on the private side of the houses, giving the sequence: access–house–private open space–communal open space. The houses are disposed round the perimeter of the site, largely making use of the existing roads with the exception of Beckton Road. This has been screened by a high brick wall and houses have been kept well back from it. Three-storey houses for larger families have been introduced at certain points to help the composition of the terraces.

A social survey of families living in houses of similar space standards in the district showed the need for the two living-spaces indicated in *Homes for today and tomorrow* to be one associated with the kitchen, acting in part as a dining area, and one a room for leisure, cut off from general activities. The survey also showed the need for the maximum number of single bedrooms, and because this increases the overall area, bedrooms are of minimum functional size but include space for a table or desk. One bedroom is on the ground floor, where it can more easily be used for other activities. This room is generally on the access side of the house, and the kitchen is then on the private side to provide a pleasant outlook and to make it easier for the mother to supervise children playing in the private or communal open space.

APPRAISAL

This scheme of thirty-nine houses was the second project of the Development Group of the Architects Division of the Ministry of Housing and Local Government and was built for the then West Ham (now New Ham) Borough Council. Design work on the scheme was planned to coincide with the publication in November 1961 of the report *Homes for today and tomorrow* prepared by the subcommittee of the Central Housing Advisory Committee with Sir Parker Morris as chairman, and the intention was to investigate ways of applying the recommendations of this report in practice. The results have been published in a design bulletin[2].

Before designing began a social survey was made, organised by the sociologists in the ministry with the architect and administration member of the team taking part. A random sample of thirty-nine families with young children was interviewed and though a small sample such as this could give no definitive assessment it did show the character of family life in this area. Most of the men were manual workers employed locally, with a large proportion of dock workers. Many of the wives also had jobs. Shift work, varied hours and meal times, relatively high income and a high proportion of mechanical equipment: the pattern was varied but definite and underlined the report's recommendations.

It was agreed with the local authority to provide approximately 30 per cent four person, 40 per cent five person and 30 per cent six person houses at a density of 198 persons per hectare (eighty per acre).

As in many parts of London the scattered industry in this area makes satisfactory residential development very difficult. There is a general lack of social amenities—particularly of open space. The site of one hectare (2·5 acres) is north of the docks in the Canning Town area, surrounded by Victorian terrace housing. It is bounded on the south by New Ham Way (formerly Beckton Road), which is a main traffic route subsequently widened—a source of noise and dirt both day and night. The relationship of this road to the site was considered very seriously by the architects. Ravenscroft Road, which originally cut the site in two has

been closed and the remaining roads surrounding the site are typical residential roads.

The main considerations which influenced the site layout were the need to provide one car space per family; the desire to give each house a private garden space with a communal landscaped area; the proximity of the main road.

Using the encircling roads for access, the houses are grouped around the edge of the site enclosing a central space, with the houses along Beckton Road well set back behind a high wall. The variation in types is clearly expressed in the freely grouped masses both in plan and section, yet the whole group reads very successfully as a unified whole. A fine combination of individual expression with collective unity. Some houses have integral garages with visitors' or second car space, some garages are grouped and similarly some houses have individual parking spaces, while others have them grouped. Each house is approached either from the pavement or from a pedestrian court and is provided with a front garden space, with a partially enclosed garden leading onto the communal space. The unfenced front gardens are not very successful and, particularly along Kildare Road, look very shabby and bare except for the occasional tenant's own fencing which shows how much better some form of uniform fencing would have been. Apart from the access gate for gardeners, which is normally kept locked, it is only possible to enter the central space through a house. This space is landscaped and contains various items of play equipment and though it is not intended that older children should play here, it is ideal for smaller children: safe, close to the house and in most cases observable from the kitchen. The gardens leading onto the central space vary in size and the small ones are not very private. But again the tenants have erected their own screens and many of the gardens are attractive. With the development of the general landscaping, this space was destined to form a very pleasant communal centre for the group of houses.

Parker Morris standards

All these aspects of the site layout follow the lines of the Parker Morris report's analysis of the home in its setting. The various types were developed to investigate ways of making provision for extra floor space, flexibility of floor space, two living spaces and improved heating, all at a cost representative of current costs as modified by the report's recommendations. What is most commendable about these aims is that they incorporated the very important point made in the report that the standards set were minima and should not be treated as maxima. All house types are slightly above the minimum areas, but two (4z, 6z3) are substantially larger and have higher heating standards. In order to achieve flexibility of plan layout all the house types incorporate demountable partitions in various positions giving the choice between one big or two smaller rooms or a variation in layout. The housing manager can store these partitions and move, add or remove them as required, but requests have been few.

The design of this sort of partition raises a number of problems. Here the architects decided on a fairly solid partition with reasonable sound reduction but needing a fair time for any modification, because they felt, rightly as it happened, that it would not be changed very often. In this case it is a pity that with its timber finish and full height door it contrasts with the rest of the interior and looks temporary. Also where the partition divides two bedrooms the cupboards have not been incorporated as originally intended and are supplied as separate wardrobes. Built-in cupboards present a wall face and are fairly negative, but as soon as a separate cupboard is supplied it becomes a piece of furniture and as in this case the cupboards are standard

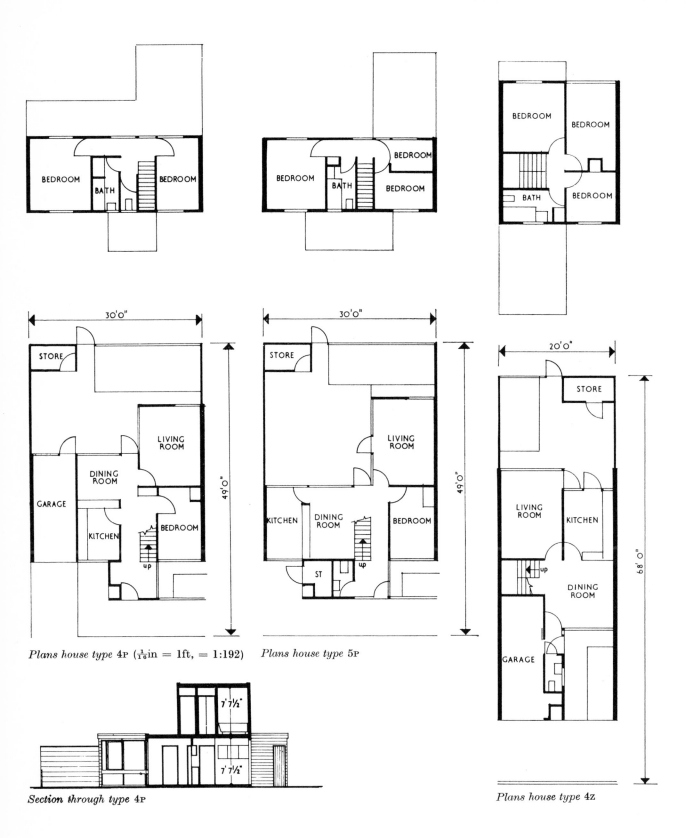

BEDROOM
BATH
BEDROOM

BEDROOM
BATH
BEDROOM
BEDROOM

BEDROOM
BEDROOM
BATH
BEDROOM

STORE
LIVING ROOM
DINING ROOM
GARAGE
KITCHEN
BEDROOM
up

30'0"
49'0"

Plans house type 4P ($\frac{1}{16}$in = 1ft, = 1:192)

STORE
LIVING ROOM
KITCHEN
DINING ROOM
BEDROOM
ST
up

30'0"
49'0"

Plans house type 5P

STORE
LIVING ROOM
KITCHEN
DINING ROOM
GARAGE
up

20'0"
68'0"

Plans house type 4Z

7'7½"
7'7½"

Section through type 4P

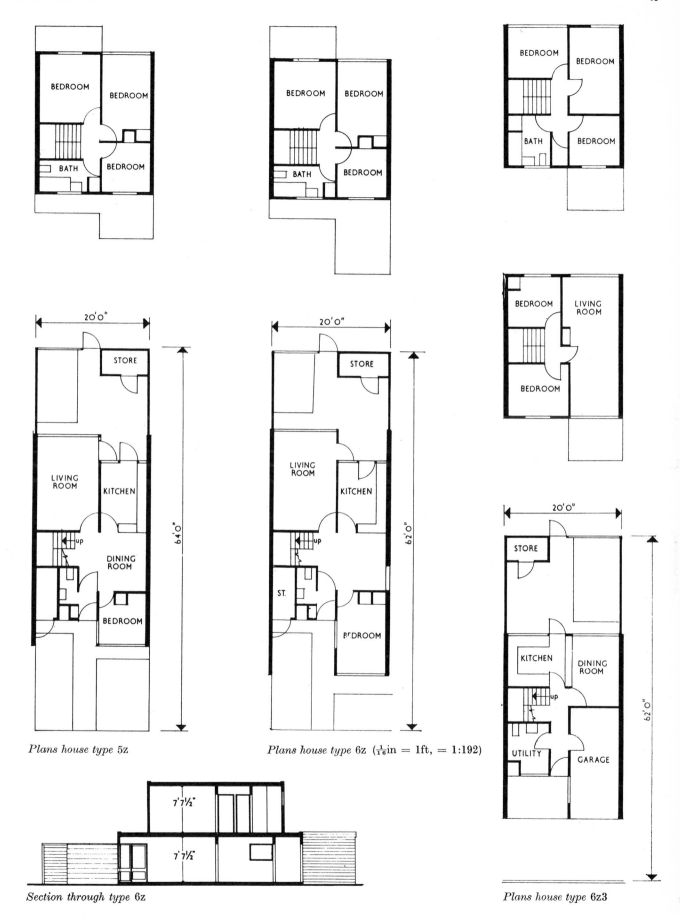

Plans house type 5z

Plans house type 6z $(\frac{1}{16}\text{in} = 1\text{ft}, = 1:192)$

Section through type 6z

Plans house type 6z3

whitewood wardrobe units they tend to clash with the more elaborate and better finished furniture that most of the tenants have. The housing manager will remove these wardrobes and store them if the tenants wish, as a few have, but this does not really solve the problem or conform to the report's recommendations on clothes storage.

One of the wishes revealed in the survey in West Ham was for two living spaces, one of which would cater for meals, but each being able to take the whole family. To achieve this bedroom sizes are kept down, though still allowing space in most cases for a table or desk and chair and the dining area is used as circulation space.

An inseparable aspect of the larger floor areas and the use of the spaces made available is the method of heating. All the houses conform to the recommended standards and two types have higher standards. Considering the pattern of living shown by the survey it was thought that an economical method of heating requiring little attention, capable of a quick heat response but giving some continuous background heat was necessary. Controllable fan-assisted electric block storage heaters were chosen. The installation as planned was found to be unsatisfactory and modifications had to be made during construction, involving a change in the positions of some heaters and the fitting of extra ones. This is unfortunate as it has meant in some cases that the heaters have been moved from convenient positions under the stairs or in bedrooms into the corners of the living-room. These heaters are rather bulky and not very beautiful and seem to require space all around them, so that, as well as sitting rather aggressively in the room, they present a difficult floor covering and cleaning problem in the gap, with its attendant lengths of cable, between them and the wall.

Generally speaking the tenants are very satisfied with the scheme. The space standards, gardens, communal space and whole house heating are all very much appreciated and most tenants are happy to pay the cost of the heating, although there has been some criticism of the amount of glass used, especially around the entrances of some types, and the draught and condensation resulting from this.

House types

Two types were developed, the z and the P with variations in size.

z *type* This type was developed for use around the perimeter of the site and has a relatively narrow frontage. The 4z, designed for four persons, is one of the types planned well above minimum recommendations. There is an extra wc, the net floor area is 82·31 m² (886 sq ft), and heating is provided in two bedrooms. The garage is large and connects to the small entrance lobby which leads into the spacious dining area. There is no clothes cupboard by the entrance. The kitchen is 8·36 m² (90 sq ft) and has the recommended sequence—worktop, cooker, worktop, sink, worktop, but the sink is not positioned near the window. Space is allowed for additional equipment. On the first floor two of the bedrooms can be made into one long room by removing the partition and two of the tenants have asked for this arrangement.

The 5z and 6z are similar plans but with a car parking space instead of a garage and an additional bedroom on the ground floor. This is a very useful room with a variety of uses and has the added possibility of removing the partition and extending the dining space; some tenants of each of these types opted early for this open arrangement. But with the large window, which is right on the front of the house, this space—especially if used as a bedroom—is not very private. A clothes cupboard is provided off the entrance lobby in these cases.

1

2

The kitchen remains the same size in all plans and is probably rather small for the larger families. The upper floor also remains the same. In order to provide a type for the large family which was above the minimum and also to provide a taller element in the composition of the dwellings, a three storey version of the z type was developed. The floor area is 112·88 m² (1 215 sq ft), one bedroom is heated.

1 *View across communal space to north-west. The fences and stores provide a rather grim enclosure, enlivened a little by the planting and fences erected by the tenants*
2 *Enclosed pedestrian access to 5P type houses*
3 *Entrance to 6Z type house. The projecting bedroom with large window is not particularly private*
4 *Projecting glazed entrance to 4P type house*

3

4

The house also has potentially five bedrooms. The dining-room on the ground floor is separate from the entrance hall, and the living-room on the first floor can be in two alternative positions or can be increased in size to include one of the bedrooms. Though not so spacially interesting on the ground floor as the other plans, this house seems to work very well and offers a useful variety of arrangements for a large family.

P type These houses are of a wide frontage type forming the terraces to the southern part of the site and set back from Beckton Road. The 4P house has an integral garage and a ground-floor bedroom and does not follow the pattern of the other plans, having the kitchen on the front of the house

5

6

5 *North elevation to Kildare Road. The planted areas are not very successful and are used as parking places by some tenants, but where tenants have erected their own fences and planted the area the bleakness is relieved*

6 *Elevation to Douglas Road showing the interesting massing with the introduction of the three-storey type*

7 *Path between gardens and wall to New Ham Way—the busy main road—that combines children's play area with access to the communal space*

7

8

9

10

11

8 *Living area house type 5p*
9 *Interior of 5p type showing stairs and dining space beyond. There is no lobby between the front door and this space*
10 *Interior of 6z type showing dining/circulation area with movable screen to bedroom beyond*
11 *Interior of 5p type showing dining area with kitchen beyond*

with the dining space separate, but not cut off from the main circulation. This arrangement is not as successful as that adopted for the z type and includes a lot of circulation space which cannot really be used for any other purpose. There are no movable partitions.

The 5P house is similar but has no garage. The first floor is the same area as the 4P but by combining the wc and bath an attempt has been made to provide an extra bedroom. This results in a 'cabin' bedroom of 3·25 m² (35 sq ft) and a small bedroom of 8·36 m² (90 sq ft). This is probably preferable, for some families, to the larger room being shared and in fact it was intended that this scheme should provide as many single bedrooms as possible. But the method of achieving it with an L-shaped demountable partition, doors close together and loss of space for circulation gives the appearance of an afterthought. A plan which allows for variation should work well whichever choice is made and if it was the intention to accommodate this fourth bedroom the flexibility of the construction on the upper floor, which was one of the aims of the scheme, should have made a more workable plan possible.

This plan also omits the coat cupboard by the front door. But what would seem to be a much more important fault is the lack of an entrance lobby between the front door and the open dining space and staircase. In modifying the heating system an additional heater was placed in the dining area, but this will not alleviate the discomfort every time the front door is opened in winter.

By-laws

Certain by-laws were relaxed for this scheme. These were by-laws relating to party walls in houses with combustible external walls; three-storey dwellings; open space to the front and rear of buildings. The procedure for relaxation under Section 63 of the Public Health Act 1936 was used with the proposals advertised for one month and then confirmed by the minister.

External appearance and construction

Although it was not the intention in this project to explore any new technical approach, as the house plan types developed it became obvious to the architects that some form of construction was needed that allowed for variation of the first floor plan shape in relation to the ground floor. A combination of loadbearing brick and timber columns and beams is used with an infilling of timber studs faced externally with stained softwood weather boarding and internally with aluminium foil backed plasterboard giving a u value of 1·19 (0·21)

This continuous use of boarding for the first floor cladding helps to give the scheme its unity of form, and where relieved by the white brickwork at the ground floor it looks very crisp. But on many elevations the boarding predominates at ground level as well, and all this black timber tends to be a little grim—especially in dull weather. Yet the recessions and projections, with the lively skyline, contrast pleasantly with the rather dull surroundings, and the whole scheme has a unity and clarity of expression that are great assets to the district.

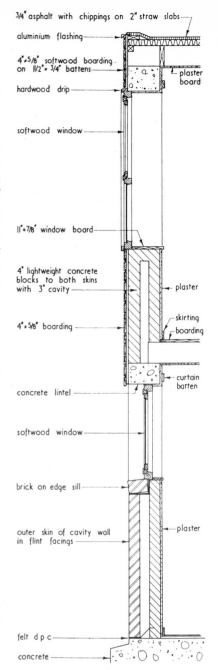

Typical external wall detail (scale 1:32)

SUMMARY

Ground floor area: 2 224 m² (23 942 sq ft).
Total floor area: 3 819 m² (41 108 sq ft).
Type of contract: RIBA.
Tender date: January 1963.
Work began: March 1963.
Work finished: February 1964.
Tender price of foundations, superstructure, installation and finishes including drainage to collecting manhole: £102 185.
Tender price of external works and ancillary buildings including drainage beyond collecting manhole £19 595.
Total: £121 780.

4 Houses at Frome

This complex of twelve low-cost houses was the first part of a proposed development of twenty dwellings which was the winning design in a competition for architects in the south-west of England sponsored early in 1962. In the conditions the basic requirement was for three-bedroom houses to be let at rents comparable to those which could be paid for local authority housing. Although controlled by this strict cost economy the architects produced an attractive development by disposing identical double-courtyard plan units in an interesting relationship within a mature site

designed by	Whicheloe & Macfarlane
staff	Bryan Latty
	Brian Tucker
quantity surveyors	Faithful & Gould
main contractor	T. Holdaway & Son Ltd

CLIENT'S REQUIREMENTS

Skilled technicians are scarce in the printing industry in Britain today, so as a means of attracting senior craftsmen the Somerset firm of Butler & Tanner decided to build houses to let to their staff. Twenty houses were required to be built in two stages—the first of twelve houses, the second of eight—and they were to be economically built to allow rents comparable with those of local authority housing.

A rigid space standard was not laid down in the client's brief. Instead a description of accommodation was given: a living area that lends itself to division by movable screening and that will allow space for meals; three bedrooms—one double, two single; a bathroom with separate wc (the wc might be in the bathroom if an additional cloakroom was provided); good storage facilities for solid fuel, waste bins, prams etc; a garage for every house; heating to the living area by an open fireplace; a means of providing a continuous hot water supply throughout the year. Emphasis was given to the importance of the design of external spaces and landscaping.

SITE

Frome is a north Somerset town with a population of 12 000; it has a market and a diversity of small industries. The 2 hectare (5 acre) site lies on the northern boundary of the town, about 0·8 km (half a mile) from the client's printing works; formerly the garden of a large house, it contains various mature trees planted informally. The land slopes generally towards the south with distant views.

PLANNING

Low cost housing at a low density in an existing woodland site is a brief that is unfortunately all too rare. The first decision was to arrange the houses in such a way that existing planting should be affected as little as possible; this was done by threading the houses around the edge of the existing clearing in the centre of the site. The second aim was to express physically a close-knit community, at the same time designing into the houses the means of escape from too close a contact which can become oppressive in rural housing. This is particularly relevant in a scheme for families whose members work for the same firm. Other aims were to effect complete separation between the circulation of vehicles and pedestrian spaces; to provide a spacious common area for children to feel safe and free to play without restraint; and to design a layout that initially would be satisfactory for twelve houses and would allow for growing into a larger group without extension being apparent.

APPRAISAL

The scheme called for a development of twenty dwellings to go on a gently sloping site, formerly gardens surrounding a large Victorian mansion. In the event, only the first stage of twelve houses has been completed. The houses are arranged in two rows running in line with the contours of the ground, enclosing a space about 21·34 m (70ft) wide which forms an avenue down the centre of the site. The view upon this avenue reveals the essence of the scheme: the avenue itself, of generous width and pleasantly paved, turfed and planted, provides the centre of communal activity. It is here that the residents meet and talk and that the children can play under the discreet supervision of

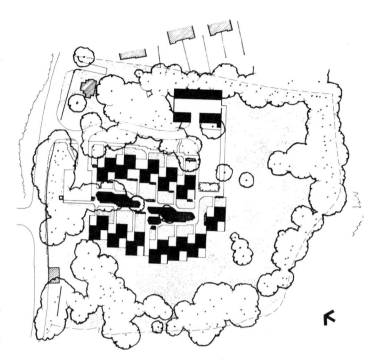

Site plan (1:1750). *The twelve houses shown solid black are complete and form the completed first stage, together with the garages.*

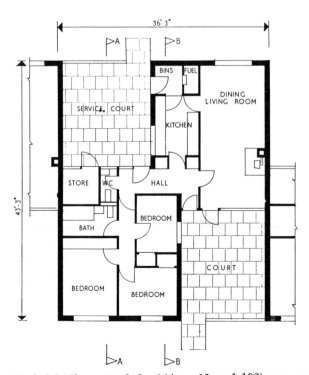

Typical double-courtyard plan ($\frac{1}{16}$in = 1ft = 1:192)

parents in the houses. Although arranged in terrace formation, the houses are planned with deeply recessed courtyards providing a private outdoor space to each unit. In the spacious rural setting, the rhythm of advancing and receding planes along each terrace produces the correct sense of scale while quietly asserting the limits of the individual house unit. In pursuing this problem of integrating the external form of the house with the site the architects were led to adopt low pitched roofs which in turn rise up and fall away from the contours, giving the single-storey units the necessary size in relation to the openness of the surroundings and thence leading the eye gently upwards to the tall trees that encircle the site.

Externally the design of the individual units is reminiscent of Danish domestic architecture in simplicity of detail and careful reduction of scale. It may be noted that the underside of the eaves is 2·057 m (6ft 9in) above floor level (window height being correspondingly reduced).

Solid walls throughout the scheme consist of a light grey sandlime brick; apparently these bricks tend to vary in size, so that the intention of presenting finely detailed brickwork with recessed jointing has sometimes gone astray. The other material used externally is painted timber for doors and windows. These are purpose made, permitting the architects to choose an appropriate size and design for their units, yet keeping within the overall limit of cost (see detail drawings). The only external feature which betrays the tight budget is the bituminous felt roof covering, otherwise the quality of the exterior design is rewarding, giving no sense of the careful economy that must have been exercised.

The houses are all based on the same design which is planned in two wings with courtyards enclosed to front and back. The entrance is from one courtyard which leads into the main living area. There is a second entrance from the other courtyard which fronts the sleeping zone. The entrance hall forms the pivot area joining both entrances and the wings together, producing a very simple circulation system.

Arising from the requirements set out in the competition, the disposition of space within the house is somewhat paradoxical. While the living area, comprising living-room, dining area, kitchen and store, is reasonably spacious, the sleeping area includes three bedrooms of minimal size yet provides, in addition to the bathroom, a second separate wc with handbasin and a second store. More rigorous planning might produce an equally satisfactory plan providing a single storage space and eliminating the duplication of the wc, perhaps allowing the bathroom an external window. This is a question of priorities, and one may question whether the extra space could be allocated to other uses or the saving put towards the cost of a house heating system, in view of the considerable external walling resulting from the courtyard plan. (The Parker Morris report suggests that one wc in a separate compartment is sufficient for a three-bedroom, five-person single-storey dwelling but stresses the importance of a satisfactory heating installation.)

The total floor area exceeds the minimum standard set down in the Parker Morris report for a four-person dwelling. The living-dining area measures 7·32 × 3.35 m (24 ft × 11 ft). The length is generous, but the width could favourably be increased, for, planned as the space is on a long axis with a door at each end, the inevitable traffic flow across the room is obstructed by furniture arranged round the fireplace.

Ceilings in the houses follow the line of the roof; in the living-room this slopes from a high point facing the courtyard to a low point above the dining table, making an attractive feature in this room.

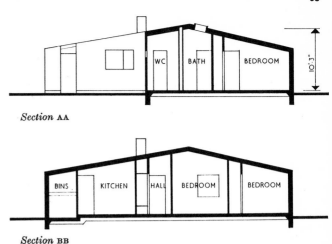

Section AA

Section BB

Section across typical double courtyard (plan on preceding page)

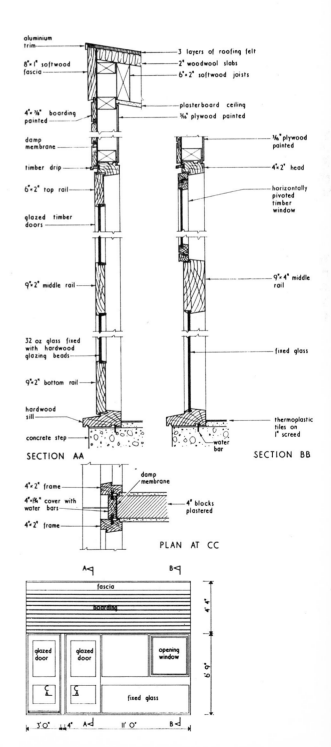

1

2

1, 2 *Upper terrace of five dwelling units. Note the careful reduction in scale of the main design elements.*

The protruding screen wall might have been raked as a continuation of the roof slope

3, 4 *The two internal courts. These are integral to the design of each dwelling.*

The detail design is simple and comprehensive while avoiding awkward junctions

The kitchen is reasonably spacious but, considering the beauty of the surrounding site, has been given an unfortunately dull outlook into the corner of the service court. Internal finishes reflect economy in design; they comprise plaster for walls and ceilings, softwood for joinery and thermoplastic tile floors. Heat insulation is assisted by the use of 50 mm (2in) wood wool slabs on the roof and 76 mm (3in) insulating block in cavity walls. Domestic hot water is provided by an electric immersion heater; the only provision for space heating is a solid fuel stove in the living-room. The site layout includes a separate vehicular access across the top of the site, with an enclosed area with garages for twenty cars at the end of the access road. Thus the major part of the site has sensibly been kept clear of vehicles. The external landscaping has also been carefully considered.

SUMMARY

Ground floor area: 83·7 m² (901 sq ft).
Total floor area: 1 004 m² (10 808 sq ft).
Type of contract: RIBA.
Tender date: December 1962.
Work began: April 1963.
Work finished: June 1964.
Tender price of foundation, superstructure, installation and finishes including drainage to collecting manhole: £30 806.
Tender price of external works and ancillary buildings including drainage beyond collecting manhole: £14 845.
Total: £45 651.

5 *Roofscape view illustrating care for detail and the junction of elements in the design. Only the felt roof is indicative of a tight cost budget. Window units are purpose made and of robust construction.*

6 *Garage block showing the consideration given to elements of the landscape design. The brick screen wall encloses the garages; at the right is a communal tv aerial and beside it a communal dustbin enclosure with capacity for two weeks' refuse from half the dwellings*

7 *Living-room. Note how the ceiling slopes down over the area used for dining. Inevitably the separate pieces of loose furniture make circulation in this room difficult. No doubt in the future the public will accept the sensible solution of built-in furniture for minimal size rooms*

8 *Kitchen. The sink and worktop unit were designed by the architects. This room regrettably looks onto the back of the service court instead of the attractive site*

6

7

8

5 5M Housing at Gloucester Street, Sheffield

designed by	Ministry of Housing and Local Government Development Group H. J. Whitfield Lewis, chief architect in succession to Cleeve Barr Oliver Cox, assistant chief architect
job architect	Patricia Tindale
architects	John Bartlett Adrian Cave David Embling John Girling Martyn Haxworth John Noble Bill Spooner Terry Standley Alan Watson
in collaboration with	Sheffield City Council J. L. Womersley, city architect
quantity surveyors	D. W. Nunn, principal quantity surveyor Bernard Critchlow Arnold Rayner Richard Sharp
main contractor	Sheffield Public Works Department

Two housing schemes are analysed which although using the same 5M system developed in the early 1960s by the Development Group of the Ministry of Housing and Local Government, provide an interesting comparison in respect of size of development, house types and treatment of sites as residential environments.

Introduction

Design work on the 5M shortlived modular system by the Ministry of Housing and Local Government's Development Group was started early in 1962 and extensively exploited during the 1960s.[1]

The ministry had decided to develop a building system which would not only be a first contribution to the solution of the housing shortage in terms of economy and productivity but would also allow inclusion of a variety of house types and answer the problems of flexible planning shown up by various attempts to apply the recommendations of the Parker Morris report of 1961.

Supply of components was to be organised under a system of bulk ordering from nominated suppliers. Prototypes were required not only to develop the system but also to obtain a programme by selling the system to potential clients. As Sheffield, Leeds and Hull were at that time setting up their Yorkshire Development Group to rationalise housebuilding, the MOHLG approached each city for a site.

Four prototypes adjacent to a Sheffield site were completed at the end of 1962 and developments included in the first programme included York University (sixteen houses) Hull (100), Leeds (150), Catterick (370) and Sheffield. At Sheffield the ministry was to carry its work further by developing the small Gloucester Street site (39 houses) itself, while Sheffield Corporation was to use the system in a scheme of 162 dwellings at Woodhouse.

The system used at both Sheffield sites was a considerably revised version of the prototype system, and is known as mark 1A. A mark 1B, with minor modifications to the detailing of external walls and windows, was used in a later programme of 2 500 houses at various sites in the city. The 5M system is a lightweight system for one- and two-storey houses based on a planning grid of 508 mm (1 ft 8 in) —5M—and consisting of a series of standard components which can be used to produce a variety of house plans and external treatments. All components can be man-handled.

A frame of steel stanchions, perimeter plywood box beams and internal timber flitch-beams is erected on a lightly reinforced site slab. Floor and roof joists, spanning up to 4.572 m (15 ft), are slotted onto hangers on the beams and the roofing is completed. Floor-to-ceiling timber cladding frames, boarded panels and windows are fixed between perimeter beams, and other external claddings such as tile hanging and concrete panels are fixed to the frames. A weatherproof shell is thus provided within which internal work can proceed.

The first floor is boarded, the staircase fixed and ceilings and external walls lined with plasterboard. Party walls— probably the most significant technical advance in the system—are then erected.

Each party wall consists of two leaves of solid laminated plaster board, each 38 mm (1½ in) thick, with a glass fibre quilt hung in the cavity, providing sound reduction and fire resistance to the required standards. Stud partitions with a plaster-board finish are then fixed, and preassembled internal doors and frames positioned. Timber trim is restricted to skirtings, window and door architraves in precut lengths.

CLIENT'S REQUIREMENTS

The project was undertaken by the ministry's architects, sociologists and quantity surveyors, as part of the Sheffield city slum clearance programme. Because of the smallness of the project—the site of 0.94 hectares (2.355 acres) was a part of a large future redevelopment area—the city did not think it important to maintain the precise proportions of house sizes required in the city generally. Moreover, because the project was to be a pilot scheme for the 5M housing system, it was not possible to provide within this part of the redevelopment scheme the one- and two-person accommodation usually contained within flats. In the event, the following scheme was agreed within the city:

Four-person houses	12
Five-person houses	23
Six-person houses	4
	—
Total	39

This produced a density of 198 persons per hectare (eighty persons per acre); the average of 247 persons per hectare (100 ppa) for the redevelopment scheme as a whole was to be obtained by the inclusion of flats in other parts of the scheme.

One car space was required for every house, a proportion to be provided in the form of garages. Additional parking for visitors' cars was required off the perimeter road.

SITE

The site lies about a mile to the west of the city centre and was part of an area of back-to-back and other mid- or early-Victorian housing surrounded by larger houses and by the new university and hospital buildings. The site is 0.94 hectares (2.335 acres) in area and has a cross fall of 7.315 m (24 ft), almost 1 in 10, from west to east. The ground to the east continues to slope away giving fine views over the city centre to the range of hills beyond. The site is bounded on three sides by roads; on the fourth by Victorian housing due to be cleared.

Although the site was formerly covered with back-to-back houses, the courtyards contained several trees, four of which were fine enough to retain.

PLANNING

In the development of the site layout the objectives were as follows:

1 That the road access should be confined to the existing road pattern, and access to an adjacent school and university building maintained. It was envisaged that at some future date the road, which is at present a complete loop, might be broken at any one of a number of points at the south-east corner of the site to provide a pedestrian route through the later parts of the redevelopment scheme. The layout should be designed to allow a choice for future development.

2 As many houses as possible should have views over the valley from the living-rooms.

3 That gardens and living-rooms should have sunlight during the afternoons.

4 That the sequence road, house, private garden, public open space should be maintained.

5 That the existing trees should be retained.

The houses were designed in the light of the recommendations of *Homes for today and tomorrow* and as a result of experiences on the West Ham project (Chapter 3) a social inquiry was conducted at Sheffield among tenants in post-war housing.[2] Among the conclusions drawn from this were the following:

1 That the four-person houses were likely to be under-occupied and space standards should therefore be the minimum recommended by *Homes for today and tomorrow;*

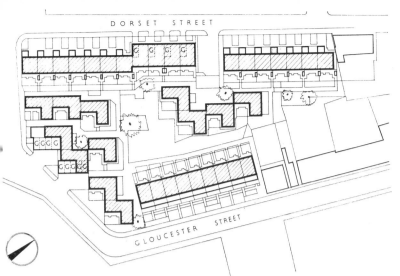

2

Gloucester Street site. This was a pilot scheme by the MOHLG *and incorporated four house types (see plans)* 1:1536

2 *Typical street adjacent to west site boundary*
3 *Ramp down from*

visitors' car park. Where standard unwrought fencing becomes a ramp balustrade

it is capped by a wrought hardwood fillet. Type 6B houses are on the right with

full height glazing to first floor living-room. Ahead is an expertly pruned tree

2 That two living-rooms were required, and the one which was likely to be used as a dayroom and for dining should be closely related to the kitchen. This is particularly important for large families, and their houses should not have a dining-room used for through circulation because meals are going on all day.

3 That the main living-room should not be a through room.

4 That an upstairs living-room would be acceptable provided that one living-room is on the ground floor.

5 That tenants welcomed innovations in house plans.

6 That a high standard of furnishing and decoration should be expected in Sheffield.

7 That privacy in gardens is appreciated.

APPRAISAL

Site treatment

The first quality of this scheme that becomes evident is its ability to stimulate visually by means of surprises and variety of form and texture. This may not be the aspect one considers first in the planning process, but it is always a quality one is pleased to find in the final solution.

The site can be entered from a number of directions. From the visitors' car park off Dorset Street one drops, by a robustly-detailed ramp 3, into a small courtyard from which a group of single-storey (type 4c) houses can be entered. One of the seven preserved trees stands here, expertly trimmed to a good shape. To right and left run distribution paths overlooked on the north by a 1·83 m (6 ft) bank to the terrace of 5A and 6B houses which line the top of the site 1. Concrete steps give access to the gardens above and it was noticed that a few tenants had tied up the garden gates at the top This may have been simply to keep small children in, but the steps—178 mm × 254 mm (7 in × 10 in)—may have been considered too steep for safety. The bank is planted with bushes because it is too steep for easy mowing. From the south-west corner of the site there are three accesses through a group of type 4c houses. One is along the path mentioned above. The second runs between a 1·54 m (5 ft) garden retaining wall and a blank house wall (the electricity substation is integrated into this block 4) and leads into a small courtyard 5 from which access is gained to one of the houses and from which another alley 6 leads into the central open space. The third access leads off the forecourt of one of the two groups of garages which are concentrated in this corner. Since the site is small, maximum walking time from garage to house is about two minutes, the average about forty-five seconds.

From the south-east boundary ramps run up on both sides of the terrace of type 5D houses (7 and 8) and are linked across the back of the terrace to give garden access. The scheme has the tight-knit quality and intimate spatial variety appropriate to urban housing and its success in these terms can be attributed to a number of factors. Full advantage was taken of the steep fall of the site—almost 1 in 10—to achieve sharp changes of level 9 and, with the use of a good deal of cut and fill, retaining walls are formed which help to enclose spaces and circulation routes, as well as giving privacy to gardens above these routes. This approach can be fruitfully contrasted with that employed on the Woodhouse site. The cost allowance, system whereby money allocated to site works is justified by site conditions obviously was of help.

The materials used on site works—precast concrete paving slabs, dark brick retaining walls and substantial three-rail timber garden fences—produce a richness of texture that is complemented by the grassed central open space and the exposed aggregate finish to the precast concrete panels of the houses.

The colours of the finish to the boarded panels on the houses at ground floor level—red and yellow ochres—strike perhaps the only discordant note. These were used at the instigation of the city architect at the time, who thought that these small developments in drab areas needed some highlighting to avoid being swamped. Yet, time and again, in the gloom and soot of a British industrial town one comes across these attempts at gay splashes of colour, looking, somehow, more tawdry and drab than their surroundings. Sheffield is unlikely ever to have a Mediterranean atmosphere, however many clean air Acts are passed, and in a town with the magnificently grim and entirely indigenous Park Hill and Hyde Park blocks, the choice here was an unfortunate deviation. All the private gardens are quite small—mostly about 4·88 m (16 ft) deep—and some tenants expressed a desire for larger ones. This depended, however, on whether gardening happened to be one of the husband's hobbies. The only way to solve this eternal problem would be to arrange for a garden boundary which could vary between a maximum and minimum—although it would probably disturb the housing manager and introduce another initial planning condition. Despite the substantial character of the garden fences mentioned above, some tenants expressed a desire for even more privacy. It is, however, surely reasonable to expect a tenant to provide whatever absolute screening, in the way of hedges and so on, that he feels he needs, as long as the architect, by siting and levels, provides the situation in which this can easily be done. At Gloucester Street the situation has been provided: a 914 mm (3 ft) hedge would give absolute screening to most gardens—and anyway some tenants require to supervise their children playing in the central open space and therefore prefer semi-open fencing.

Even though the gardens are small, the central open space is still fairly restricted and the size of the scheme prohibits much flexibility in the use of space. It would therefore be unreasonable to complain that no specific children's play space has been provided—certainly there is no room for a paved area for ball games—and the site itself is almost an adventure playground with its ramps, steps, grass banks and narrow alleys, its sense of intimacy and enclosure and the copious provision of walls and corners.

Looking back again over the site from the elevated level of the car park, one sees that the drabness of roofscape so common to low-rise flat-roofed buildings is largely alleviated by the variety of plan shapes and changes of level. This is fortunate for the tenants of the type 6B houses with their first floor living-rooms at the top of the site. At least the roofs are noticeably clear of tv aerials, a master aerial being provided in the car park, cabled to tv jacks in the living-rooms.

It is worth noting that the compactness which is the key to the success of this layout has been achieved with no relaxation of planning regulations for space about buildings.

Type 4c

This is an L-shaped, single-storey two-bedroom house. It was planned within the minimum Parker Morris net area since a preliminary survey showed that this size of house was likely to be underoccupied. The re-entrant angle encloses a south-facing garden on two sides and all windows to habitable rooms face into this garden.

The main entrance door is set into one of the blind walls and the public access path can therefore run adjacent to this wall without disturbing tenants. Since the blind wall of an adjacent house usually forms the third side of the garden, the minimum of screening is needed to give privacy from the south. In fact, on this site privacy is almost built-in since there is either a substantial drop beyond the garden boundary, as in the group at the south corner of the site, or the ground slopes steeply away, as in the group set on top of the grass bank in the central open space.

The second bedroom can be split into two and provision is made for a second door in this event, but no clothes storage space is provided to either bedroom apart from a cupboard in the corridor.

A difficult question to answer here was whether to provide specific heating to the bedrooms. Since these were on the same level as the living areas there was unlikely to be much convected overspill. Ducting of warm air from the heating unit with associated fans and ducts, or provision of a second unit in the bedroom area, would have involved extra capital expense reflected in increased rents. It was considered that since the bedrooms would rarely be used as bedsitters, provision of socket outlets for the tenants' own electric heaters was a more reasonable solution.

First floor plan house type 5D

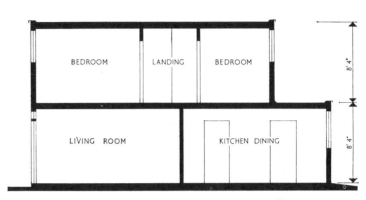

Cross section house type 5D

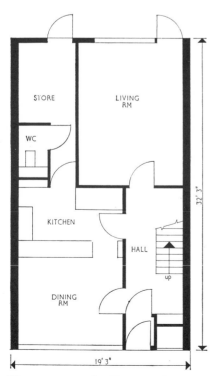

House types on the Gloucester Street site are shown on this page and opposite.
Ground floor plan house type 5D
($\frac{1}{10}$in = 1ft = 1:120)

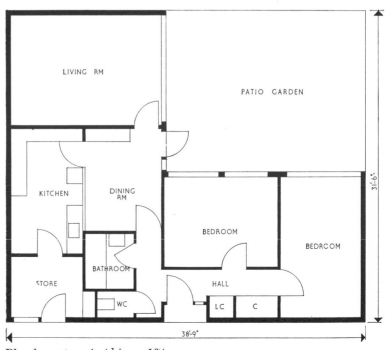

Plan house type 4C ($\frac{1}{10}$in = 1ft)

4

5

6

7

8

4 *South-west boundary of site showing, left to right: type 5A terrace; access to site; L-shaped type 4C with steps up to garden; access leading to courtyard shown in 5; electricity substation*
5 *The court from which access is gained to main door, store door and dustbin recess of a type 4C house. Face fixing of the asbestos cement fascia—one reason for the use of plywood at Woodhouse—is evident here. One waits impatiently for the tree to grow*
6 *Alley from court, shown in 5 to central open space. Retaining wall to type 4C garden is on left. This photo shows how absolute privacy could easily be achieved in these houses*

7 *Alley along north flank wall of 5D terrace looking towards prototypes on the other side of Gloucester Street. Although eight different textures can be seen, there is visual cohesion because of the tough uncompromising character common to all*
8 *Access to site by ramp along south flank wall of type 5D terrace, showing first floor set-back and bold restriction of space up to the point of entry to the central open space*
9 *Looking west towards central open space with type 4C house on left. There is ample evidence here of the imaginative use of materials and exploitation of natural features on the site*

The kitchen layout is not ideal, the cooker being separated from the sink by through circulation to the store. The kitchen is separated from the dining area by a screen which stops below eye level, thus allowing a view through the glazed wall into the garden and supervision of children playing there. Natural light to the kitchen had to be supplemented by a rooflight, which is a small price to pay for the overall advantages of this type of plan.

Internal access to the dustbin is provided from the store by means of a lid over the dustbin recess. Access from the outside, through the store to the kitchen, is useful in the depositing of bicycles, but garden tools and materials have to be brought through the kitchen and dining-room: this problem is solved elsewhere either by providing a separate garden store or, where bicycle access is possible through the garden, by placing the store on that side. The wc and bathroom are internal, naturally ventilated through grilles in the roof.

At the main entrance no cupboard is provided for outdoor clothes—a noticeably useful provision elsewhere—and the recessing of the door, to bring it a little off the public path, has meant the loss of a reasonable entrance space. Prams

First floor plan house type 5A. *The bedroom on the right is divisible into two with the addition of a door*

First floor plan house type 6B

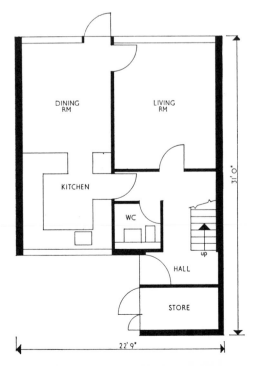

Ground floor plan house type 5A (1:120)

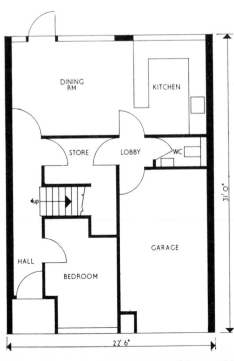

Ground floor plan house type 6B ($\frac{1}{10}$in = 1ft)

10

11

10 *Terraces of types* 5A *and* 6B *from Dorset Street. The cladding of the projecting store to type* 5A *is detached for access to the dustbin recess, but this is now under the kitchen window. The master tv aerial is the only protuberance of this sort on the whole site*

11 *Type* 6B *balustrade between living-room and staircase. Entrance to bedroom 2 is just round the corner on left. Note typical pendent lighting fitting adapted to low ceiling*

would be particularly difficult to manoeuvre, although the preliminary social survey showed that this size of house tended not to be chosen by couples with very young children.

These houses were being designed at a time when the ministry was interested in the possible use of prefabricated plumbing units in the upgrading of slum housing. The Development Group therefore developed a heart unit with a large contractor and installed it in half a dozen of this house type. This was an experiment quite outside the 5M system because, in principle, all 5M components could be man-handled while the heart units required the use of a crane.

Type 5A
This house type is incorporated in the two terrace blocks running along Dorset Street on the north-west boundary of the site; it has three bedrooms for five persons.

The entrance is sheltered by a projecting store **10**, accessible only from the outside: a separate garden store on the other side of the house solves the multiple problem of general storage. The entrance hall could be pleasantly spacious but is visually constricted by a hefty slatted screen to the staircase. A cupboard under the stairs provides adequate storage for outdoor clothes and footwear. A wc, with wash-basin, is available at this level, without a window but with natural ventilation.

12 *Kitchen from dining area. The duct below the ceiling discharges warm air under the living-room window above. Sink and cooker are in a continuous run alternating with work tops— the ideal arrangement—but the sink corner is rather cramped with washer and refrigerator in front of the draining board*

12

The kitchen is well planned with the sink and cooker in a continuous run of ample work top. An interesting device here is the lid set in the work top, through which rubbish can be dropped directly into the dustbin below; the dustbin can be removed from the outside. Although there were initial suspicions that the arrangement would be un-hygienic, there has been no problem with smell and the tenants find it extremely convenient. Obviously its success relies on the adequacy of the seal around the lid and such a device in production could probably use something like a flexible plastic lipping: the wood section used here, even if well executed, may be liable to damage and subsequent unpleasant leakage.

The heating unit stands between kitchen and dining-room, on the living-room wall, discharging into these three rooms and into bedrooms **1** and **3** over. Bedroom 2 is a twin with two doors, and half the houses are provided with a demountable partition to form two small rooms of .5·11 m² (55 sq ft) each. Clothes storage is provided to bedroom 3 only. The bathroom is clearly planned, with easy access to opening lights. As this house has a frontage of 6·55 m (20 ft 10 in) all rooms including kitchen and bathroom are on an outside wall.

Type 5D

A terrace of nine houses of this type encloses the site on its east boundary. The angle between Dorset Street and this boundary means that while living-rooms facing downhill from Dorset Street have a south-east aspect, here they would be facing almost east. There was an obvious advantage, therefore, in placing the living-rooms on the uphill side facing into the site so that they get the afternoon sun.

This is the only house type with a draught lobby to the main entrance door; in principle, this is a valuable provision. With a restricted allowance of space, however, the conflict is always between providing a trim lobby which knots up the entrance and a recessed porch which gives some protec-

tion to callers but little to the heating system in a winter gale. Pram access into the hall would be direct and simple. With a house frontage of .5·33 m (17 ft 6 in) the kitchen receives indirect light and tends to be a little gloomy on a dull day.

The downstairs wc is arranged off a lobby between the kitchen and the store, a sink having been provided in the latter space. Washing facilities are therefore available for the husband returning from work (the major industries in Sheffield tend to be rather grubby ones) and the store could alternatively be used as scullery or laundry. The kitchen, as in type 4c, suffers from the splitting of the work area by through circulation. With the internal kitchen and the store on the garden side, it was not possible to arrange internal access to the dustbins.

No flexibility is provided in the bedroom arrangement— the shape of bedroom 2 would invite division into two but is without twin access—but ample clothes storage is available. Again owing to the narrow frontage, the bathroom is internal, ventilated by a roof grille. Heating provisions are as for type 5A.

The first floor set-back caused no structural problems because of the lightweight, framed character of the 5M system.

Type 6B

This is the largest of the house types; planned with four bedrooms for six persons, it has a frontage of 6·35 m (20 ft 10 in) and a net area, to Parker Morris standard, of 92·50 m² (1000 sq ft). It is the only house type with its own garage and is found in the Dorset Street terrace.

The most interesting planning point is a first floor living-room which the tenant interviewed found pleasant, since it commands a fine view of the site and the city beyond, and very useful because her children could play upstairs on a wet day and were 'safely tucked away' while she worked in the kitchen. The arrangement also allows a south-east aspect to all three living-working areas. The staircase is left open to the living room **11** so as to maintain continuity with the living areas downstairs and to provide supplementary light to the stairs.

With this arrangement, one of the small bedrooms is dislodged from the first floor and is placed next to the main entrance, making an ideal bedsitter for an older child who would almost have his own front door.

The entrance hall for a house of this size is rather mean, being a mere passage, but this has allowed a very generous work bench in the garage which the husband found an absolute delight. Internal access to the dustbin is also gained from the garage.

The kitchen is well-planned with uninterrupted work area **12,** and lobby access to the internal wc, as in type 5D, is found here.

The heating unit is placed in the internal store and with circulation through the store from hall to lobby, little usable floor area remains—unfortunately—as this is the only space for outdoor clothes.

Warm air is taken across the dining-room ceiling in a rather obtrusive duct **12,** to discharge in the ideal position under the living-room window. Warm air is also provided to kitchen, dining-room and bedrooms 1 and 3 although, as discussed in a subsequent section, the heater capacity is sufficient to heat all other areas when doors are left open. Although this bedroom is slightly smaller in area than bedroom 1, the tenants interviewed used this as a master bedroom, which is probably the most sensible arrangement, since the husband and wife would be the last to retire. However, in the case of illness or a late sleeper, the access from bedroom to bathroom past the living area could be an embarrassment.

The two other bedrooms and the bathroom are *en suite* off a lobby entered through a door from the living-room. The internal bathroom is well planned and the linen cupboard generous, but very little clothes storage space is provided and the tenant confirmed that a cupboard in bedroom 1 or 2 would have been useful.

6 5M Housing at Woodhouse, Sheffield

designed by	W. L. Clunie, city architect in succession to J. L. Womersley Jesse Dean, assistant city architect in succession to Bernard Warren
job architects	Don Kendrick Roger Wallis
assistant	Fred Illingworth
quantity surveyors	A. W. Lancaster, chief quantity surveyor T. A. P. Barker, chief quantity surveyor (housing) Charles Higginbottom
main contractor	Sheffield Public Works Department

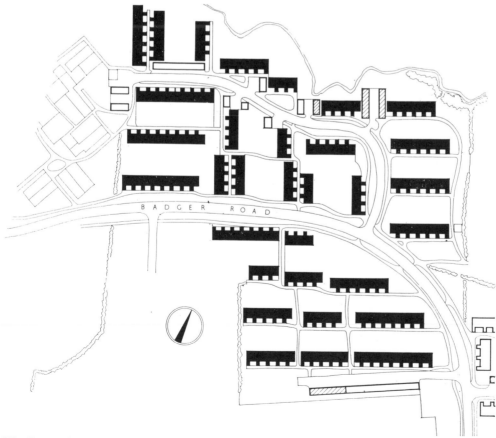

Woodhouse site plan. Garages are indicated with heavy enclosing line and only those shown hatched have been completed to date (1: 2500)

CLIENTS' REQUIREMENTS

The scheme was part of a larger project for the extension of Woodhouse Village within the Sheffield boundary. To compare the 5M system directly with other forms of industrialised construction it was decided to use one house size and plan throughout the scheme. This was to be a three-bedroom five-person type and there were to be 162 dwellings with a net density of 150 pph or 60 per acre.
One car space was to be provided for each house, and one quarter to be provided initially in the form of garages.
The layout was to be simple with the minimum of site works to allow speedy erection of the components and completion of the work.

SITE

The site lies within a new housing area north-east of the village centre of Woodhouse, approximately 6·5 km (four miles) south-east of Sheffield and within the city boundary. The whole area slopes to Shirtcliffe Brook, the northern boundary of the site, at a gradient of approximately 1 in 9. The other boundaries are the main railway line to the east, and a fringe of private development to the south. The site was originally agricultural land with no trees except for those bordering the stream. The railway is on an embankment which blocks any view eastwards; the prospect to the north is across fields to a distant private housing estate, and north-west to a local landmark, Handsworth Church. There is a new spine road through the area and the housing is grouped in culs-de-sac off this road.
Other housing is mainly of an industrialised type with some traditionally built maisonettes south of the spine road. Most of the area has been subjected to subsidence from coal mining and the land, although stable, was considered unsuitable for any but light structures.

PLANNING

The 5M housing area is divided into two parts by the spine road; to allow the greatest freedom of pedestrian movement access generally to be by footpath with the links between each house group. The main planning aim was to provide pleasant private housing groups segregated from traffic. Since the slope of the land northwards provides views from the upper floors, and this aspect gives better privacy, living rooms on this side provide a more pleasant arrangement than on the south where they are rather overshadowed. Daylighting is supplemented by a glazed screen between kitchen and living room.

APPRAISAL

Site treatment
Although the same building system was used at both Gloucester Street and Woodhouse, there is a marked difference of approach reflected in the house plans and in the site treatment and layout.
The difference in house plans reflects mainly a difference of attitudes, and this also accounts in part for the disparity in quality of site layouts. But the comparative bleakness of the Woodhouse site is due in the main to the previous bold, and entirely commendable, support that the Sheffield Corporation gave to J. L. Womersley in Park Hill, Hyde Park and other developments. By the time Woodhouse came to be financed, the housing revenue account was tight. The consequences can be seen in the largely monotonous

siting of blocks, primarily on the basis of economy, **1** background; avoidance of site modelling, resulting in uncomfortably sloping gardens; fencing **1**, **2** which is so flimsy that tenants immediately supplement it with their own trellis work **3**; absence of any play areas except the unbroken stretches of grass between blocks; pacuity of garage provision; in-situ concrete paths **4** and not a tree in sight (to be remedied in future landscaping).
Another reason for the siting arrangements and for the use of one house type throughout was that the scheme was to be an exercise in cost and productivity to complement the pilot scheme at Gloucester Street. In the pilot scheme the ministry naturally wanted to test the limits of the system, and the scheme itself was small with only thirty-nine houses; it was unlikely therefore that it would show any savings on traditional construction or give reliable information on productivity.
The problem facing the designers of the Woodhouse scheme at drawing board stage was that, as the system was completely new, there were no comparative cost or manhour data to enable them to decide how rigorous they needed to be. In the event it appears that they played too safe, for the final cost of the Woodhouse house was £376 below the tender estimate, which itself was comparable with the cost for traditional construction.
Now that these and other schemes have provided comparative data, it is hoped that architects will be able to achieve a better balance between the quality of the environment and cost and productivity.

House type
The one house type used at Woodhouse has three bedrooms and is for five persons. It has two storeys with a net area of 88·26 m² (950 sq ft)—over Parker Morris.
Very little attempt was made, however, to follow up any of the more radical recommendations of the report. The now traditional living-dining area, for instance, adopted at a time when we were trying to accustom ourselves to the more restricted spaces of economy housing, cuts right across the recommendation on provision of multiple living areas where different kinds of activity can be carried out. No attempt has been made to provide flexibility in bedroom sizes or numbers. As far as their use as bed-sitters is concerned, the capacity of the heating unit could prove to be inadequate, as is the provision of only one socket outlet to the small bedroom. The entrance to the house is screened by a freestanding store. This is not built in system construction as the steel frame would have been uneconomical in this situation, but it is regrettable that the junctions of the self-supporting concrete panels, with their crude timber cover plates, do not equal the standard of the system detailing. And with the main garden on the other side of the house, the position of this store necessitates carting garden tools and materials through the living-room.
Turning into the entrance porch, formed by a roof link between house and store, unbelievably one comes face to face with a dustbin standing in the open next to the front door. Despite the low timber screen on the line of the party wall, one can see more of these sentinels guarding the entrances to the next four or five houses.
Inside the front door, the hall is comfortably generous and a wc with wash basin and coat hooks is immediately available. There is also a cupboard in the wc where wellingtons, umbrellas and coats can be neatly stored. Pram access into the hall and the parking space under the stairs is reasonably easy, but some tenants complained of the 178 mm (7 in) riser to the front door step.

1 *and* **1a** *Site planting not yet complete but grass already looking unable to prevent the medley of fences and uncontrolled contour making a disturbing outlook.*

The kitchen **5** is quite a large room of 11·61 m² (125 sq ft) with a continuous L-shaped run of working surface and space in the opposite corner for a small dining area. It seems perverse to allocate space to duplicated dining areas (a kitchen is hardly the ideal place to carry out any other activity such as homework) when the main dining area is also unsuitable for a second activity.

The living-dining room, with its oddly detailed heating unit, faces north, south, east or west—as the case may be. Two-thirds face north.

The first reason given for this is that the view in this direction is better—if you go upstairs so as to see over the adjacent terrace downhill. An arrangement which took advantage of this (such as the first floor living-room to the Gloucester Street type 6B) may have justified the argument but here it is small compensation for loss of sun in the living-room to see a view by starlight before turning in. One could do that anyway, whichever way the living-room faced.

The second reason is that the rooms are more overlooked from uphill on the south side, and this is probably true, accepting the practically undeveloped site and minimal site works provided. Where living-rooms face north, in order to allow sunlight to penetrate the wall between dining-room and kitchen is glazed—in that rippled glass that makes people moving on the other side appear to flow like amoeba.

On the first floor, the plan is very compact and clothes storage cupboards quite generous if a little misplaced—a cupboard is invariably required in bedroom 3, where the furniture is made up of bits and pieces, but rarely in bedroom 1 where a full suite is displayed. One wonders what motives lay behind the provision of three lights to the windows of the smallest bedroom (and bedroom 1) but only two to bedroom 2, which looks underlit. External aesthetic seems to be the only answer. The linen cupboard is heated by warm air which filters through a perforated hardboard panel from the flue housing.

1 a

Technical comment on both schemes

Heating system

The heating system used throughout both schemes is gas warm air, ducted from a heating unit in the dining-room or kitchen to living-room, landing and some bedrooms. The discharge grilles are closable in all cases but at Woodhouse a cut-off is provided to all upstairs rooms. This is operated from the heating unit and is undoubtedly useful where bedrooms are not used largely as bedsitters, as it obviates

Ground floor plan of house type used at Woodhouse
($\frac{1}{10}$in = 1ft, = 1:120)

First floor plan

Cross section ($\frac{1}{10}$in = 1ft, = 1:120)

2 *Not one foot of excavation was carried out to master the natural site levels, and these strange warped gardens are a typical result*

the closure of individual grilles and avoids heat loss from ducts. A thermostat is provided in the living-room only, which means that if bedrooms are to be heated at night, the living-room must be continuously heated to operate the thermostat. Capacities of heating units vary considerably between the two schemes. At Gloucester Street, type 4c (single-storey, 162 m³ = 5 700 cu ft) has a unit with a capacity of 6·75 kW (23 000 Btu/h); types 5A and 5c (two-storey, 195·5 m³ = 6 900 cu ft) 10·25 kW (35 000 Btu/h); and type 6B (two-storey, 215 m³ = 7,600 cu ft) 12 kW (41 000 Btu/h). At Woodhouse (two-storey, 203·7 m³ = 7 200 cu ft) the heating unit capacity is only 6·75 kW (23 000 Btu/h), which must be a minimum for the heated areas and cannot allow overspill to those areas not specifically heated, ie small bedroom, hall and wc.

A factor which is probably relevant to the tenants' satisfaction is that most tenants came from houses heated by traditional open fires with multifarious supplementary units such as paraffin heaters and electric fires—after which any form of central heating was probably a thermostatic heaven. All tenants interviewed confirmed that running costs, as far as they could tell so far, were comparable with those of the traditional set-up.

In all cases the positions of grilles were chosen on the basis of economy of ducting. The housing manager mentioned that trouble had been experienced with warping of doors where grilles were too close.

External finishes

The two standard finishes to the external boarding were Solignum, and Arpax, the latter being used at Gloucester Street only. Arpax has a considerably longer guaranteed life in normal weathering conditions (some difficulty was experienced at Woodhouse with shrinking and warping of boards), but since it is a skin type of finish it would be, although tough, susceptible to chipping and impact damage where used at ground floor level as at Gloucester Street.

At Woodhouse, plywood fascias were substituted for the asbestos cement used at Gloucester Street to avoid visible face fixing.

Internal finishes

Floor finishes are thermoplastic tile to the ground floor and softwood boarding to the first. A number of tenants expressed a wish for brighter colours on the kitchen floor—usually the only area exposed anyway—and perhaps the small extra cost of this provision would have been justified.

Plasterboard walls at Gloucester Street are finished with a skim coat of plaster (a pity that there was this wet work above ground slab) because of fears (from experience) about the quality of taped joints. At Woodhouse the architects persisted with taped joints and were rewarded by quite satisfactory results. Concern was expressed that tenants, when redecorating, may unwittingly strip off the paper surface of the board and the tape with old wallpaper, but this could be avoided by good sizing of the original finish or warning the tenants against trying to strip off the old paper while it is dry.

The wall finish generally is bound distemper with pva emulsion in the kitchen—some tenants complained of the difficulty of removing grease over the cooker and thought that a more easily cleaned surface was justified.

3

3 *The result of inadequate initial provision of boundary fencing—this is not for privacy but to stop trespassers stepping freely into the garden. Dustbins are not quite visible from here*

Joinery

The quality of joinery work at Gloucester Street is noticeably poor in two situations.

First, in two house types (5D and 6B) a bold attempt has been made to deal with bathroom plumbing by means of a duct across one whole wall. This houses the soil stack and

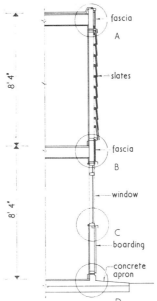

Key section through typical 5M *house external wall* ($\frac{1}{6}$in = 1ft, = 1:72). *Details are given below.*

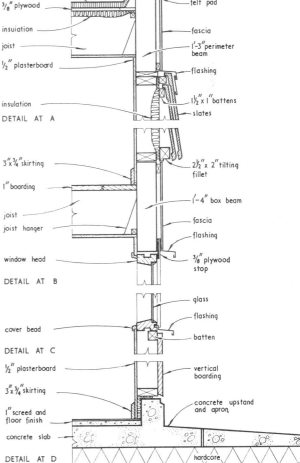

soil runs to wc, bath and lavatory basin, with the wwp and the cold water storage tank. Access panels are provided where required; these panels are simply sheets of plywood screwed to the duct wall. It is difficult to see how the architects were persuaded to accept the workmanship here: the edges of the panels seem to have been cut with a ripsaw, screws are crooked and even the panels themselves are often out of true. The flimsy detailing was obviously overoptimistic with regard to the craftsmanship expected, and is not helped by an ill-considered detail in type 5D, where the bath slots into the duct space and creates more chaos at junctions of panels and cover fillets.

Details at A, B, C, *and* D (*see key section above*)

At Woodhouse a less 'holistic' approach has been adopted, with exposed wwp and a skirting duct under the washbasin to carry wastes across to the main stack which is housed in a cupboard at the end of the bathroom. One has to admit that, largely owing to better joinery work on site, the finished product is easier to look at.

The second situation occurs around door frames, which were made up in the shop and brought onto the site (braced by a permanent threshold), architraves being fixed in-situ. These architraves are precut in length and sometimes fall as much as 6 mm ($\frac{1}{4}$ in) short if a junction; when they meet it is often at peculiar angles. Those at Woodhouse are very much better but this, the architects affirmed, was the result of persistence—nearly all architraves were sent back at least once. It was worth the effort. The permanent threshold to all doors allows a close fit at the bottom while allowing clearance over carpets and rugs without the aid of rising butts. In Scandinavia, it is common practice actually to rebate the threshold, giving a positive draught seal, and groove the head of the frame to allow ventilation in a comfortable position.

4 One of the face-to-face pairs of terraced blocks which run downhill, mainly at changes of contour direction. These stores are non-system for economy: compare corner treatment and roof detailing with standard projecting stores at Gloucester Street
5 The kitchen in the Woodhouse type of house is a large room with space for dining, left, good working arrangements and ample storage space

Ironmongery and electrical fittings

Ironmongery was generally well chosen, the closing device to top vents, although slightly Art Nouveau in appearance and with inadequate sash depth for the fixing plate, having a particularly firm closing action.

Socket outlet provision in both schemes was generally up to Parker Morris recommended standards and a jack provided in the living-room for tv reception from the master areial.

Ceiling roses were provided generally, although where pendant fittings were used they had to be so ridiculously short **11** (Chapter 5) [floor to ceiling height is 2·31 m (7 ft 7 in] that one wishes tenants could be persuaded to take a less traditional approach. The housing manager pointed out that where batten holders had been provided in previous schemes, tenants had often enclosed them with elaborate but unventilated fittings which caused a serious internal heat build-up, eventually damaging cables and fittings.

Batten holders are provided in bathrooms to allow for enclosed fittings which would discourage tenants from using portable electrical appliances, but in most cases the tenant has just left the naked bulb.

Construction

It is a pity that the architects of Woodhouse, who were persistent enough with the joinery finally to obtain decent results, were not sufficiently persuasive on the question of party wall construction to convince the contractors that the revised 5M lightweight party wall could be built without too much trouble. The difficulty appears to have been that the contractors (ie the corporation's own Public Works Department) also built the 5M prototypes at Gloucester Street where the party wall was constructed of two plaster-board skins with a sand-filled cavity and lead curtain. Considerable difficulty was experienced with this form and the contractors shied away from further untraditional methods. Further, in the Public Works Department organisation, a balance of trades had to be maintained which would have been upset by the entire elimination of bricklayers from a scheme as large as Woodhouse.

It was therefore agreed at tender stage that at Woodhouse (the second scheme) the party walls should be of concrete blocks. The fact that at Woodhouse architects and contractor were working within the same organisation is also obviously

relevant.

As it turned out, the revised 5M lightweight construction used at Gloucester Street caused the contractor no major difficulties and the experience of a tenant in the 6B house, who lived next door to a family with eight children but heard nothing, was an isolated but fairly positive field confirmation of the acoustic tests carried out by the Building Research Establishment.

Summary

The contract periods for both schemes were of about the same length for the thirty-nine houses at Gloucester Street and the 162 at Woodhouse, and this seems to be of some significance. Probably the most important factors were the greater variety of house types on the smaller Gloucester Street site and that this was a pilot scheme. It was roughly estimated at Woodhouse that productivity increased substantially after about twenty houses had been erected and the labour force had become acquainted with the components. No one house type at Gloucester Street reached this figure—the greatest number of one type is the fourteen type 5A.

Other factors are obviously the more complex layout and site works at Gloucester Street and the size of labour force that could be employed on the restricted site.

Cost analysis of thirty-nine houses at Gloucester Street and 162 at Woodhouse

SUMMARY

Ground floor area: 10 256 m² (110 282 sq ft).
Total floor area: 18 426 m² (198 240 sq ft).
Type of contract: RIBA firm price.
Tender date: September 1963.
Work began: September/November 1963.
Work finished: October/November 1964.
Tender price of foundation, superstructure, installation and finishes including drainage to collecting manhole: £499,670.
Tender price of external works and ancillary buildings including drainage beyond collecting manhole: £32,570.
Total: £532,240.

7 Canada Estate, Neptune Street, Bermondsey

The high density housing development is situated at the heart of what was once London's dockland, in an area originally zoned for industry. As such it posed problems of integration within an industrial environment but brought new life to a part of London that has largely excluded the resident for many decades. Vandalism, however, is a continuing problem

designed by	architect to the then LCC
deputy architect	F. G. West
principal housing architect	K. J. Campbell
assistant housing architect	J. G. H. D. Cairns
section architect	C. A. Lucas
job architects	P. Bottomley
	J. Robinson
design team	M. Richardson
	Mrs. M. Nesovic
	R. Hatton
	D. Heal
senior planning officer	J. C. Craig
quantity surveyor	Mercer and Miller (preparation of bills)
principal quantity surveyor LCC	M. F. Rice (cost planning analysis and management)
structural engineer	J. H. Humphreys
engineering and electrical services	P. F. Stott, acting chief engineer LCC
chief officer, Parks Department	F. Hallowes
main contractor	Tersons

CLIENT'S REQUIREMENTS

The then London County Council wanted nine one-room, sixty-four two-room, 128 three-room, sixty four-room and twelve five-room dwellings, as well as an area maintenance depot and car parking space for 25 per cent of the dwellings.

SITE

The site is situated next to the now closed Surrey Docks and has remarkably fine views at a high level, though the ground level has been confined by the surrounding buildings and dock walls, pending redevelopment of the dock sites.

To take advantage of magnificent views across London and to accommodate the smaller two- and three-room dwellings, two twenty-one storey point blocks are sited towards the east end of the site where they cause the minimum amount of overshadowing. The lower blocks are arranged in an open space which is free from vehicular traffic and therefore reasonably quiet and secluded. The larger dwellings are accommodated in four four-storey cluster blocks and maisonettes. In addition there is a three-storey block of old people's dwellings.

PLANNING

The site is an area zoned originally mainly for special industry but later for residential purposes at a density of 336 persons per hectare (136 ppa); the density achieved is 341 pph (138 ppa). The total number of garages and parking spaces represents 31 per cent of the number of dwellings, a figure slightly in excess of the standard of 25 per cent existing in 1960 when the scheme was approved.

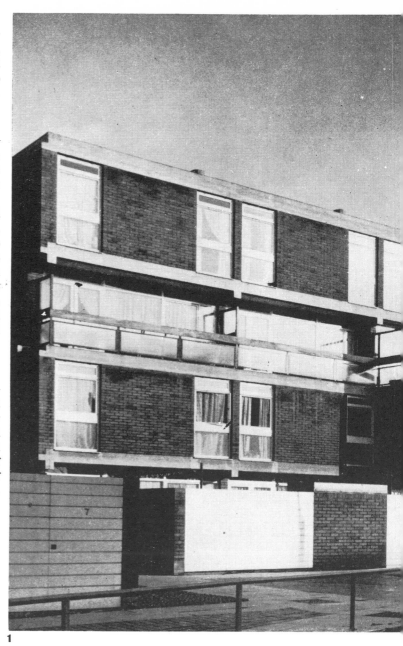

1 *Looking east from grassed area with enclosed gardens to ground floor maisonettes in the foreground*

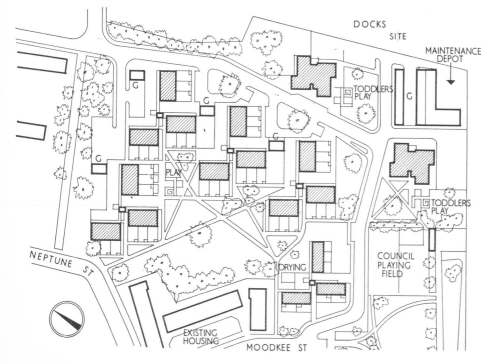

Site plan (1:1152) showing two point blocks of flats, four groups of maisonette blocks each linked to a central staircase, and old people's dwellings to the south-west G = garage areas

APPRAISAL

The site's closeness to the Surrey Docks offered the possibility of interesting views of river activity combined with rather grim immediate surroundings. The scheme comprises two 21-storey point blocks, four 4-storey groups and one 3-storey group. The plans used were LCC type plans and the scheme illustrates how type plans can be used imaginatively to produce a layout with individual character. The grouping of the low blocks is very formal, but the spaces produced are various and freely related to one another. All these spaces are pedestrian with an interesting variety of paving and connect with a small piece of open space, producing a relatively quiet traffic free environment which is a great asset to the neighbourhood. Unfortunately the two point blocks are separated from the pedestrian movement by the service road. This is not heavily used by traffic (though it is used by the maintenance depot), but it forms a barrier that breaks the informal interlinked quality around the low buildings and tends to

push the point blocks into the corner with the garages and maintenance depot (see site plan below).

The point block has been held to have many advantages in high density schemes, freeing the layout planning and allowing the ground to be used in a variety of ways, but it presents problems. One is the town planning problem of their relationship to one another and to the townscape as a whole; the other is their integration with other buildings and the movement of human beings at ground level. On this relatively small site it is a pity that the pedestrian spaces linking front doors and staircases and giving the scheme a sense of place did not include and assimilate the ground level entrance to the point blocks.

The separation of the point blocks is not helped by the treatment of the ground level entrance. This is arranged three-dimensionally in a very interesting way, with a wide ramp up to the main lift hall. Nearly all the walls, however, are exposed, rough board shuttered concrete and the buildings have not been very well finished.

As a result what would have been a smart, exciting entrance looks drab and sordid **5**. When done well, rough shuttered concrete can look marvellous. But it is a risky finish to use in this country, especially if, as in this case, it forms such a major part of the design. Many builders have great difficulty producing it in large areas and it can so easily result in an effect opposite to that intended.

Apart from the general opportunities for toddlers to play in the paved and grassed areas, there is a playspace with a maze-like wall arrangement and varying levels that is positioned among the low blocks close to the grassed open space, and two smaller playspaces—one at the base of each point block. Also adjoining the site to the south is a borough council children's playground with play equipment.

The low blocks

Each block comprises three arms extending from a central staircase with each arm in the four-storey block containing six maisonettes. The three-storey block for old people provides one- and two-room dwellings in a similar grouping. The maisonettes are mostly four-room dwellings, the ground level type with a garden, the upper level with a full-width balcony. The ground level dwelling at the end of each arm is a five-room type. This mixture of dwellings is used to break up the façade and model each arm. This quality contributes to each three-armed group a unity which would have been lost if each arm had been a short length of straightforward four-storey maisonettes. Internally the planning is competently organised in detail to pre-Parker Morris standards. The living-room of each dwelling is heated by an open fire.

The staircase tower **5** contains, in addition to the access stairs, the water tanks, drying cabinets and refuse chute. The simple planning of these elements produces an elegant sculptured form which in isolation seems a very satisfactory architectural solution. When seen as one of a number of similar elements, all of which are parts of the total group, the form appears overworked-- particularly the proliferation of chunky concrete rainwater spouts. But once again it is the use of rough boarded concrete that detracts from both the elegance of the architectural conception and the homeliness of a place to live, and makes it rely on being in use and planted with trees, shurbs and grass for the sensitive grouping of these buildings to override criticism and produce a pleasant environment.

Second and third floor plans of maisonette blocks

Ground and first floor plans of maisonette blocks (1:288). There are three blocks linked to a staircase tower (see 2 and site plan) in each maisonette complex

Cross section through larger maisonettes

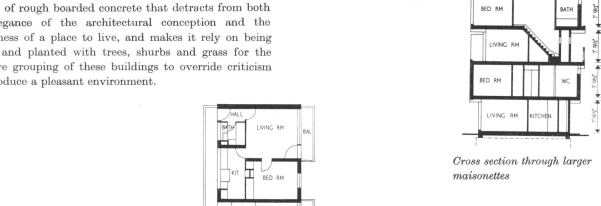

Upper floor plan of old people's dwellings situated at the south-west of the site ($\frac{1}{24}$in = 1ft, = 1:288)

Cross section through smaller maisonettes

The point blocks

Point blocks are difficult elements to incorporate into a townscape. Almost any large area of rehousing at high density would benefit in layout by using point blocks and in most cases it is difficult to say whether a particular site is right or wrong for them. And how expressive should a point block be? Each one a monument richly encrusted with balconies and topped with flying tank rooms? Or a simple, no-nonsense stack of dwellings appearing rather self-conscious of its arbitrary exposure above its neighbours? This site is one on which the placing of point blocks can be justified. The views are fascinating and the views of the point blocks themselves as part of the river scene call for a bold expressiveness. The blocks are strongly

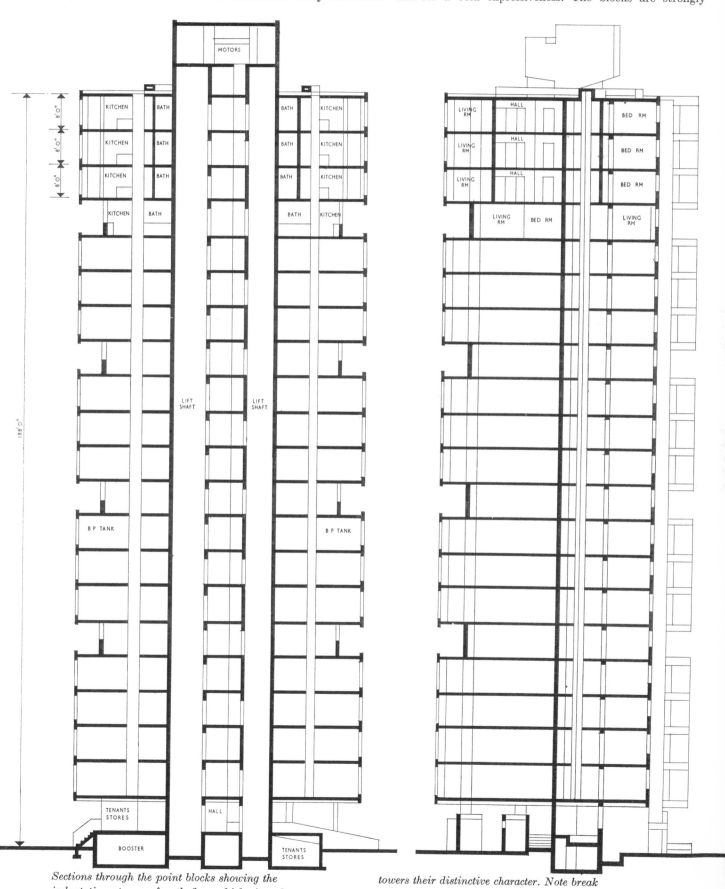

Sections through the point blocks showing the indentation at every fourth floor which gives the towers their distinctive character. Note break pressure (BP) tanks on the eighth floor 1:300

2

3

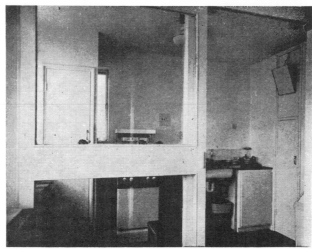

2 *Garage area with point block beyond. Many tenants have found it difficult to curtain the long sliding window satisfactorily*
3 *Interior of point block living-room showing freestanding column with kitchen beyond*
4 *Glazed wall and sliding door between kitchen and living-room*

4

Plan of floors 5, 9, 13 and 17 (where the indentation occurs)

Plan of upper floors other than 5, 9, 13 and 17. Note column at centre of living-room areas

Ground floor plan

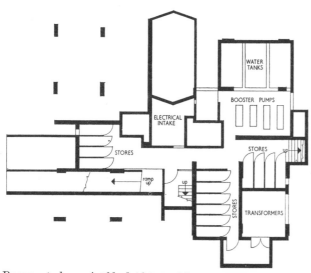

Basement plan point block ($\frac{1}{24}$in = 1ft, = 1:288)

modelled by inserting between every three floors of three-room flats a floor of two-room flats. This produces an interesting silhouette that reads well even when seen from a distance (there is a particularly striking view from Tower Bridge). But apart from this outward formal expressiveness, is there an inward requirement in the organisation of the elements that produces this relationship? This would be more difficult to rationalise. There appears to be no advantage socially in mixing the types in this way and the floor area left over where the plan is reduced is not used—it would seem illogical for the smaller dwellings to have a larger balcony anyway. The only reason then for this arrangement is to produce a modelled form. In theory this approach could be questioned, but it is justified by the result on this site.

The structure is in-situ reinforced concrete with brick and panel infilling. It is arranged with a basic simplicity giving equal floor spans and accommodating the requirements of the different floor layouts. This is difficult to accomplish satisfactorily and in this case it has resulted in a 711 mm (28 in × 13 in) column in the middle of the living-dining area of the three-room flat. These flats are small—the original area was reduced to save cost and it could be argued that the architectural effort and money spent was not worth it for such tiny dwellings—and this column dividing up an already small space must produce an almost impossible furnishing problem **3**.

The living-dining area of each flat has a narrow window-cleaning balcony outside a large window with a low sill. Part of this window can be slid open giving panoramic views of the river. This element is very successful and gives a luxurious quality to the space.

Two high speed lifts are provided, one of which will take a stretcher, and there is a single escape staircase. As is usual in these blocks the central lift hall is permanently ventilated to the open air on both sides providing a 'blow through' which, when the wind is in a certain direction, tests the strongest door springs and cancels most of the value of a central enclosed lift hall in a tall building.

The internal bathrooms and wcs are artificially ventilated

and each flat has electric floor heating, plus an electric fire in the living area. The main water storage is in the basement and water is automatically pumped up to tanks at roof level when required. Drinking water is also pumped up to special tanks in the roof. Refuse is collected at the bottom of two chutes in containers on two standard LCC five-container roundabouts.

A transformer chamber is housed in the basement. Groups of tenants' stores are placed at basement and entrance levels. All these elements at the base of the block are arranged tidily within the structural pattern without any straining or contradiction and form an interesting series of entrance spaces and enclosing forms that are part of the total unity of the block. This solution appears simple, but in many cases the problem of the combination of utility elements and ground level structure overshadow the important quality at this level—the pleasure of entering a building.

Externally the structural organisation is clearly expressed, dividing the elevations into well proportioned elements. It is a pity that these striking and carefully considered buildings have not been very well finished.

There is provision for garaging and parking cars for 31 per cent of the number of dwellings; slightly in excess of the standard obtaining at the time of planning. Small groups of garages and parking spaces are placed among the low blocks and a large group adjoins the maintenance depot close to the point blocks. The maintenance depot comprises a number of workshops and stores arranged around two sides of a A standard solution—four-storey maisonettes with high blocks—has been handled in this case with imagination and original thought; the scheme is a worthy addition to London's river views.

5

POINT BLOCK OF FLATS

SUMMARY

Ground floor area: 219 m² (2 358 sq ft).
Total floor area: 6 194 m² (66 682 sq ft).
Type of contract: LCC with fluctuations.
Tender date: November 1961.
Work began: February 1962.
Work finished: February 1965.
Net habitable floor area: 4 449 m² (47 901 sq ft).
Gross floor area: 6 194 m² (66 682 sq ft).
Tender price of foundation, superstructure, installation and finishes including drainage to collecting manhole: £260,764
Tender price of external works and ancillary buildings including drainage beyond collecting manhole: £82,688

8

6

7

5 *Link stair to a four-storey group of maisonettes*
6 *Paved way between blocks leading to proposed pedestrian way*

7 *View from second floor access level showing children's playspace, enclosed private gardens and paving layout*

8 *Entrance level of point block. Despite the sculptural planning and the careful detailing the drab concrete creates a sordid atmosphere*

9 *General view showing the grouping of the four-storey maisonettes*

9

8 Housing at Winstanley Road, Battersea

This housing scheme was large enough to develop its own character and this potential has been realised to a high degree. Remarkable care and money was spent on environmental aspects of groundscape, landscape, sculpture, car parks, social amenities and integration generally of tenants and children into their surroundings. This concern for the tenant as a person has taken precedence over the more formal and academic aspects of the architecture and the comparative restrictions of the industrialised method of building

designed by	George/Trew/Dunn
associate in charge	A. Artur
job architects	J. Williams
	M. Burke
	G. Janssens
assistant	D. Abbiss
quantity surveyor	E. C. Harris & Partners
consultants	
structural engineers	W. V. Zinn .
	Ove Arup & Partners
electrical and	
mechanical engineer	A. E. Mohring & Son
heating engineer	Andrews-Weatherfoil Ltd
landscape architect	Michael Brown
main contractor	Wates

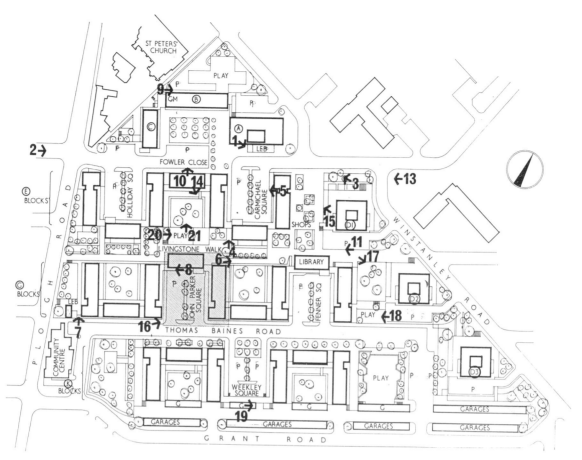

Site plan ($\frac{1}{192}$in = 1ft, = 1:2304). The area in tone indicates that part of maisonette blocks shown in detail plan and section on pp 92-3. Bold numerals refer to photo viewpoints. GM = *gas meter,* LEB = *London Electricity Board substation*

APPRAISAL

Housing is tied more closely to people's needs than are many other types of building: this is true especially of local authority work. Despite this the housing built by local authorities is often based on formal architectural concepts and effects and little money and interest is left for the environment after the buildings have been designed and costed, either in detail or in the larger sense. In fact it is often true that the needs of 'pure' architecture and the needs of the environment in human terms are incompatible.

This is certainly true of the Winstanley Road project which George/Trew/Dunn has designed, consciously or not, in human and informal terms, sometimes at the expense of what is usually called architecture. This human concern expresses itself in the shaping and interplay of the urban spaces and volumes, the introduction of workshops, tenants' rooms and play decks, the individuality of the planning and access to the dwellings, the informality of the elevations, but above all, in the shaping and creation of usable spaces and visual interest at ground level. This is architecture scaled down to the human being.

Site and area
The triangular site of 5 hectares (12⅓ acres) is next to Clapham Junction station in a run-down area which has now been redeveloped. To the south lie the wide acres of railway track raised from 4·57 m to 7·62 m (15 to 25 ft) above the level of the housing site **1**. Comparatively new housing— mostly by the same architects—forms the north-eastern boundary behind Winstanley Road which has been diverted

to reduce its importance as a through route and turn it into an estate road, while a main road, Plough Road, runs along the western side of the site.

The general atmosphere of the area was lively, sordid and very intimate in its sense of enclosure in spite of the houses and shops being usually no more than three storeys high **2**. This intimacy does not exist in buildings to the north-east some of which are two-storey houses facing generous lawns

Existing planning
In 1960 when the first stages of the scheme were planned, there was no plan for the area and GTD had only the indeterminate pattern of its own housing to the north-east and the existing urban pattern as starting points. The former streets on the site were small terrace houses lining four streets running parallel with the railway.

Basis of new layout and staging
The line of these streets formed the basis for the replanning which was a neat though not absolutely necessary restriction in the replanning (see site plan). Basically, the scheme is three superblocks of four to five storeys each culminating in a detached eleven-storey tower. A twenty-four-storey tower with a short four-storey block stands in the northern corner of the site.

The layout was determined further by the phasing of the site clearance, making it necessary to build high blocks for easy rehousing. These blocks were built first, thus enabling easy staging and allowing existing roads across the site to serve as construction and service roads.

The scheme was originally planned in 1960, extended in

1 *View from top of twenty-four-storey tower: network of pedestrian, planted and vehicular spaces flows into pattern of surrounding streets. In distance is Clapham Junction station and raised railway tracks. Untidy roofs of lower buildings are obvious to many people in flats; a completely dark finish would have been preferable. Chequerboard patterning has been applied to garage roofs alongside railway. Boiler houses form successful rooftop termination to tower blocks*
2 *Looking from west down a typical street at the time of completion. Tower block has a roof playdeck and a tenth storey playdeck and workrooms, now-locked because of lack of supervisory staff. (Photo viewpoints are marked on site plan earlier*

1

2

Section through circulation areas
and lift motor room

First floor plan

Typical cross-section through
five-storey block
($\frac{1}{32}$in = 1ft, = 1:384).

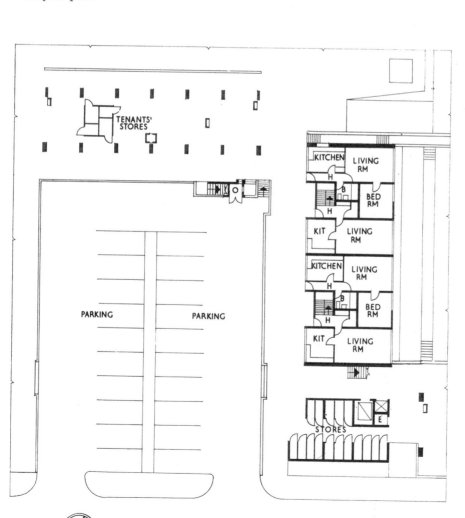

Ground floor plan maisonette blocks G ($\frac{1}{32}$in = 1ft, = 1:384).
Site plan shows relationship between these two blocks and
rest of development.

scope in 1961 and partly replanned, because of the change to industrialised methods, in 1963. Considering the time at which the scheme was planned its planning principles compare well with present principles of layout and traffic segregation. Its greatest success however lies in creation of a pleasant environment by a combination of many factors: Spaces are similar in feeling to the former streets, tightly knit and friendly without being overpowering **3**. There is a lot of space available for pedestrian use but nowhere is there the sense of desolation associated with many new housing areas. The only criticism is that of monotony in the variety of scale, many of the squares being the same size. Most vistas are closed and the few long views are narrow and curtailed. The planning and the shape of the site throw up several alleyways which add to the mystery of the site. Several of the blocks have their ground floors open to allow further spatial penetration **4, 5**.

The grouping and arrangement of the buildings is introvert because of the general nature of the district and the close-ness of light industry and the railway. More than twenty areas can be called urban spaces, although the interplay is such that there is no definite number and they all form part of one connected space. Many spaces are treated imagin-atively although their variety is not strong enough to counterbalance completely the similarity of volume of these spaces. It may be significant that visitors to the site find the layout confusing.

The theoretical pedestrian flow is along a main east-west promenade—Livingstone Walk to two of the superblocks with a wide pavement access to the third superblock **6**. In practice the vehicular culs-de-sac are so planned that vehicles do not intrude and there can be a successful coexistence between car and pedestrian on the access roads. Access to the individual dwellings varies in planning techniques but all methods depend on a small number of dwellings reached by a staircase and short balcony or cor-ridor access. Additional staircases at the second floor level reach the upper maisonettes and access to these staircases has led to the creation of a 1·83 m (6 ft) wide access gallery at second floor level which connects all the buildings in superblock **8**. Each gallery has what is unfortunately considered as the luxury of two lifts, which must be useful for pram and wheelchair access. This gallery appears at first sight to be important in linking all the blocks, but does not, in fact, appear to be used to traverse the scheme but only as a means of getting to the nearest staircase to reach the ground. The towers are fairly standard in terms of access, but since they are towers, the access remains intimate on each floor.

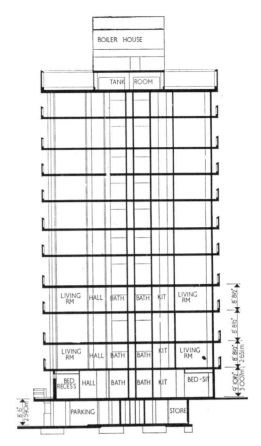

Typical section through D *blocks* 1: 288

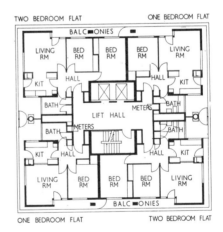

Typical upper floor plan

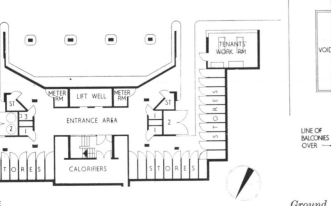

1 BULK REFUSE
2 REFUSE CHAMBER
3 CLEANER

Lower ground floor plan D *block*

Ground floor plan D *block*

Roof plan

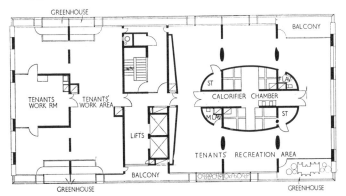

Tenth floor plan

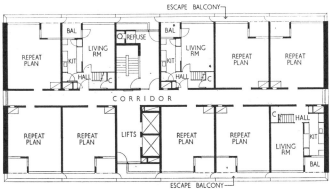

Typical bedroom level plan (see section right)

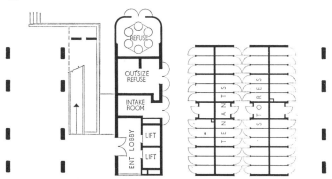

Typical access level plan (see section right)

Ground floor and entrance hall level tower block A
($\frac{1}{32}$in = 1ft, = 1:384).

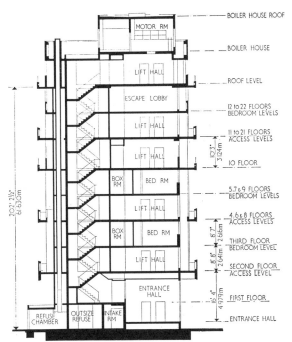

Shortened cross-section through tower block A
($\frac{1}{32}$in = 1ft, = 1:384).

towers are fairly standard in terms of access, but since they Garages and parking provision were low by the standards then applied by some local authorities—68 to 70 per cent for the site overall—though they were raised sharply in the final stage. Nevertheless the 373 cars which can be accommodated on site are not as dominant as they might be on many schemes. Most of the garages are relegated to the edge of the scheme where they give a depressingly bleak effect. Parking near the towers is hidden below ground level, the area at the foot of the tallest tower block being covered by a play deck **9**. The uncovered parking is split into nine small groups each of not more than twenty cars. With the addition of plentiful tree planting the cars are not oppressive in what is a very tight-knit scheme **9**, **10**, **11**.

The local council happily has included four shops and a children's library in the middle of the scheme although these were an afterthought in the planning. The architects have provided sixteen tenants' workrooms scattered through the site. A large workroom and a play deck originally took up all of the tenth floor of the twenty-four-storey tower **12**, and there was a safe play deck on the roof. The roof play deck, however, is locked because the borough cannot provide supervision for it, and the tenth floor subsequently turned into an additional six flats because of vandalism The tightness of the planning makes privacy very difficult to achieve, and the plan form of interlocking squares makes it even more difficult, even though the dwellings are so planned that there is little overlooking corner to corner **13**. Many flats and maisonettes at ground level are next to the pedestrian ways and generally speaking the incidence of overlooking is high. On the other hand, it can be argued that many people traditionally use net curtains and expect to do so. Sixty-six small private gardens have been won from the scheme; these are all overlooked but do give some feeling o separation and are mostly well used **14**.

The groundscape, lighting, sculptures, railings, small changes of level and the minor environmental urban details are carefully considered although not always consistent **15**. All the hard landscape is heavily patterned in bricks, setts and a variety of other materials and this, with the great complications of detailed forms in the ground treatment and the changes in level, forms a rich liveliness approaching

3

4

5

3 *There is a happy scale to spaces even in this central area, Huitt Square. All details are made to 'work' for scheme—transformer station at foot of tower has a long low roof and planting to integrate it into*

surroundings. Both high and low blocks are broken down in scale but there is no link between the two types either in materials or colour
4, 5 *Two links between interlocking spaces demonstrating attention to detail and variety of techniques and views*
6 *View along Livingstone Walk, planned as main pedestrian route through site. Seats, handrails, planting and lighting are all carefully considered*

chaos throughout the scheme. Many of the details have had to be mastered by forming other details and many architects would shudder at the variety of forms and treatment that can be tolerated here because of the obvious loving care and craftsmanship lavished on them and the intimate scale of the various parts of the scheme. Most of the external lighting is fixed to or integrated with the buildings but there are also three types of lamp post used through the scheme. There is an abundance of seats and an obvious thought for the minutia of everyday life. The scheme must be unique in the extent of its artwork and wall decoration. There are sixteen pieces of external wall decoration by William Mitchell & Associates **16**, one freestanding piece of formal sculpture by A. K. Bobrowski **15**, and four pieces of play sculpture designed by the job architect A. Artur.

The task of the landscape architect Michael Brown was the

6

96

7 *Looking north along Plough Road from end of Thomas Baines Road. Here tendency to use too many materials overwhelms detailing. Throughout scheme boundary walls and retaining walls use different bricks in contrasting yellow and red while a third, blue-black, brick is used on building. Downpipes are neatly detailed but incompatible* with cantilever. Note scale of adjoining Victorian housing along Plough Road at time of construction

8 *Second floor gallery with individual access to top maisonettes*

Three techniques of integrating cars:
9 *Under playdeck near tower block. Beyond, two-storey houses of an earlier scheme*
10 *Within Fowler Close—viewpoint taken from*

7

8

9

11

10

12

13

beneath one of the E blocks
(compare with site plan
p 89)
11 *Sunken parking near
eleven-storey towers with
workroom in far corner and
first shops in Huitt Square.*

*On the left library is nearing
completion*
12 *Children's gay playdeck
in tower block, now closed*
13 *Tower blocks inevitably
cause overlooking problems
but balconies tend to control*

view
14 *The sixty-six small
gardens are generally well
kept. Gallery access runs
very close to many windows*
15 *Patterning of Huitt
Square.*

16 *Wall sculptures by
William Mitchell &
Associates obtained by
lining shuttering with
expanded polystyrene*

14

15

16

detailed interpretation of the architects' scheme and this has been carried out conscientiously. The raising of the greens between blocks is most successful in providing well kept patches of grass while allowing enough access for children to use them without undue wear. More than 300 trees have been planted **17**.

The character, forms and spaces created by the layout are a joy to the children but there are also special facilities for them. The play sculptures are well used as are the constructions of pipes, walls and Wendy houses scattered throughout the scheme **18, 19, 20**. Play decks are on top of two banks of garages and a sunken area for ball games is still being built. Lavatories have been built at ground level but these are kept locked because of misuse and lack of supervision. There are three caretakers—housing managers on The informality of the elevations to the four- and five-storey buildings adds to the intimacy of the scheme. This informality stems from the expression of the planning which integrates several types and sizes of dwelling in each building **21**. A wide range of materials is used—concrete columns and beams, pebbledash, floor beams, blue-black sandlime brick end walls, and infill panels of white unglazed ceramic mosaic, grey-green glass, ply finished in dark green cement paint, or white painted horizontal boarding. As is often the case the towers are strangers to the lower blocks, different finishes and colours being used—concrete aggregate panels with painted panels on the recessed decks

Internal planning

The individual buildings are intricately planned to enable the variety of dwelling types to be accommodated within the restrictions caused by industrialisation and some north-facing blocks **22**. Detailed planning is adequate but less care has been spent on the details of the flats than on the external environment—the plumbing especially is ill-considered The standard of finish is high.

Industrialisation

Although the scheme is industrialised it is some measure of its success that the method of construction does not appear to have overwhelmed the planning and the buildings' appearance as is so often the case. This appraisal has

Conclusion

The vagueness of the original brief and the many changes in the planning since the scheme began in 1960 have allowed more flexibility than is usually the case. This flexibility and the imaginative setting aside, at an early stage, enough money for landscaping and external works has led to an unusually high standard of environment.

SUMMARY

Ground floor: 349·8 m² (3 766 sq ft).
Total floor area: 3 670 m² (39 513 sq ft).
Type of contract: RIBA with fluctuations.
Tender date: May 1963.
Work began: August 1963.
Work finished: March 1965.
Net habitable floor area: 2 273 m² (24 467 sq ft).
Gross floor area: 3 670 m² (39 513 sq ft).
Tender price of foundation, superstructure, installation and finishes including drainage to collecting manhole: £157 384. Tender price of external works and ancillary buildings including drainage beyond collecting manhole: £20 465. Total: £177 849.

17 *Small patches of grass are kept to a good standard by treating them as walled beds. Children are not supposed to play on greens but this is not rigidly enforced* **18, 19, 20** *Provision of*

17

18

19

facilities for children
18 *Play sculpture—here by Michael Brown, landscape architect*
19 *Wendy houses on garage roofs*
20 *Steps and poles used for sliding and balancing*
21 *The intricate planning of building forms elevations whose informality dominates industrialised method of building*

21

22 *Living/dining-room in large maisonette*

20

22

9 Housing at St Mary's Redevelopment Area, Oldham

This housing scheme of 520 dwellings is the result of a development project in the classical tradition by the then Ministry of Housing and Local Government Research and Development Group. In collaboration with town planners and a progressive local authority, the group investigated social, economic and construction needs of a *central area slum clearance and redevelopment site, evolved design criteria on the basis of this investigation and tested validity of criteria in design of a housing scheme which was used as a prototype for the application of Laing's 12M Jespersen system to local authority housing*

designed by	Ministry of Housing and Local Government Research and Development Group in collaboration with Max Lock & Partners and T. Cartlidge, borough architect, Oldham
quantity surveyor	Ministry of Housing and Local Government quantity surveyors
consultants	
structural engineers	Ove Arup & Partners
heating engineers	John Laing & Son Ltd Building Services Design Department with Steensen Varming Mulcahy
main contractor	John Laing Construction Ltd

CLIENT'S REQUIREMENTS

Extensive areas of Oldham are scheduled for slum clearance
and redevelopment. This was the first phase of the St Mary's
Ward to be completed and it acted as a suitable case study
in industrialised building for the Research and Development Group at the then Ministry of Housing and Local
and associated consultants at a density of 272 bsph (110
bspa).

SITE

The site lies just north of the centre of Oldham and is
bounded by Horsedge Street to the north-east, Burnley
Street to the south (this is the line of the proposed orbital
ring road), Lord Street to the west and Rifle Street to the

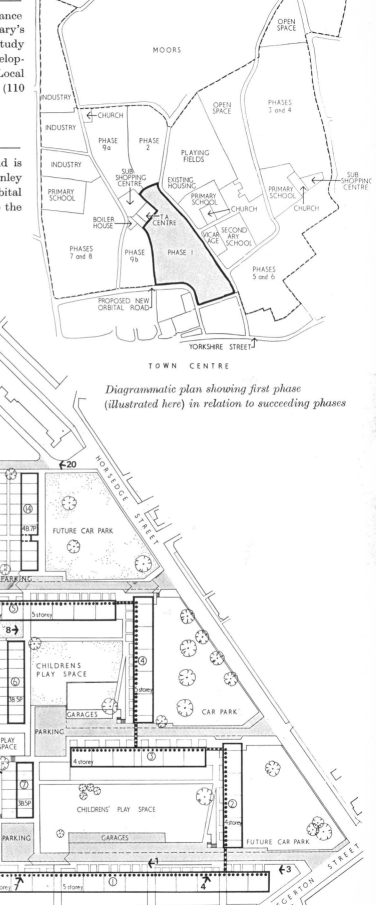

*Diagrammatic plan showing first phase
(illustrated here) in relation to succeeding phases*

*Site plan ($\frac{1}{48}$in = 1ft, = 1:576). Photographic viewpoints are shown (F = photo on p 100 . Dotted line indicates pedestrian
circulation within flats at deck level (compare with diagrammatic section p 103). Areas of tone are vehicular circulation within
boundary of site*

north-west: all these were existing roads. It was the first stage of a major redevelopment of St Mary's Ward and lies on the south edge of the moors at the highest point in Oldham, 228·6 m (750 ft) above sea level.

PLANNING

The main points affecting site layout in a report submitted to the Oldham Borough Council were as follows:

1 One-level segregation was to be provided for pedestrians and vehicles, no through roads were to be within the site boundaries and spur roads were to provide service access.

2 The largest dwellings for families with children were to be houses with attached private open space arranged in short terraces following contours of the site, enclosing small public play spaces for young children and near larger spaces for older children.

3 Smaller dwellings were to be flats grouped in composite blocks: single workers and married couples past child-bearing age would be first to be placed in these dwellings. The natural slope of the ground was to be used to provide access by covered decks running out from ground level with all front doors thus accessible from ground level. Access decks, so far as possible, should give onto the through pedestrian way.

APPRAISAL

The primary subject investigated in this development project by the Ministry of Housing and Local Government Research and Development Group was slum clearance and reconstruction of a central urban area. A typical case study had to be found under a progressive local authority willing to collaborate in extensive preparatory studies.

In St Mary's Ward, Oldham, 121 hectares (300 acres) of sub-standard housing were due to be redeveloped and the ministry acted as architects for the first ten phases. This first phase, which replaced the worst buildings, was originally to cover only two hectares (five acres) but it was realised that this would be too small for economic use of a building system and the site was increased to six and a half hectares (sixteen acres).

Max Lock & Partners, appointed by the borough council, prepared apart from planning proposals, a condition survey of dwellings within the 121 hectares (300 acres): from this it was decided to retain about 750, or 15 per cent of the houses.

Meanwhile the development group worked at two levels: Sociologists surveyed tenants in the slums of St Mary's and in three recently redeveloped high density central urban residential areas in Leeds, Liverpool and London: from this they evolved social and design criteria for the development project brief.

At the same time, the architects identified an industrialised building system—12M Jesperson—suitable for the density and building heights likely to be required, working with the licensees of the imported system to make it more flexible and bring it into line with national regulations and standards.

Mechanical engineering consultants also studied costs and functional implications of a district heating scheme and quantity surveyors examined cost implications of the proposed outline redevelopment. Reports of design, engineering and cost proposals were submitted to Oldham Borough Council.

The ministry's sociological surveys mentioned resulted in a number of Design Bulletins: *Living in a slum*,[1] is a study of the people living in the original substandard dwellings on the site of the scheme, and the development of the project is reported in other bulletins.[2]

In brief, houses were found small, damp, cold and underserviced, and larger families were grossly over-crowded. Social facilities used most within St Mary's were small shops and pubs; most people appreciated the neighbourliness of the district and friendships were mostly within the same street. Three-quarters of the residents wanted to remain in the district after rehousing and the longer they had lived there the more they wanted to stay: reasons were mostly social dependence and physical convenience (such as easy travel to work). Nearly all tenants insistently wanted to be rehoused in a house or bungalow.

This last point was of particular concern in a complementary design bulletin, *Families living at high density*,[3] in which were examined design issues for redevelopment of central urban residential areas. Tenants in three such redeveloped areas in Liverpool, Leeds and London were studied. In particular it deals with special problems of multi-storey dwellings; the relative merits of high and low blocks and of flats and maisonettes; and the attitude of tenants to being moved away from their original dwellings.

No consistent differences in satisfaction were found between housewives with children living in block dwellings and those living in houses on the same estate: opinions were more affected by siting, physical and social characteristics of the estates; by the dimensions, design and amenities of their home. A high density of 321 persons per hectare (130 people per acre) did not appear incompatible with satisfactory family life.

Nevertheless there was an overwhelming preference for living in houses rather than block dwellings, especially among families with young children, although many of the disagreeable features of living in a block were not due to intrinsic features of multi-level living. Low space standards, damp, noise, poor thermal insulation, inadequate heating, poor refuse disposal and clothes drying arrangements all seemed more prevalent in block dwellings than in houses although the technical problems involved are not insuperable Some difficulties however were found inherent in block dwellings: these included remoteness of children's play areas and difficulty in maintaining communal access stairs and balconies. On the other hand, house dwellers suffered from overlooking and lack of privacy and, since houses were larger, heating was more of a problem: both these deficiencies of course could be overcome.

The report concluded that families with children should, if they wished, be provided with houses but this did not mean that they need be banished to low density housing far from the city centre. Mixed high and low development could provide the proportion of houses required for families with children if the housing cost yardstick did not prevent it. Low rise high density development were not discussed in this report.

The survey concluded with detailed design implications which were taken as part of the brief.

Tables I and II (p. 104) show the content of the scheme.

The density of the site is 272 persons in 72 dwellings per hectare (110 people in thirty-two dwellings per acre).

There are 110 parking spaces and thirty-three garages

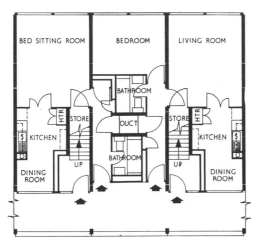

Flats at public access level with private staircases to flats above. Left, standard deck plan—bedsitting room and one-bedroom two-person flats. Right, ground floor in four-storey flats—bedsitting-room and one-bedroom two-person flats ($\frac{1}{16}$in = 1ft, = 1:192)

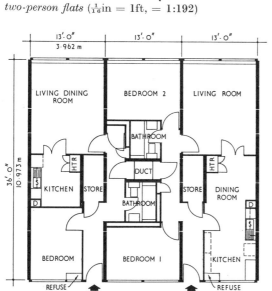
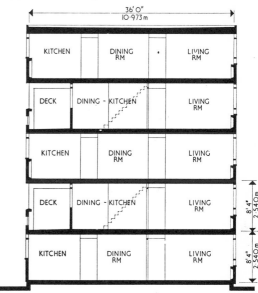

Ground floor level in three- and five-storey flats— one-bedroom two-person and two-bedroom four-person

Section through typical flats

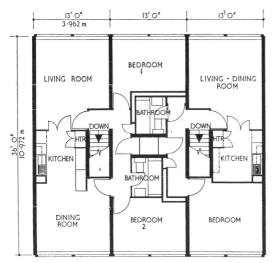
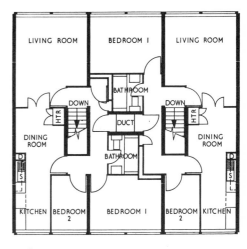

Flats above access level with private staircases from below. Left, two-bedroom four-person and one-bedroom two-person flats. Right, a pair of two-bedroom three-person flats ($\frac{1}{16}$in = 1ft, = 1:192)

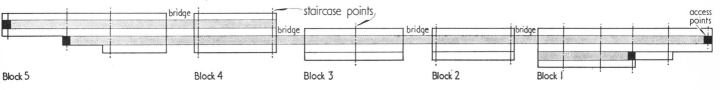

Diagrammatic section through flat blocks showing access decks in tone, bridges, access points and vertical circulation. Compare with site plan

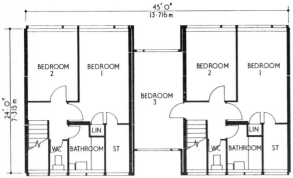

Upper floor of house where third bedroom spans pedestrian way ($\frac{1}{16}$in = 1ft, = 1:192)

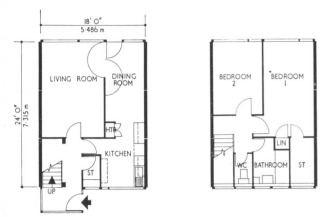

Ground and first floor plans of two-bedroom four-person house. Compare with plan above where a third bedroom is added between houses to span pedestrian way

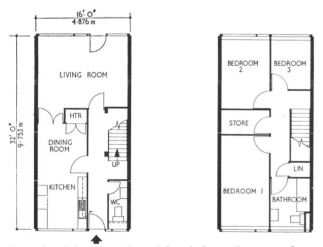

Ground and first floor plans of three-bedroom five-person house

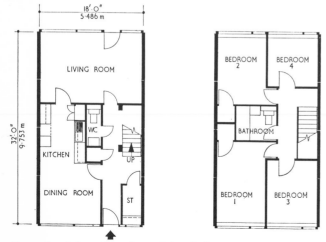

Ground and first floor plans of four-bedroom seven-person house ($\frac{1}{16}$in = 1ft, = 1:192)

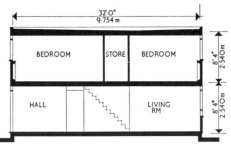

Typical section through house ($\frac{1}{16}$in = 1ft, = 1:192)

throughout the site—provisions for 143 vehicles at an average of 0·28 per dwelling. Sites for shops and a pub were provided at the outset.

Site and layout

The site is very exposed and although the prevailing wind is south-west there are frequent cold north-east winds off the moors and the average number of degree days for Oldham is 4 250 a year. In addition the average annual rainfall is high at 40in over an average of 225 rain days.*

The area of the site is six and a half hectares (16·12 acres) and there is a fall of 12·12 m (40 ft) from north-west to south-east.

Incorporated in the town planners' proposals for redevelopment of St Mary's ward as a whole was a network of pedestrian ways which, on the phase 1 site, runs from

* A degree day is the number of degrees between 65°F and the daily mean temperature when this is lower. Degree days are usually expressed as a yearly total.
A rain day is a period of twenty-four hours between 9am and 9am Greenwich Mean Time in which ·01in (·2mm) or more rain is recorded

Table I Distribution of dwelling types

Dwelling type	No of dwellings	Percentage of dwellings	No of people	Percentage of people
Two-storey houses				
Two-bedroom four-person	60	12	240	13
Three-bedroom five-person	90	17	450	25
Three-bedroom six-person	5	1	30	2
Four-bedroom seven-person	25	5	175	10
Five-bedroom nine-person	2	0	18	1
Total	**182**	**35**	**913**	**51**

Average size 5 people per dwelling

Flats				
Bedsitting-room	53	10	53	3
One-bedroom two-person	126	24	252	14
Two-bedroom three-person	97	19	291	16
Two-bedroom four-person	42	8	168	9
Three-bedroom five-person	19	4	95	5
Three-bedroom six-person	1	0	6	0
Totals	**338**	**65**	**865**	**49**

Average size 2·6 people per dwelling

| **Grand total** | **520** | **100** | **1 778** | **100** |

Table II Summary of dwelling sizes

Size	No	Percentage
One-bedroom and bedsitting-room	179	34
Two-bedroom	199	39
Three-bedroom	115	22
Four-bedroom	25	5
Five-bedroom	2	0
Total	**520**	**100**

1

2

Radcliffe Street in the north down to the southern boundary. When the proposed orbital ring road is complete along the line of this boundary, the pedestrian way will cross it at high level to give access to the town centre.

The four longest spur service roads (see plan) run from Horsedge Street on the east boundary and penetrate deeply into the site. Access decks to the composite blocks **2** are provided at three levels as shown on p103

The middle level serves all the blocks, which are connected by pedestrian bridges **3**, **4**; access points are at the west end of block 1 and in the middle of block 5. A higher level, accessible from the west end of block 5, serves this and block 4. A lower level serves only the east end of block 1. For convenient access, decks are arranged to discharge onto or near the through pedestrian route.

With the use of access decks, lifts can be omitted from a scheme of this size. In larger schemes such as Park Hill, Sheffield, lifts are still necessary because convenient access onto the decks at ground level cannot be gained from all approaches to the site. Furthermore of course the system can be employed only where the ground slopes steeply. Even in this scheme, it is questionable whether a lift at say the junction of blocks 1 and 2, may not have substantially cut walking distances for pedestrians approaching from the east. The degree of inconvenience experienced is doubtless one of the points which will be investigated in the follow-up study.

Since the building system employed–12M Jesperson–requires houses and blocks of flats has been influenced by the desirability of providing straight runs during construction. At Gladsaxe, Denmark, where the original Jespersen system was used, the stark result of allowing the discipline of a tracked crane to dominate all others can be seen: at Oldham

3

4

1 Spur service road next to block 1: Cars parked at top of rise are blocking turning circle in cul-de-sac—but are justifiably at nearest point to owners' homes
2 Access point at west end of block 1: Hand tamping of surface aggregate of precast concrete panels, rather anomalous anyway in this industrialised system, is sometimes betrayed by rather poor quality as here

3 Pedestrian bridge between blocks 1 and 2: Very neat zoning of elements, characteristic of this system, is particularly evident here
4 Closer view of pedestrian bridge: Timber is so sympathetic a material that it is tempting to use it even in situations such as this where larger-scale sheet materials, more in keeping with rest of system, would have been preferable

relationships of elements, enclosure of spaces and proper siting of facilities such as play spaces, parking and pubs have obviously been primary considerations.

All house terraces run north–south: in this way terraces can line both sides of pedestrian routes, and living-rooms and bedrooms, facing onto back gardens, still receive sunlight from east or west. The minimum distance between front faces of houses is about 9 m (30 ft) but this applies only to the two-bedroom four person type which has no bedroom or living-room at the front (see photograph on p 100). Between faces with living-rooms and bedrooms the minimum distance is about 13·5 m (45 ft) and, while overlooking from bedroom into living-room is technically possible, complaints are few and net curtains rare.

While toddlers' play spaces have been reasonably distributed throughout the housing complex, an attempt has been made to provide facilities nearer to home: some of the semi-private access paths between back gardens have been provided with self-closing gates at each end **5** and the paths widen at intervals to form small play alcoves. Whether these areas, which cannot be seen from the houses, will be regarded as safe remains to be seen. If the Englishman were not so addicted to his high garden fence (designed here with the garden sheds by Max Lock & Partners) then an arrangement of this sort would be more obviously workable. Surface drainage is proving difficult. The outdoor space around the high density houses originally on this site consisted mostly of concrete yards. The resultant made-up subsoil is hard to drain and Oldham is also about the wettest place in England.

Many back gardens to the houses slope up from a concrete terrace outside the living-room (note line of fence in **6**) and inches of water lie in this valley during rainy spells. Land drainage pipes are having to be installed. Similarly, district heating distribution ducts have been flooded.

6 Paved area with play facilities between blocks 6 (right) and 9 (higher level on left): While paving details are generally well considered it is sometimes difficult to see reason for use of deterrent varieties in a position such as that of tilted setts under ramp retaining wall. Outdoor lighting was chosen by the borough engineer

5

5 Steel gates enclosing semi-private access path and play alcoves between pairs of house terraces are self-closing

6

7

8

9

7 *Block 3 from upper access deck in block 1: It can be seen that landscaping money was spent on extensive ground moulding and turf was bought rather than seed. Trees, on* *other hand, are only small saplings although they have survived quite well so far* **8** *Blocks 5, 4 and 6 (left to right): This is only situation where privacy of living-rooms* *and bedrooms is threatened, ie on ground floor non-access side of flats as in block 5 here* **9** *Block 5 on right, block 10 on left: Handrails are* *thoughtfully provided to ramps as well as staircases*

Landscaping of the site is well considered throughout with a basis of considerable ground moulding (**7, 8, 9**). In general, larger public spaces are surfaced with grass and have substantial tree planting while subsidiary areas are hard surfaced and have some smaller scale planting. Turf was used rather than seeding—wisely, since the topsoil tends to remain soggy and liable to damage. Trees are subject to recurrent vandalism. Play areas have been provided with a certain amount of equipment.

The usual oddities of microclimate in the vicinity of slab blocks are noticeable—in particular, microgales between blocks 1 and 2—but the very exposed position of the site has compensations in magnificent Lowry-like views of Oldham and some splendid glimpses of the moors **10**.
A site for one public house next to the main pedestrian route was designed to attract through as well as local traffic. On the same principle, the sites for corner shops were reserved at the west end of block 5.

10

10 *Looking east across site,*
with block 1 on right, to
moors beyond
11 *Block 10: Way through*
between two-bedroom

four-person house types with
additional bedroom above,
making three-bedroom
six-person link version
12 *Ground floor flat in*

block 1 (five-storey):
Entrance to one-bedroom flat
showing use of door-
mounted refuse sack which
is neat but not under cover

13 *Public staircase to flats.*
Good robust detailing
14 *Rooflights over public*
staircase. Central rod braces
balustrades at each level

the result partly of the way the system was used and partly of the modular planning discipline.

Car parking at an average of 0·28 cars per dwelling was low in comparison with the norm at the time, and even of this, less than one third was in garages with no workshop space provided. Two potential additional parking areas were available along the east boundary: if both these had decks for two-level parking, there could have been one space per dwelling.

The boiler house 18, designed by Max Lock & Partners, was sited to the north of the housing development and planned to cater for 2 500 dwellings in various phases.

Dwellings

All dwellings are to Parker Morris standards, except thirty-two houses and forty-five flats in which room areas, particularly storage provision, are slightly below. This was

Certain criteria were proposed for allocating bedrooms and living/dining-rooms:

Bedrooms Of the one-person pensioner households, half were to have a separate bedroom; half a bedsitting-room.

All single persons of working age were to have a separate bedroom and sitting-room.

Married couples were to share a bedroom and each other adult in households with less than five people was to have his own bedroom.

Not more than two people were to occupy one bedroom.

Young married couples were to have a spare bedroom; growing families of three or four people were to have an extra bed space.

Living-rooms All except half the one-person pensioner households (see above) were to have separate living-rooms.

All households with three or more people were to have a dining-area, not necessarily separate from the kitchen.

All kitchens were to have some room for informal eating.

All houses are two-storey and there are three standard types of house each having its link version in which an additional double bedroom is provided over the adjacent public way through at ground level 11. The standard two-bedroom four-person (link version three-bedroom six-person) is 5·486 m (18 ft) to centres of party walls and 7·315 m (24 ft) deep; the standard three-bedroom five person

11

(link version four-bedroom seven-person) 4·877 m × 9·754 m (16 ft by 32 ft) deep; and the standard four-bedroom seven-person (link version five-bedroom nine-person) 5·486 m × 9·754 m (18 ft by 32 ft) deep.

In the standard two-bedroom four-person house, the usual problem of small houses—need for greater ground floor than first floor area—has been met by allowing the entrance hall to project and shelter the entrance door (see photograph on p100). It is regrettable that no canopies have been provided.

In the standard three-bedroom five-person house, which has a narrow frontage, the dining-area is planned between kitchen and living-room, taking light indirectly from the kitchen. (This arrangement was also tried in the single-

12

13

14

storey 5M housing at Sheffield, see pp 57- 78, although rooflighting was available there.) Artificial light seems to be used in this area during daytime but comments are not very adverse. An additional wc on the ground floor is provided for this type and for the standard four-bedroom seven-person. Bedroom 1 in this type is a rather awkwardly elongated shape and some difficulty was observed in furniture arrangement: the situation is aggravated by the corner position of the door which sterilises half the short wall.

The standard four-bedroom seven-person house is planned with the dining-kitchen arrangement reversed, the dining-area being on the outside wall and the kitchen in the centre.

One would have thought the first arrangement more acceptable than the last: the kitchen does not directly overlook the public areas where children may be playing, or front door for identification of visitors; the working area of the kitchen has the worst light; and privacy is probably more valuable in the dining-area than the kitchen (although this was not borne out at Sheffield). In this type, both the ground floor wc and the bathroom are internal and vented by mechanical extract fan. None of the house types has a satisfactory method of dividing the second double bedroom as children grow up. Certainly planning for this possibility requires more circulation space and presumably it was felt that the need has not yet been fully proved. Fortunately some completed housing schems do incorporate this facility and its use will, one hopes, be observed over the next few years.

In all house types the generous staircase width [1·016 m (3 ft 4 in) overall, 0·940 m (3 ft 1 in) tread width], resulting from the 0·305 m (1 ft) structural increments is appreciated

by tenants and gives an air of remarkable spaciousness to the entrance hall **19.**

The key to the arrangement of flats lies in planning of access levels (ie all deck access levels and the ground floor level in four-storey blocks) where a one-bedroom two-person flat and a bedsitting-room flat are each wrapped around an entrance lobby and staircase serving a flat above. The one-bedroom two-person and bedsitting-room flats on the access levels are entered on either side of a central service unit which houses an internal bathroom and drying cupboard to each flat with a common extract duct.

Each of these two-flat complexes is three structural bays in width and it would probably have made planning this level easier if the two staircases had been placed in the central bay. However the architects were uncertain whether it was structurally advisable to place two staircases within one structural bay although it was later apparent that this would have been feasible. As it is, the planning of the small flats at access levels does not seem to have suffered too much except that the route from kitchen to front door is about 10·5 m (35 ft).

If it is objected that the 12M Jespersen system which Laings had available has been well tried in Denmark and that the architects therefore need not have landed themselves in such difficulties, it should be noted that the situation just discussed is a typical example of the way in which our planning requirements differ from the Danes'. The architects are providing—not for the first time—an access route to flats which is intended to be more akin to a street than a gallery: but a route of such a width cannot be provided economically on every floor. Further, since access to flats on floors without decks is made by means of a staircase in the centre of the block, these flats can be planned with rooms on both frontages without the lack of privacy resulting from gallery access. None of this is new but it is not common practice in Denmark and the system was not, therefore, designed to cater for these situations.

The ground floor plan in four-storey blocks is identical to the access deck plan except that the bays on either side of the entrance come out to the face of the building. This allows the dining-room and kitchen to be rather larger—probably, in fact, rather lavish for a one-bedroom two-person or bedsitting-room flat. The entrance lobbies to the upper flats incorporate pram storage spaces.

On floors immediately above those just described (ie gaining access by private staircase from below) the three-bay unit contains either two two-bedroom three-person flats or one two-bedroom four-person and one one-bedroom two-person. The two-bedroom three-person flat has its dining-room sandwiched between living-room and kitchen; the two-bedroom four-person flat has a large dining-room and sandwiched kitchen.

In three- and five-storey blocks, the ground floor **12** contains no access to flats above and each three-bay unit contains a one-bedroom two-person and a two-bedroom four-person flat.

All the basic types described above are augmented when they are next to public staircases by additional bedrooms. Some public staircases **13, 14** also contain a refuse chute and there is an incinerator **15, 16** on each access level and a drying-room on the top floor.

Criticism, particularly at this early stage of occupation, is most easily directed at the internal detailing. There is a certain lack of co-ordination for instance between the sizes of the built-in fittings and the structural openings, with frequent gaps of an inch or so at the sides of the cupboards. Similarly, between high-level cupboards and the ceiling is a rather half-hearted gap of 152 mm (6 in) in which few items can be stored and which is probably difficult to clean **17**. Night vents in the bedrooms tend to blow open (although the exposed situation must be taken into consideration) and are sometimes screwed shut by tenants. Pipe work in the bathrooms and wcs is generally exposed and rather messy, and the hardwood strip used as a splashback around baths and sinks is already deteriorating.

From the tenants however there are hardly any complaints so far about basic arrangements of dwellings or the amount of space provided. That such items as refuse chutes, incinerators and heating equipment have been used properly is largely owing to the care taken by the architects in ensuring that tenants have been properly instructed: in collaboration with the housing manager, a handbook explaining these points was produced and distributed to all tenants. The fact that one of the housing manager's staff has an office on the site and is on call daily for advice has helped considerably.

15

Heating

A coal fired boiler in the boiler house **18** on the other side of Horsedge Street supplies high pressure hot water to mains which feed each building. Inside the building, mains pipes branch to heating circuits and to calorifiers for domestic hot water.

The boiler house, at present containing two boilers of 15 825 000 kJ (15 000 000 Btu) and 25 320 000kJ (24 000 000 Btu) capacity, has a space for a further 25 320 000 kJ (24 000 000 Btu) boiler and will serve 2 500 dwellings in the first five phases. Finely graded soild fuel is delivered in 14 tonne loads directly into a fuel boot below ground. A conveyor/elevator lifts the fuel as required for topping-up three reinforced concrete hoppers at roof level. From here

16

15 *Hopper to refuse chute and adjacent incinerator Public staircase beyond*
16 *Access ramp and doors to refuse chamber: Chute discharges into refuse container which is wheeled out and mechanically handled by refuse vehicle. Access to public staircase is on left of refuse chamber*
17 *Kitchen of four-bedroom seven-person house: Built-in cupboards appear distinctly unintegrated. It may be found that where kitchens such as this require supplementary artificial lighting, traditional central rose will be inadequate*

17

18 *Boiler house: Cladding is consistent with that on housing. Concrete fuel hoppers on roof are mentioned in text, but their dramatic balancing act is spoilt by masking from normal points of view*

18

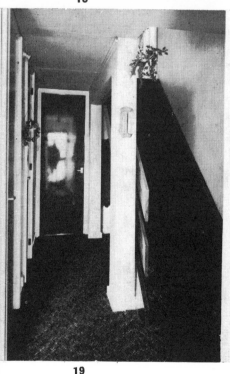

19 *House staircase: Generous width, resulting from 305 mm (1ft) increment in span lengths, is appreciated by many tenants*

19

the fuel is gravity-fed to the boilers and after combustion in the form of a fine fuel ash is removed by suction to two cylindrical steel storage tanks above the delivery bay.

The reinforced concrete hoppers **18** are each of 60 tons capacity and are supported as point loads at the intersections of a diagonal grid beam—which seems a triumphant solution to a rather unnecessary problem. The precast concrete cladding panels have the same finish and texture as those in the housing development.

The amount of heat and hot water consumed by each tenant is metered: a weekly standing charge is collected with the rent and the tenant receives a rebate or surcharge when the meter is read. Space heating in the dwelling is by fan-assisted warm air heat exchangers heated by hot water, controlled by thermostats and time clocks.

The design temperature is a constant 18·3°C (65°F) in living-rooms, dining-rooms and kitchens regardless of the outside temperature.

Construction
The ministry chose John Laing & Sons to link with in evolving the structural system because of Laings' experience of similar types of construction and its strong research organisation. Laings already had an interest in the Jespersen system, evolved in Denmark by the engineer P. E. Malmström and it was decided to make this the starting point for the work since the thinking behind it was similar to the ministry's and conformed closely to the requirements of central area slum clearance sites. It allows medium and high housing densities to be achieved with the use of one- and two-storey houses as well as low rise flats.

The MOHLG (with Ove Arup & Partners as its structural consultants) and MOPBW collaborated with Laings in modifying the system to conform more closely with the requirements of housing design in this country—the basic difference being a greater variety of plan types.

The primary modifications made to the original system were the conversion to imperial measure—during which the spans were stretched rather than reduced—and the introduction of some standard variations (made in the same mould as standards) and a few specials.

The detailed brief for the modified 12M Jespersen system included the following:

off-site factory production of concrete walls and floors to reduce site labour and speed up construction;
medium-size units to provide a balance between standardisation and planning flexibility;
use of mobile cranes on sloping sites giving a maximum unit weight of 2½ tonnes;
omission of screeding and plastering implying a high degree of accuracy and good finish on walls and floors;
suitability for blocks up to five storeys;
accommodation of a variety of cladding panels, partitions and floor finishes;
a U value of 0·2 or better for external walls and grade I sound reduction to party walls and party floors;
use of alternative forms of heating;
price within MOHLG cost yardstick;
dimensional and performance standards as recommended in the MOHLG Design Bulletin 8 *Dimensions and components for housing.*

Three horizontal planning grids are inherent in the system: The 1200mm (4ft) or 12M grid. This determines the width of floor and wall panels, the former being 1200mm wide and the latter 1200mm and 2400mm. A dwelling's depth is therefore a multiple of 1200mm. The 300mm grid (1ft). Floor panels may be any width up to 5400mm in 300mm increments and spacing of cross walls (the only load-bearing element) is therefore in 300mm (1ft) increments to centres. The 100mm grid (1ft). Used in positioning partitions, kitchen fittings and doors. Partitions have one face on a grid line. Floor to floor height is 2500mm. Floor and wall panels are 178mm (7in) thick, wall panels unreinforced. Steel moulds are used for all concrete panels. Service or duct holes can be cast through walls.

At St Mary's, wind bracing is provided in the flats by spine walls to ducts. Foundations are concrete rafts to houses and piles to flats.

Concrete cladding panels are faced with exposed white calcined flint aggregate tamped onto the top of the concrete in its mould. Above sill level are glazed timber units, and cladding on access decks is the same, with boarded timber

112

20

22

21

20 *Present boundary between old and new at end of Dorothy Street. Block 16 (four-bedroom seven-person) is on left*

21 *One of the more daunting views: Block 1 from south. Unfortunately this is most common approach direction from town centre*

22 *Sometimes integration of elements, such as road-retaining wall-steps-footpath-gable wall situation in this area, reaches a very high standard*

units below sills. Timber is finished with black preservative stain, opening lights being painted white.

Internal partitions are lightweight concrete slabs 3in thick with wallpaper applied directly to them and the Jespersen concrete walls. Concrete soffits to floor slabs are decorated with a stippled plastic finish. Flooring is of timber boarding on battens. Where the floor is a party floor the battens are on strips of sound insulating quilt.

At first assessment the system appears to have accomplished all that it set out to do and doubtless achieves a very high technical standard. Duccio Turin has pointed out that the cost of a building comprises 20 per cent to 25 per cent labour and 60 per cent to 65 per cent materials. We can hope to affect costs only marginally while we retain the use of traditional materials and, in the same way, reduction in total labour content (including factory labour) is limited by the nature of materials such as those used in the 12M system. It will be a breakthrough at the level of materials technology which will presumably bring the big rewards. Meanwhile, as a product of our semi-traditional industry, this system is one of the better examples and is a clear demonstration of the advantages of close collaboration between the client's architect and the manufacturer.

The system was also employed on 520 houses in one further phase of the St Mary's Ward redevelopment, and has also been used at Glenrothes, Aldershot, Gosport and Livingstone New Town, Scotland.

FLATS: SUMMARY

Ground floor area: 5 017m² (46 662 sq ft.)
Total floor area: 24 346m² (225 491 sq ft) (including shop).
Type of contract: Negotiated lump sum with bill of quantities.
Tender date: August 1965.
Work began: January 1966 (superstructure).
Work finished: January 1967 (superstructure).
Net habitable floor area; 22 396m² (208 212 sq ft.)
Tender price of foundation, superstructure, installation and finishes: £389 919.
Tender price of external works and ancillary buildings including all drainage: Part of larger contract—total price £59 689.

HOUSES: SUMMARY

Ground floor area: 9 028m² (83 965 sq ft.)
Total floor area: 18 669m² (175 627 sq ft.)
Type of contract: Negotiated lump sum with bill of quantities.
Tender date: August 1965.
Work began: January 1966 (superstructure).
Work finished: January 1967 (superstructure).
Tender price of foundation, superstructure, installation and finishes: £513 369.
Tender price of external works and ancillary buildings including all drainage: Part of larger contract—total price £59 689.

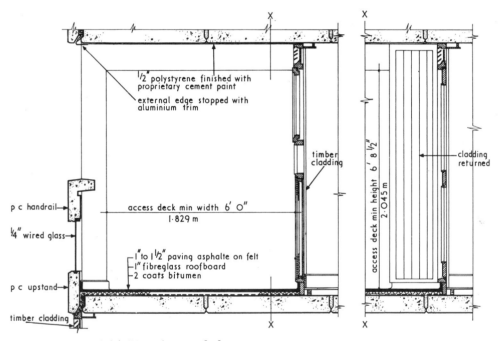

Dimensioning and detailing of access deck

10·Housing at Laindon, Basildon

This housing scheme of
862 dwelling units was
included in MOHLG Design
Bulletin 10 Cars in
housing 1.[1] In this it could
hardly have been a better
choice, containing as it
does most approaches
recommended in the Bulletin
to provision of parking
facilities, organisation of
pedestrian and vehicular
circulation routes, and
grouping of dwelling blocks.
The scheme is also
significant as an exercise
in the use of Siporex
lightweight concrete panel
construction: formally and
aesthetically it is more
interesting than most
examples seen in the system's
country of origin, Sweden.

designed by	Anthony B. Davies of Anthony B. Davies & Associates, in succession to the Department of Architecture and Planning, Basildon Development Corporation
associate in charge	R. Thomas
quantity surveyor	E. C. Harris & Partners
consultants	
foundations	C. F. Bath
superstructure	A. C. Ross
associate	J. D. Bedwell
landscape	Department of Architecture and Design, Basildon Development Corporation
main contractors	W. C. French & Costains

1 *Spurriers cul-de-sac entry. Direction signs for pedestrians are clear, some however cause users to cross vehicular routes*

2 *Further into Spurriers. An easy transition from parking to landscaped areas . . . shortly leading to one of the children's enclosed play areas*

2

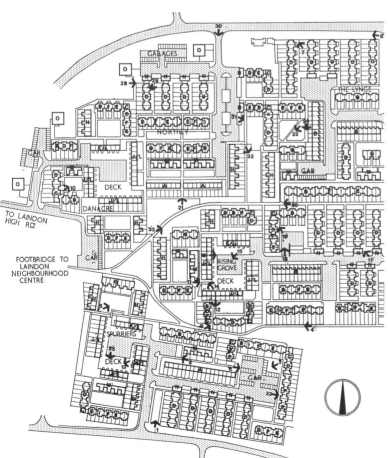

Site plan of Laindon housing areas 1, 2, 3, Basildon (1:2 000). House type references are given by letters. Numerals show photo viewpoints

CLIENT'S REQUIREMENTS

The first new housing area in the existing suburb of Laindon was to be developed to inject new population into a depressed area of the town and create initial support for a new neighbourhood centre to be built as the next part of the programme on the western boundary.

Because at the time this project was conceived in 1963/64 saturation in the building industry was slowing down production of houses by traditional methods, it was decided to consider parallel use of non-traditional methods of construction to maintain the programme of 1 000 houses a year.

SITE

In the Laindon neighbourhood of the new town of Basildon. The site is bounded to the west by Laindon High Road, to the north by St Nicholas Lane, to the east by Leinster Road and to the south by Laindon Link. It is served by a county primary school at its south-eastern extremity and the new Laindon neighbourhood centre has been constructed to the west. It slopes considerably from west to east.

PLANNING

All the recommendations of the Parker Morris Committee in *Homes for today and tomorrow*[2] relative to the house and its environment were to be implemented. Progressive segregation of vehicular and pedestrian traffic had evolved in the new town layouts over the previous five years or so but with the pedestrian circulation secondary to the vehicular. In this layout, the formula was reversed so that it was designed with primary pedestrian circulation enabling mothers and children to walk from all parts of the area to and from the neighbourhood centre and school with minimum involvement with the motor car.

3 *The short cut already worn across the planted surround indicates need to adjust the pavement layout*
4 *Under a bridged passage*

into a potentially interesting open space, at a change of direction and inclination of a primary route for pedestrians.
5 *Further up this primary*

route a small play square is passed. Ramp on right leads up to one of the deck blocks. Paving is extremely well handled here

6 *But not so well at this point where one of the main pedestrian ways stops abruptly. In terms of circulation priority, the path*

3

4

5

6

7

to the left is of equal importance to that on the right. The irregular central area has been covered with 'municipal' asphalt

7 *A left-over space at end of* *an access path. From a distance the impression is that here is an exit (See site plan for photo viewpoints)*

APPRAISAL

This scheme showed promise early as a significant example of a well handled medium density layout. It is full of interest and variety, and should be a pleasure to live in. The handling of the problems of pedestrian/vehicle relationships make the scheme a textbook example of the principles propounded in *Cars in housing*[3]—too much so at times.

Second floor plan house type B

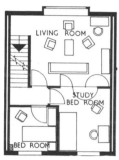

First floor plan house type B

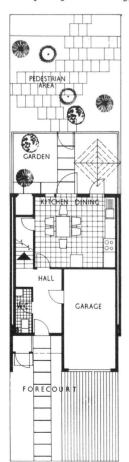

Ground floor plan three-bedroom five-person house type B
(references given on site plan—cost outline p 127)

$(\frac{1}{16}\text{in} = 1\text{ft}, = 1:192)$

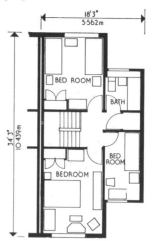

First floor plan house type D

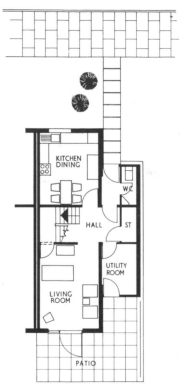

Ground floor plan three-bedroom five-person house type D
($\frac{1}{16}$in = 1ft, = 1:192). See cost analysis on p

Section through house type B—*plans left*

Second floor plan house type J

First floor plan house type J

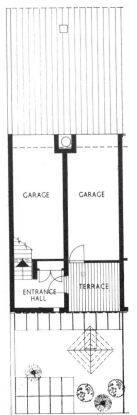

$(\frac{1}{16}$in $= 1$ft, $= 1:192)$

Ground floor plan three-bedroom five-person deck house type J

much so at times

Pedestrian priority has been established as far as the demands of the engineer and the then Ministry of Transport road width requirements allowed. Progression through the pedestrian ways is already a stimulating experience. One passes from narrow passages into a series of differently sized and treated open spaces; vistas are continually opening

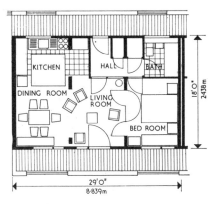

Plan of one person one-bedroom flats type L
(*above deck dwelling*)

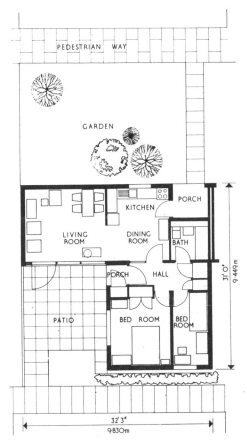

Plan of two-bedroom two-person house type M

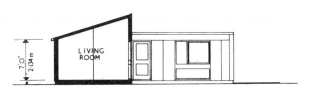

Section through two-bedroom two-person house type M

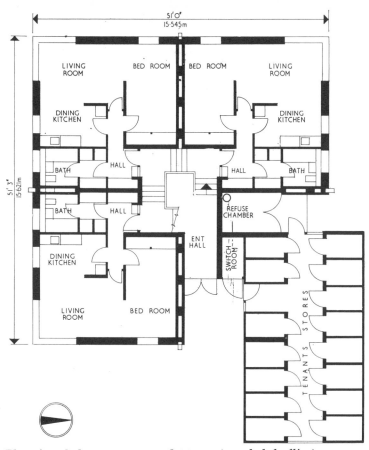

Plan of one-bedroom one-person flat type L (*over deck dwelling*)
($\frac{1}{16}$in = 1ft, = 1:192)

and closing; glimpses down side routes frequently afford views of small squares and play areas. A sense of anticipation has been sustained throughout.

Transition from vehicular to pedestrian routes has also been sensibly treated. At several points the cardinal sin of the separationists has been advantageously committed; play areas spill into parking areas, and why not? Dad can tinker with the car, while junior plays near at hand: neither constitutes a danger to the other. The initial plan for provision of five different forms of parking proved in the event too complicated and was subsequently stream lined.

A scheme of this type certainly shows the need for a new set of design criteria for vehicle access route sizes. As mentioned above, this scheme has been severely compromised by the imposition of traditional road requirements; suburban widths complete with sidewalks are the order of the day. Attempts at achieving satisfactory environmental conditions are negated by these outdated regulations. If narrower carriageways had been permitted, with humped entries and speed deterring surfaces, a higher degree of safety would have been achieved, a better scale between bordering house blocks would have been possible and of course land would have been released for more open space or slightly increased densities.

The fact that it is possible to park anywhere along the wide carriageways, while still leaving room for two lanes of traffic, raises the question as to why the corporation has accepted the specially designated parking areas yet at the same time has insisted on road dimensions which make them unnecessary.

The free use of hard ground surfaces is a heartening depar-

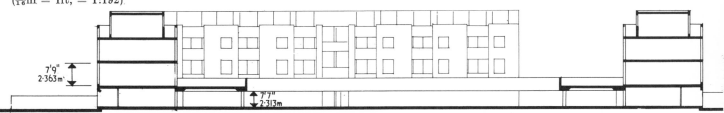

Section through typical deck block. See detailed plans p 118 ($\frac{1}{32}$in = 1ft, = 1:384)

8 *A confusion of fencing materials. If concrete blocks alone had been used, with fewer steps down slope, closer relationship between house and landscape would surely have been achieved*

Food preparation, eating and refuse disposal checked against Safety in the home (*see text on p. 127*)

Dwelling type and number of persons	B (6)	D (5)	J (5)	M (3)	L (2)	O (2)
Work sequence 1 Arrangement of working area should provide uninterrupted sequence of work surface—cooker—work surface—sink—work surface, closely related to storage and eating areas (para 14)	**Sequence** No **Relationship** Yes	No Yes	Yes Yes	No Yes	No Yes	No Yes
Position of cooker 2 Cooker should not be immediately next to a window or door (para 15)	OK	OK	OK	By window	OK	OK (marginal)
Doors 3 Doors to kitchen should be placed to minimise through traffic (para 16)	Yes	Yes	Yes	Yes (main circulation)	Yes	Yes
4 Swings of all doors and cupboard doors in kitchen should be planned to avoid collision (para 17)	Yes	Yes	Yes	Yes	Yes	Yes
Work top height 5 Work tops on each side of cooker should be same height as boiling plate or rings (para 18)	Yes	Yes	Yes	Yes	Yes	Yes
Fittings above cooker 6 A ceiling mounted airer or a cupboard should not be fixed directly above cooker or boiler (para 19)	Not applicable	Not applicable	Not applicable	Not applicable	Not applicable	Not applicable
Lighting 7 Lighting of working areas should be arranged to avoid shadow (para 20)	Yes	Yes	Yes	Yes	Yes	Yes
Storage 8 Storage space within normal reach should be provided for all articles in daily use (para 21)	Yes	Yes	Yes	Yes	Yes	Yes
Play space 9 Play space for children should be planned within sight of kitchen (para 22)	Yes	No	No	Yes (not generally applicable)	Not applicable	Not applicable
Dining space 10 There should be enough table or counter space in kitchen for a casual meal to be eaten (para 23)	Yes (part of dining-room)	Yes (part of dining-room)	Yes	Yes	Yes	Yes

10

11

12

9 *Corner and bridging houses are well handled however. Experience with lightweight autoclaved aerated concrete on an earlier project at Lee Chapel North, Basildon, proved the need for a wall protecting rail (seen in passage) to protect walls from abrasion by prams, bicycles and so on*

10 *Another enclosed play space. Children can play hopscotch here on specially laid out paving. Again they have taken the logical direct path to swings across planted plot*

11 *Pram access to deck blocks is possible by ramp or . . .*

12 *by well detailed stair runners*

ture from the norm. For once practicality has prevailed over the usual romantic desire of architects to create country in the town by setting off the buildings with 'children keep off' grass. Children have been permitted on the grassed slide mounds and before long turned them into mud hills.

A disturbing aspect of the scheme is its lack of coherent overall form. Despite the good handling of the immediate ground plane, there is no feeling of place and there are no obvious points of reference. An overriding fear of monotony has led the architects to overwork the positive qualities of interest and variety. To an already busy composition of one-, two-, three-, and four-storey blocks on a sloping site, they have added a variety of conflicting roof slopes and colour changes on identical blocks and in infill panelling. Each has probably been employed for a very good reason but the sum of them all does not add up to an identifiable environmental form.

This shows one lesson that architects engaged on large scale housing are slowly learning. Design decisions must be considered concurrently at more than one level. The English architect with his preoccupation with detail is certainly master of the individual dwelling unit, but is less able to handle combinations of these units on the broader environmental scale.

In this project, the individual dwellings combine well into blocks. They retain their identity through obvious elements, such as porches and stores, but their individuality is appropriately subservient to the whole. The architects

13

14

15

16

17

18

13 *But decks when reached are interesting mainly for their views out to countryside. Paving treatment does however succeed in breaking down expansive scale of these areas*
14 *View down into scheme . . .*
15 *to (not quite) under-deck parking . . .*
16 *and to access roads . . .*
17 *Down access roads there are toughly detailed car ports . . .*
18 *and parking courts. This one leads off in the centre*
19 *under a bridged house to . . .*
20 *one of the primary pedestrian routes . . .*
21 *and further across between blocks . . .*
22 *Later comes a pleasant grassed square which is*

19

20

22

perfectly in scale with its perimeter two-storey houses
23 *Entry to these houses has been carefully considered with an integrated door canopy and refuse bin store roof; privacy from adjacent house and an easily manageable front garden. Honest articulation of wall and floor panel joists is seen clearly here . . .*
24 *as it is in three-storey blocks including change in level . . .*
25 *and also in deck blocks. But here both at deck level and on access balconies above, canopies over front doors would have apparently upset the crispness of the design. Should 'design' take precedence over user convenience ?*

21

23

24

25

have shown commendable restraint in the use of materials for the dwelling blocks, a factor which makes their colouring exercises even more inexplicable. Three materials have been consistently employed throughout: lightweight autoclaved aerated concrete for the walls; timber for porches, external stores and some infill panels; and tile hanging for the remaining infill panels.

In their use of lightweight concrete, the architects have shown a clear understanding of the characteristics and inherent aesthetic qualities of the material. There have been no attempts to 'ice the cake' (the simple slab-on-wall construction is clearly expressed): joints have been clearly articulated and vulnerable areas are adequately protected. It was unfortunate that the contractors were not able to see their way to solve the technical problems of the few four-storey perimeter blocks and thus use lightweight concrete throughout. These neo-*brut* brick and concrete blocks, although pleasant in themselves, are certainly strangers to the area. The contrasting form of these blocks could have been employed to advantage by locating them at the entry to each cul-de-sac where they would act as much needed points of reference for the whole scheme.

In the detailing and choice of materials for private and public fencing the sure handling of the dwelling blocks has been lost. The dwellings and their courtyards read as independently considered elements. Three materials are employed for fencing and none bears any affinity to those employed in the dwelling blocks. If one material had been used for both solid and perforated walls, and it was of a colour which related to the adjacent dwelling blocks, closer integration between the dwelling, its own open space, and the overall environment would have been achieved.

The deck blocks are good tough urban elements which appear out of place in this project. As formal elements they do not work as points of reference within the site, not being high enough to contrast with the terrace blocks around. Only one of them is at a logical focus of pedestrian or vehicular routes. As undercover parking elements they are highly inefficient although admittedly they keep the weather off cars. As the section indicates, the garages require free space immediately in front of them for access, space which although under cover cannot be fully used for additional parking to justify the undoubtedly expensive structural decking. A more satisfactory solution would have been to provide non-lock-up parking alone, with efficient parking arrangements dictating the form of the block above.

The deck surfaces also appear to be wasteful elements. If they were parts of the main pedestrian circulation routes in a dense urban situation, each would be a pleasant piazza to pass through. But in this project the decks are inappropriate. Generally being a floor above the level of the pedestrian routes with adequate open space provision, they are dead ends, of use only to the perimeter dwellings which on three of the four sides also have their own ground floor private open spaces. It is intended that these deck areas will be landscaped when their role in use has been determined. This will certainly be a taxing exercise.

The relationship between family composition and provision of private open space is a critical factor present in many similar projects, highlighted in these deck blocks. Here the perimeter dwellings have open space provisions, scaled from $88 \cdot 26$ m² (950 sq ft) through $22 \cdot 30$ m² (240 sq ft) to zero.

These sizes appear to have been dictated by location of pathways and orientation, rather than family size, which will here be predominantly composed of couples with three young children.

26 Dilemma of full height glazing: does this resident really want to display the workings of his refrigerator, his drier and his vegetable rack?

27 Is this resident modest about displaying such material possessions or does he prefer to pay less for curtaining and achieve a tidier appearance to his home?

28 Coming into the site from another direction a pedestrian route passes under bridging houses—note here protective cobbling in front of lightweight autoclaved aerated panelling

29 Car ports and access paths are on either side of this route with an easy transition from one to the other. At bottom this route links up with . . .

30 one of the vehicle culs-de-sac which is approached past one of the brick and concrete mini-towers. Here all characteristics of typical suburban road patterns are shown even down to kerb parking

26

27

28

29

30

31

31 *Through car ports on left there is one of the most pleasant play areas, from which one catches a glimpse . . .*

32 *of another potentially good space between rows of terrace houses. At the top of this passes one of the primary pedestrian routes . . .*

33 *leading towards the main central grassed area at the confluence with the other primary route*

34 *Two-storey three-bedroom house (type D, cost analysed p812–814). Semi-open plan* *has a general feeling of spaciousness—stair landing and storage below it, left, have been treated in a novel way*

35 *The kitchen looks workmanlike and benefits from undersill daylighting when owner has only a few appliances*

36 *Stairs are soundly detailed and . . .*

32

34

33

35

36

126

37 well lit
38 Staircase borrows light
from bedrooms but of course
also gives it to them at night
39 This single-storey
two-person type M patio
house kitchen shows need
for appliance and fitment

manufacturers to
co-ordinate dimensions. Note
unsafe position for cooker by
a doorway and without
work top provision on both
sides
40 Home is always, in the
end, what you make of it,

as in a type M patio house,
looking through the living
spaces . . .
41 or in a single-person
type L flat on the top floor
of a deck block, looking from
the kitchen into the living
spaces. Here the folding

doors into the bedroom have
been partly covered by a
shelving unit which in fact
could not have fitted
anywhere else

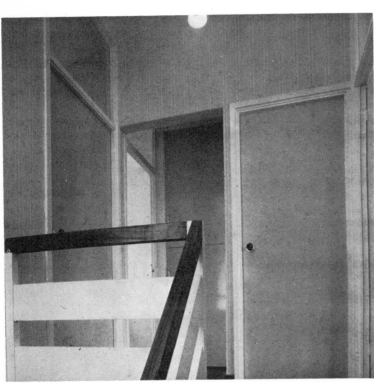

37

38

39

40

41

Changes in plan form were provided for in the design, and advantage has been taken of this provision, particularly since the sale to tenants of some of the dwellings.

Built-in storage is provided in most bedrooms but it is not entirely effective as much of it is not deep enough to hang clothes at right-angles on the rails.

A detailed check on the safety of internal planning has become possible since the publication of *Safety in the home*[4]. Application of the check list to the kitchens of the basic plan types in this project indicated only one marked fault, omission of a work surface on both sides of the cooker spaces. (See table on p 120.).

The one-bedroom flats on the top floor appear to suffer from being contained within envelopes dictated by the formal composition of the blocks rather than actual user suitability. The set-back on either side of the block and expression of the profile of these flats on end elevation is most 'architectural'. But it has dictated an unsuitable internal plan arrangement, with continuous balconies and high sills on the private side, and narrow unsheltered access on the other. Covered access, terraces of usable size and windows giving views from a sitting position are surely more important than formalistic whimsy.

SUMMARY

Ground floor area: 45·1 m² (485½ sq ft).
Total floor area: 90·21 m² (971 sq ft).
Type of contract: Negotiated—fixed price.
Tender date: August 1964.
Work began: September 1964.
Work finished: March 1967.
Tender price of foundation, superstructure, installation and finishes including drainage to collecting manhole: £2 731.
Tender price of external works and ancillary buildings including drainage beyond collecting manhole: £336.
Total: £3 067.

11 Housing at Reporton Road, London SW 6

This scheme is a prototype for infill development in an area of Victorian housing—in this case within the London Borough of Hammersmith. It is designed as high density/low rise housing to keep the scale of the neighbourhood and incorporates pedestrian decks above road and garaging level. The intention is that

redevelopment should be phased, demolition and rebuilding taking place as local conditions demand. A mark II version of this housing has been completed at Moore Park Road, opposite Fulham Broadway LT station, though plans for a much wider area were scrapped following a change of council control in 1964–7

designed by	Higgins Ney & partners
partner in charge	H. C. Higgins
associate	N. D. Hancock
quantity surveyor	chief quantity surveyor, Architect's Department, London Borough of Hammersmith
consultants	
structural engineers	Hugh Chate Associates
main contractor	London Borough of Hammersmith Building Department

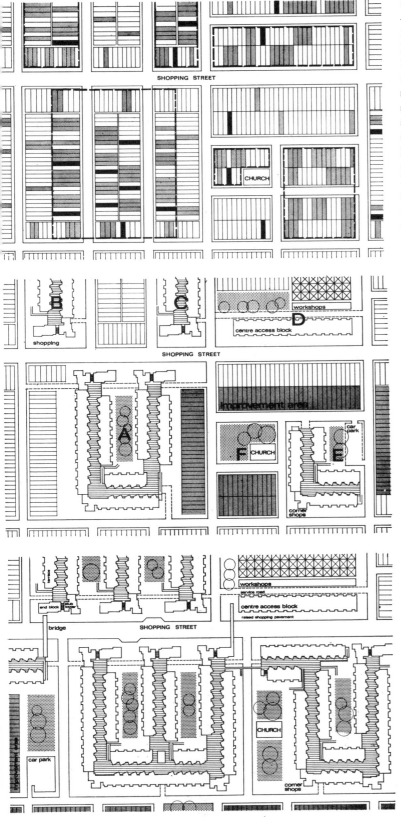

Three plans showing progressive development of a typical area of Victorian housing. Top, the old street pattern; centre, redevelopment partially completed in six areas; bottom, completion with pedestrian/vehicular segregation effected

CLIENT'S REQUIREMENTS

In 1964 the architects were commissioned by the then Metropolitan Borough of Fulham to make proposals for redevelopment of Victorian housing areas in Fulham. A pilot study produced the idea of deck housing to be used on infill sites such as blocks occupied by terrace housing. This study was continued by the London Borough of Hammersmith which commissioned a detailed study for the redevelopment of the Moore Park Road area, Fulham, then housing some 2 000 people. The Reporton Road site was made available for a prototype deck housing project. Development was to be at 336 pph (136 ppa) with 100 per cent garaging. Thirty-four dwellings (ten two-bedspace, six four-bedspace and eighteen five-bedspace maisonettes), a meeting-room, a launderette and a shop were to be included.

SITE

The site was originally composed of two bombed sites on either side of Reporton Road. By joining the two sites across the closed road an area of 0·39 hectares (0·97 acres) was achieved. To the east the site is bounded by a Victorian church and vicarage. All other approaches are lined by three-storey semi-basement terrace houses.

PLANNING

The fundamental planning objective was to produce a high density block sympathetic in scale with the low rise street environment of an inner London nineteenth century housing area. For this reason the block has been restricted to four floors and is basically in a terrace form: with two terraces backing onto a garage and walkway deck. Most of the units are wide front single aspect types (modern back-to-backs). The block runs north-east to south-west giving north-west south-east orientation to units. It is built right up to the pavement of St Peter's Terrace (see plan on p 131) to give maximum space for the green area and to shield the play area from the through road. Front doors are approached either directly from ground level or (in two-thirds of cases) from the walkway which is designed as an upper level open space—a street rather than an access gallery or corridor.

APPRAISAL

The government White Paper *Old houses into new homes*[1] has helped to intensify the study of environmental areas. This is particularly so in London and similar built-up areas where to the problem of delays and rehousing difficulties involved in totally clearing an area for complete rebuilding has been added the knowledge that the number of dwellings that will become unfit unless they are rehabilitated will increase beyond even the most ambitious new housing totals. A variety of approaches is required ranging from total rebuilding to careful rehabilitation and preservation. One important element in such an attitude is a building type in scale with the surrounding buildings to house people at similar densities. This needs to be usable as an infill on small sites as well as having a larger scale pattern to which it can develop or, if the situation allowed, be built straight away. There is also the need to fit in with the existing framework of pedestrian and vehicular movement at the preliminary stage, but also to meet the possibility of forming a new framework relating to a new road layout and pedestrian segregation.

The prototype scheme at Reporton Road, Fulham, is con-

1 *Approach from Reporton Road showing access ramp onto the raised deck*

2 *Entrance area and ramp access*

3 *North elevation onto Kilmaine Road showing access road with pedestrian deck over*
4 *Entrance to a ground level dwelling from public pavement. With the front door leading directly into the dining-kitchen there is a lack of privacy and protection from the weather*

ceived as such a building type, a more advanced version of which could be used for a larger redevelopment area.

The Reporton Road scheme illustrates the proposal in its simplest form: a four-storey development with pedestrian access off a high level walkway over a service road and parking space. The walkway gives access up and down to eighteen five-bedspace maisonettes. There are two-bedspace flats accessible from the ground and four-bedspace maisonettes in a block at one end of the walkway. The maisonettes are heated by gas fired warm air units and the ground floor flats have electric underfloor heating. All dwellings are connected to a Garchey refuse disposal system with a tank under the garage floor which is pumped out regularly by a special vehicle. A launderette is provided at walkway level with a communal meeting-room over.

In any pedestrian/traffic segregated scheme using multi-levels, the relationship between the height of the pedestrian deck and the road is crucial. If it is situated one storey up it is easier to reach from the ground, but it cannot continue over main roads. By placing the walkway over the service road in this scheme the main pedestrian level has been established one and a half storeys above pavement with access by a ramp and staircases. Having fixed the level of the access way it should be planned to function as intensely as possible to make it the vital spine of the community. Achieving segregation of pedestrians and vehicles by

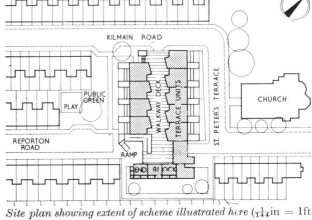

Site plan showing extent of scheme illustrated here ($\frac{1}{144}$in = 1ft = 1:1728)

Diagrammatic section explaining overlap of maisonettes with flats under. Compare with plans on facing page ($\frac{1}{48}$in = 1ft, = 1:576)

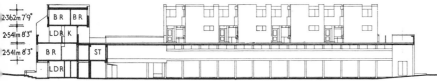

ong section showing pedestrian deck with vehicle access below ($\frac{1}{48}$in = 1ft, = 1:576)

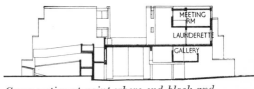

Cross-section at point where end block and terrace units meet ($\frac{1}{48}$in = 1ft, = 1:516)

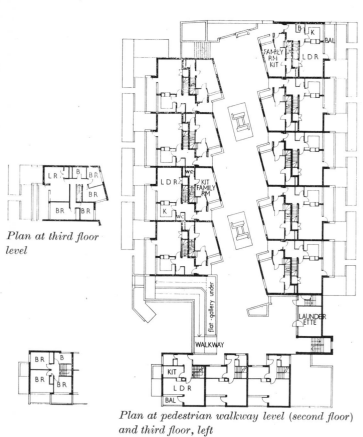

Plan at third floor level

Plan at pedestrian walkway level (second floor) and third floor, left

Plan at gallery level (first floor)—compare with cross-section on previous page

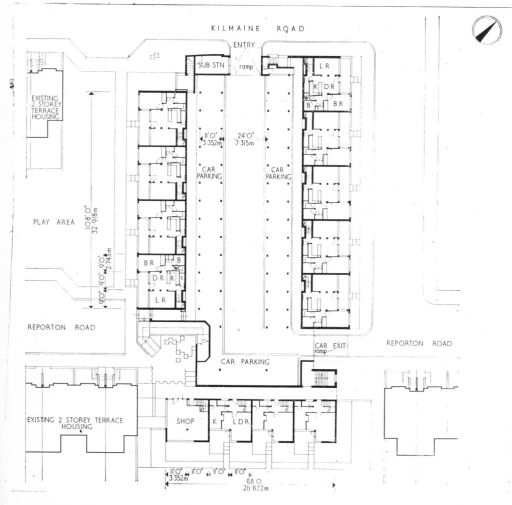

5 *South elevation of end block that forms a stop at right-angles to the deck*
6 *Covered service road with parking bays on each side. The high level windows are to the service gallery*

5

7

8

9

7 *First floor gallery serving end block*
8 *The ramp gives access to the first floor service gallery then continues up to the pedestrian deck. Is the service gallery a more convenient way into the dwellings?*
9 *Pedestrian deck looking*

south with end block in distance. Handrail in foreground contains a fluorescent lighting fitting
10 *Pair of entrance doors approached from the deck. The kitchen of one of these dwellings has a window onto the deck*

10

tunnelling the pedestrians under the roads—as at Hyde Park Corner or the Elephant and Castle, London—has been rightly condemned. But the answer is not just to put them up in the air. To be successful a pedestrian way must be convenient, sheltered and of maximum usefulness, otherwise children will continue to play around the cars and mothers will walk under the deck out of the rain.

This scheme attempts to solve the problem with a number of features. All dwellings have a 'back door' on an enclosed gallery above the car parking (see section p   ). This door will be used by postmen and so on and gives access to stores and also (via the fire lobby) to car parking below. Because it is accessible from the ramp, only one storey up and under cover, it could also become the most convenient way into the maisonettes. The main entrance at deck level is more pleasant of course and the hub or main generator of

the home, the kitchen, is deliberately situated at this level. The main entrance to the flats is at ground level which means that only two-thirds of the dwellings are served from the deck level. Of these, 50 per cent have kitchens facing onto the walkway. In other words, only one-third of the dwellings have direct visual contact with the deck. The pedestrian deck space between dwellings has a very pleasant small-scale, intimate quality and the splayed walls which allow light into the kitchens and avoid direct overlooking give interest to the space and the roofline. Would this with the kitchen location be enough to encourage people to use the space? Apparently, yes.

The type A maisonette is entered from deck level, with kitchen/dining-room at that level and stairs up from the entrance hall to living-room and double bedroom, both of which have access onto a large balcony. Also on the upper

11

12

13

14

11 *Meeting room and laundry at deck level*
12 *Dining-kitchen of the ground floor dwelling that is approached directly from outside*
13 *Living-room of ground floor flat from dining-kitchen, showing rather obtrusive columns*
14 *View from kitchen onto the walkway*

floor are three single bedrooms and a bathroom. The two small bedrooms over the kitchen/dining-room are awkward shapes because of the splayed wall and will be difficult to furnish. This has been modified in the later version of the plan. From the kitchen/dining-room there is access to an internal, artificially ventilated wc and stairs down to the service entrance.

The maisonette type B is entered from deck level with living/dining-room and kitchen opening onto a balcony at that level and stairs down from the entrance hall, which also gives access to an internal artificially ventilated wc, to one single and two double bedrooms, a bathroom and the service entrance.

The dwellings are to Parker Morris standards with, apart from lack of coat cupboards in the entrance hall, good storage provision. The least satisfactory of the plans is the ground floor flat, which is entered down steps from the pavement at ground level onto a paved area. The dining area has a fully glazed wall onto this area, and the entrance door, which is unprotected, opens directly into the dining area.

The lack of an entrance hall was one of the faults shown up by the survey of the housing designed by the MOHLG at West Ham (see pages 41-50). In the present case (using underfloor heating) the lack of privacy and excessive heat loss will be accentuated by the large glass areas. This aspect was reconsidered in the later development, together with the rather unsatisfactory relationship of the dining and living areas. The scheme provides three types of external space. Each dwelling has a 9·30 m² (100 sq ft) balcony, except the ground floor flats which have a paved area outside the entrance. The walkway provides a communal paved area with seats and planting and there are two grassed areas, the larger of which includes a children's play area.

The construction is a combination of reinforced concrete and loadbearing brickwork. The balcony fronts are exposed aggregate concrete and the external walls are brick with standard metal windows. Different coloured bricks are used each side of the walkway to allow a degree of tenant preference. This does not seem necessary as the design is very vigorous and interesting and needs no additional variety.

In general it is a pity that with a low rise scheme, none of the dwelling has a garden, although right from the start it was foreseen that, in the later versions, the ground floor flats (as a design option) could be recast as family maisonettes.

The main advantages of the established pedestrian level with a covered access road are attained only when a large development has set its own pattern onto the area. In the initial stages, as small infill elements, they have the problem of linking the new level with the old. This prototype, though it does not illustrate the developed answers to the problem to be seen in later versions, is very valuable as a means of studying some of the difficulties inherent in such a design approach.

SUMMARY

Ground floor area: 1 408 m² (15 156 sq ft).
Total floor area: 3 271 m² (35 216 sq ft).
Type of contract: Direct labour with subcontractors on fluctuating tenders.
Work began: July 1966.
Work finished: March 1968.
Net habitable floor area: 2 600 m² (28 000 sq ft).

Tender price of foundation, superstructure, installation and finishes including drainage to collecting manhole: £160 783.
Tender price of external works and ancillary buildings including drainage beyond collecting manhole: £5 835.
Total: £166 618.

12 Co-ownership Housing at Barnton, Edinburgh

designed by | Roland Wedgwood Associates
associate in charge | D. D. Quinn
staff | J. Leonard
 | A. Stungo
quantity surveyor | James D. Gibson & Simpson
structural engineers | Blyth & Blyth
heating engineers | Steensen, Varming & Mulcahy
landscape architect | John Byrom
main contractor | Weir Housing Corporation Ltd

Southfield estate in Edinburgh is a co-ownership housing society project, completed in 1968
A perimeter wall of terrace housing encloses two large communal spaces accessible only to estate residents.
Simple 3·200m square (10ft 6in) planning units are used throughout, interlocking

ingeniously to create a variety of dwelling types built up of a limited range of standard components. The appraisal examines residents' attitudes to tenure and privacy, and discusses why it is that the estate has so much appealed to architects and their families

CLIENT'S REQUIREMENTS, SITE, PLANNING

In late 1963 the Adam Housing Society was offered a 3·6 hectare (9 acre) north-sloping site on the western boundary of Edinburgh on which to create a co-ownership scheme to be financed under section 11 of the 1962 Housing (Scotland) Act.

The cost limits laid down by the Scottish Development Department proved more generous than those permitted under subsequent Housing Acts. The Scottish Development Department and the planning and lighting departments of Edinburgh Corporation co-operated on the venture.

The brief called for high quality houses, at least to Parker Morris standards, a wide variety of size and type with an emphasis on the needs of the larger family, and one garage and one parking space per dwelling. Since this was to be the largest co-ownership scheme in Scotland, special efforts were to be made to explore its potentialities, such as communal open space, district·heating, resident caretaker/ gardener and a communal tv aerial.

The scheme provides 110 dwellings and 112 garages at a density of 136 bed-spaces per hectare (55 bs per acre). There are ninety-eight one, two and three-storey houses of three to six rooms (plus dining-kitchens) ranging in area from 63·2 m² (680 sq ft) to 110·6 m² (1 190 sq ft) and twelve four-storey one and two bedroom flats of 53·9 m² (580 sq ft) and 66·4 m² (715 sq ft) respectively. Seventy-one dwellings have integral garages and the rest share forty-one grouped lock-ups.

Earlier research by the architects disclosed the shortcomings of many cul-de-sac designs, particularly in relation to service vehicles which were found to form a large and often ill-catered for proportion of housing area traffic. It also led to re-thinking of the concept of separation of vehicles and pedestrians, producing in turn some of the ideas included in the layout. Pedestrians and vehicles will mix in housing roads and the aim here has been to make this mixing relatively safe by: 1 keeping volume of traffic low by having culs-de-sac; 2 keeping speeds low by detailed design of roads; 3 designing out situations where pedestrians, especially children, could suddenly appear in the path of vehicles; 4 enabling all vehicles to turn in forward turning circles; 5 providing really safe play areas for children (particularly of pre-school age).

This last requirement coincided with a desire to provide communal private gardens in the Edinburgh New Town tradition, large enough to accommodate 'forest' trees. Although a main town footpath was being developed along the western boundary, Southfield did not otherwise form part of any larger planned segregated layout. This confirmed as appropriate the keeping of all access to one side of the dwellings while providing optional pedestrian access through the communal gardens and a lockable gate onto the town footpath.

The final solution was to lay the dwellings out as a continuous wall along the perimeter of the site, enclosing two large rectangular open spaces and two smaller ones at the extreme ends. This concept of a continuous terrace was also seen as a means of co-ordinating the wide range of dwellings and as providing the right conditions for the use of a group heating system. This latter was the subject of a special study by the consulting services engineers. They found strong economic as well as social grounds for recommending this kind of system, given the requirement for whole house

1
2

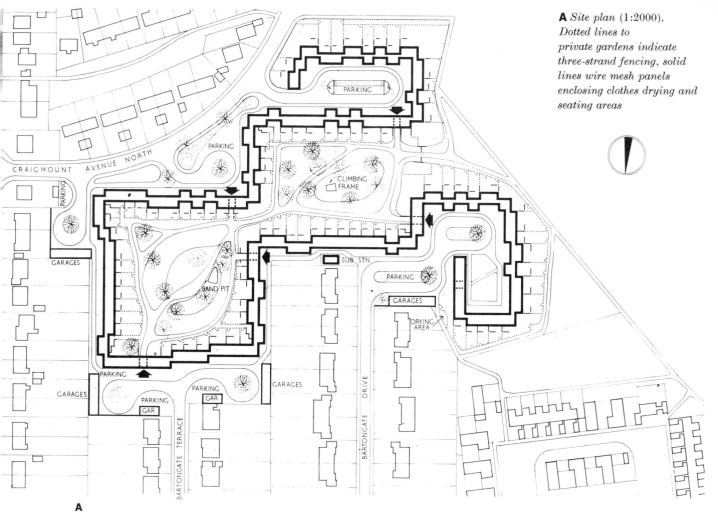

A *Site plan* (1:2000).
*Dotted lines to
private gardens indicate
three-strand fencing, solid
lines wire mesh panels
enclosing clothes drying and
seating areas*

A

1 *Aerial view of Southfield
estate from south-west.
Perimeter wall of terrace
housing encloses linked
communal spaces accessible
to residents through back
gardens. Estate tenants of
houses bottom left and
bottom right without gardens
backing onto communal
space have keys to gates of
five "pends" providing direct
access. At centre bottom is
metal gate on footpath leading
into estate; this had to be
reinforced with lateral shields
to keep out trespassing
children from neighbouring
estates. Blocks containing
flats are lower left and at top
behind district heating
chimney stack. Note
landscaped ridges of
communal spaces*
2 *Group of houses on west
side of estate, with glimpse
of open country beyond—
Southfield is on western
boundary of Edinburgh city.
Note varied roofscape and
gate from private garden
giving access to communal
space*

heating and taking both amortisation and running costs into account.

An oil-fired low-pressure hot water system was installed, with heating by radiators and hot water by individual calorifiers. The heating plant comprises two packaged oil fired boilers, with a total rating of 1 610 kw (5·5 × 106 Btu/h) using fuel oil of 35 seconds red wood, no 1 viscosity. The maximum connected load is 13 20 kw (4·5 × 106 Btu/h), but the actual maximum is less, due to diversity of use. The plant has a flow temperature of 99°C, is nitrogen pressurised, and serves the estate with two pipe distribution. Each dwelling return temperature is limited to 60°C by thermostatic control valves on the heating and domestic hot water circuits. The heat used in each house is measured by the simple and effective method of a water meter in the common return, in conjunction with the temperature limiting valves. A major oil company has lease of the society's heating plant, and charges for running costs only. A Btu meter was therefore installed in the boiler room, to facilitate charging of total heat delivered

Detailed planning requirements and increments of dwelling size were found to be closely met by combinations of 3·20 m (10 ft 6 in) square plan units. This dimension was also generally agreed to be the minimum width for a living room and the length for a dog-leg stair. Thus one square provides a stair plus bathroom, a dining-kitchen or a second bedroom. Two squares give the living room and a garage plus store or provide a dining-kitchen for larger houses plus single bedroom. Three squares give a master bedroom plus living room for the smaller dwellings.

Changes in floor level to accommodate the 12·2 m (40 ft) fall from south to north across the site are restricted to half storey heights. These enable rooms to be served by the half-landings of the dog-leg stair, permitting further variations in house types. The roofs are constructed as mono-pitches rising by half a storey height per square. They are therefore always geometrically related to each other, creating constant detailing. The slope is exposed in the rooms beneath and to improve proportions and to economise on volume the roofs spring from a window-head height of 2·06 m (6 ft 9 in). The roofs over stair/bathroom squares generally rise a further half storey height to provide clerestory sunlight and tank-space.

To keep the range of house-types within reasonable limits the depth of the terrace was restricted to two squares; this also permitted through living rooms to combine sunlight from the south with view to the north; and garage/stores also became through spaces giving direct access to gardens. Single square steps on plan cope with changes in level and provide extra parking spaces on the access side, and sheltered patios in the gardens. The seven basic house types are ordered by the use of a very small range of components as well as by the 3·20 m (10 ft 6 in) grid [with 228 mm (9 in) added for wall thickness]; thus there are two windows and two external doors all of identical dimensions and one small window of the same width; one internal door size, one joist, ceiling joist, stair flight etc. The whole scheme would have lent itself to prefabrication, but it was in fact built by traditional means. Many living rooms are upstairs, and since bedrooms were also meant to be usable as studies, all habitable rooms have windows extending to the floor.

All houses have private gardens planted with beech hedging and equipped with screened paved patios and gates colour coded to match front doors. Most devolve onto the communal open spaces which were established and planted before the initial occupancy of the houses. As found, the site was medium loam arable on boulder clay, treeless and fully exposed to the prevailing south-west winds.

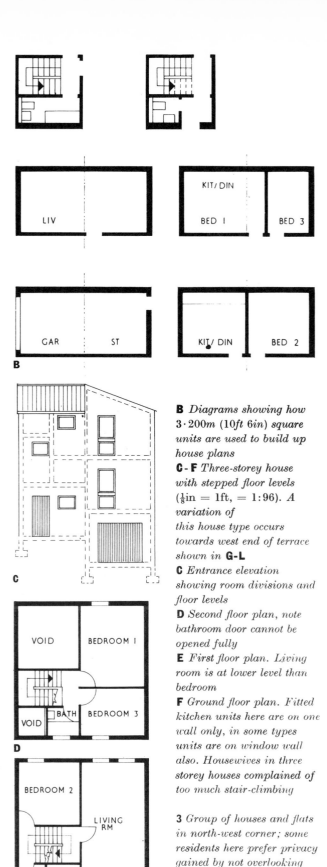

B *Diagrams showing how 3·200m (10ft 6in) square units are used to build up house plans*
C-F *Three-storey house with stepped floor levels (⅛in = 1ft, = 1:96). A variation of this house type occurs towards west end of terrace shown in* **G-L**
C *Entrance elevation showing room divisions and floor levels*
D *Second floor plan, note bathroom door cannot be opened fully*
E *First floor plan. Living room is at lower level than bedroom*
F *Ground floor plan. Fitted kitchen units here are on one wall only, in some types units are on window wall also. Housewives in three storey houses complained of too much stair-climbing*

3 *Group of houses and flats in north-west corner; some residents here prefer privacy gained by not overlooking communal area*

External walls are 229 mm (9 in) cavity construction, with rough cast common brick outer skin and 89 mm (3½ in) lightweight block inner skin. Cross walls are 229 mm (9 in) solid brickwork and spine walls 114 mm (4½ in) brickwork. Where these break through a roof to become an external wall they are sheathed in glass fibre and faced in zinc. Sound insulation is included in intermediate floors in houses and floating timber floors on precast concrete slabs are used in the flats. Heating mains are suspended below timber ground floors or in pitch fibre ducts under garages and pends. Roofs are slate-grey Redland Delta concrete tiles.

APPRAISAL

Southfield estate is on the north-western edge of Edinburgh about four miles from the city centre, adjacent to the green belt and in a high amenity residential suburb, with easy access to local shopping and bus routes. The site is on a north facing slope commanding a fine view over the river Forth to Fife in the north and to West Lothian in the west. Surrounding housing, with the exception of a neighbouring cost-rent housing society development, is mainly owner occupied, detached and semi-detached property, built during the last forty years.

during the last forty years.

Housing in this area must compete on the housing market with new speculative developments and well established residential estates of houses similar in size to those at Southfield. Who then chooses to live at Southfield, a co-ownership estate developed under the provisions of Section 11 of the Housing (Scotland) Act 1962, where a deposit of 5 per cent of the market value of the house and a monthly rent secures the tenancy of a three-bedroom house, and what do you think of the quality of housing, environments and investment which they obtain?

To examine these and other questions about forms of housing tenure a comparative study financed by the Social Science Research Council was undertaken by the Architecture Research Unit of Edinburgh University. The Southfield Housing Society scheme was studied along with an owner-occupied estate and a cost-rent estate in the same area of Edinburgh, to assess the role of co-ownership housing in the housing market and to obtain residents' reactions to the quality of housing provided. Figures quoted in the appraisal which follows are based on questionnaires completed by eighty-one residents from the 110 households and further interviews with thirty householders.

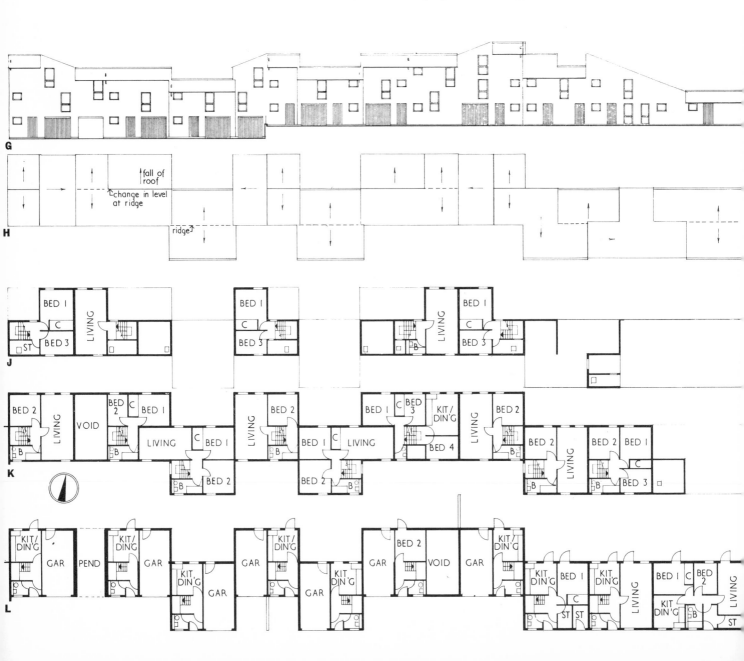

4 *Living room in one of the
houses and* **5** *in one of flats.
Horizontally pivoted opening
light over fixed light is one
of only two window types
used throughout scheme.
About one in four of all*

*the original householders on
estate were architects or
planners*
6 *Kitchen storage space in
this flat has been
supplemented by tenant*

G-L *East-west terrace facing
south onto Craigmount
Avenue North* 1ft)
($\frac{1}{32}$in = 1ft, = 1:384)
G *Elevation*
H *Roof plan. Ridge line is
dotted, continuous line
indicates change of level*

J *Second floor plan*
K *First floor plan*
L *Ground floor plan*
M-R *Part east-west terrace
facing north onto Barntongate
Terrace*
($\frac{1}{32}$in = 1ft, = 1:384)
M *Elevation*

N *Roof plan*
P *Second floor plan of houses, fourth floor plan of flats*
Q *First floor plan of houses and flats. Second and third floor plans of flats are*
repeats, on third floor end windows to kitchen/dining rooms move to side wall
R *Ground floor plan. Pend access from street to inner communal area of estate is at centre*

Residents

For the most part residents at Southfield tended to be young professional families with pre-school children. Among the householders three out of four were under forty years old, more than half of these being under thirty; by contrast only one in nine was over fifty. Nearly two-thirds were professional people and over a quarter were architects or planners. Nearly two out of five households were of two persons and a similar proportion were families with children under school age; in fact in the eighty-one households responding to the survey there were eighty-eight children.

Older householders on the estate tended to be couples nearing retirement age; the husband had been mobile for most of his working life, and now wished to settle down but was too old to obtain suitable mortgage facilities for house purchase. Although some of these couples enjoyed estate life and particularly liked watching the younger families, they did not appear to be fully integrated into the community.

The younger householders had been attracted to the estate mainly by the design and the layout of the houses and the estate in general; they were prepared to consider co-ownership as a form of tenure because it was financially attractive for a short term stay. Few of them considered making their permanent home on the estate.

Almost three out of five residents were living in Edinburgh prior to their move to Southfield and had heard about the estate by word of mouth. Many were attracted to look round by the rather unconventional appearance of the buildings, liked what they saw, investigated further and found that this seemed to suit their short term requirements. However, 40 per cent owned their previous dwelling and most of them saw the conventional form of house purchase as being a better deal financially and intended to buy their own home again in the near future. Meanwhile they found it profitable to invest the profits of their previous sale against future house purchase.

Rooms

Residents were generally agreed that overall space standards were satisfactory, and remarked very favourably on the spaciousness of the living room **4, 5** which accommodates either modern or more traditional furnishings with equal success. In the larger dwelling units additional space in the kitchen allowed the families to eat there comfortably, but the lack of this space in the smaller dwellings was often commented upon by residents.

The additional cloakroom at ground floor level was mentioned by many tenants as a good feature of their house; this compared favourably with owner occupiers on a nearby estate who unanimously criticised the lack of this amenity. Families with young children found the bathrooms rather tight, and were irritated by the fact that the bathroom door could not be fully opened without hitting the edge of the bath; some families had considered rehanging the door to open outwards.

Storage

Storage provision met Parker Morris standards but its positioning was criticised by tenants. Houses with integral garages had storage space provided in the garage, and those with garages apart from the dwelling had a store room. Generally, garage storage was much appreciated, and used for work space, bicycles, gardening equipment etc; but it did not compensate for shortage of storage in the dwelling. The most frequent comment was, that while the space was invaluable, it was not suitable for hanging clothes or sorting food and household cleaning materials, and that the houses on the whole were short of this type of space.

7

8

9

10

11

Where houses had internal stores, wardrobes were often placed there to give additional hanging space. Residents also seemed to accumulate the normal household junk in these 'glory-holes'. However, those with store rooms in the dwelling did not like to use them for gardening equipment and felt that their garages were too far away. They would have liked some type of garden store.

All residents interviewed complained about the sink and adjacent worktop and storage unit 7. Where these units overlapped in a corner position several feet of storage space become inaccessible. Some tenants reorganised the arrangement of these units to overcome this problem, but it was generally felt that this was a design fault which could have been avoided. Most of the co-owners were very keen do-it-yourself fans and built in additional storage in the kitchen, but there was some reluctance to undertake this type of work because 'it is not really our own house'.

Furniture making was a very popular hobby on the estate and the standard of workmanship very high. Many householders would be competent to build in fittings, cupboards and units but they did not do so because they were uncertain of their position with regard to the society in making alterations to their dwellings.

Tenants of three-storey houses in many cases regretted their choice of dwelling type, particularly if they have young children. Most were attracted by the layout, with first floor living rooms and bedrooms on the top floor, but found in practice that this increased the housewife's work and made supervision of children's play very difficult. One wife commented that whatever item she wanted was always at least one flight of stairs away; she tried to dissuade friends from moving into a similar dwelling type.

Decoration

An interesting topic raised by several householders interviewed was the subject of redecoration of the exterior of the houses. Nobody had a very clear idea of how arrangements for this were to be made (it was in fact to be the responsibility of the residents' management committee). While many would have liked the opportunity to choose the colour of their front door and garden gate they doubted whether they would be given the opportunity; they felt that the estate was very 'architectural' and that they would have some colour scheme imposed upon them.

Several older residents did not like the colours chosen, which they felt were rather dull. Many tenants did however mention the advantages of not having the expense of doing outside decoration, which is a responsibility of the society; they thought that in this way they benefitted over owner-occupiers who had to put money aside for such expenditure.

7 Kitchen in typical flat; arrangement of cooker suite and storage units has been criticised by tenants
8 Entrance hall of three-person flat
9 West-side communal area
10 West-side communal area, looking into east-side at left. Assorted levels, planes and angles of terraces, walls and roofs have been devised from vocabulary of simple square planning grid and small range of components
11 Sandpit (seen also in photo p 137) is major attraction to young children. Mounding behind adds interest to area, reduces scale of flat block
12 Cul-de-sac at south side of estate. Pend gate at centre is always kept locked; residents all have key to get into communal area. Keeping outsiders out has been constant battle—though many children from neighbouring estates come in (with permission) to play

12

Roofscape and heating

The distinctive roofscape **10** at Southfield was commented on both by residents and outsiders. Comments were generally favourable and most people felt that the unusual appearance of the estate distinguished it from the normal run of speculative built housing in the area.

One point of irritation, however, was voiced by several householders. In order to obtain the roof pattern some dwellings had very high roof spaces above the staircases, which tenants did not like. These were difficult to decorate, required heating and to some 'space-hungry' residents wasted an area which they feel might be of some use to them. Some of the more adventurous were considering plans to build an extra room on a platform in this area, accessible by rope ladder, to utilise fully every inch of living space. These tenants felt that their convenience had been sacrificed in an attempt to give the estate an 'architectural appearance'.

The whole estate is served by a district heating plant **11**. Tenants were most impressed by the efficiency of the district heating plant, **11**, which gave constant hot water and full house central heating. Some householders had problems with the metering system, and their bills fluctuated, but on the whole this proved in practice a cheap and efficient method.

this is in practice a cheap efficient method of heating. Heating accounts are paid to the society, who deals with the fuel company directly.

Communal open space

On an estate with so many young children, safe play space is a great advantage. All mothers of young children interviewed were happy to allow them to wander around the enclosed central area **9** without supervision. Some mothers were worried that someone might leave a pend gate open and a child wander off, but on the whole it was felt that the children were completely safe, always within view of someone's window.

With this freedom of movement children could make social contacts at an early age. There is a danger that the children can become exclusive in their contacts and restrict their choice of friends to children living on the estate, but residents thought that their children made other friends at school and playgroups, and invited them back to play on the estate. Children from the nearby houses were often found playing with the Southfield children in the communal areas.

Access to the space is through individual house gardens **2** or through the pend gates **12** which are kept shut and for which all residents have keys. Bars were later added to the top of gates to prevent outsiders, mainly children reputed to come from a nearby council estate, climbing over the gates and hoisting their bicycles over with them so that they could use the footpath system as a racetrack.

The central area is mounded, grassed and planted with trees; the residents said that the purpose of the mounding was to discourage organised ball games, but it did not seem to deter the small footballers who were generally out in great numbers. This mounding certainly adds interest to the area for the young children and reduces the scale of the flat block. A movable climbing frame and chute have been erected, swings being vetoed by safety conscious mothers. A very attractive sandpit **11** proves an attraction for young children and on fine days mothers tend to congregate there also.

A successful and well attended barbecue **13** was the first communal activity to take place in the open space. Turf was lifted to accommodate charcoal fires, and a discotheque was provided.

Privacy

Outsiders interviewed in connection with the overall study of housing tenure often commented on Southfield, and some of the cost-renters had considered living there. They seem, however, to have decided against this on the grounds that residents of Southfield suffer from a lack of privacy; they prefer their more conventional dwellings with stockade type garden fences. Residents at Southfield, however, did not complain about this, and seemed to think that they enjoyed quite a high degree of privacy. Several commented that this would be improved in the gardens **14** when the beech hedging planted along the wire fences became established and more tenants had planted climbing shrubs on their trellises.

On the whole tenants enjoyed the 'communal way of life' but some housewives said that they wasted rather a lot of time because when they went out to the garden they were bound to see a neighbour and stop and chat for a while. Residents also felt that the provision of communal open space on the estate led to increased privacy for the houses in that it separated houses from each other, avoiding their looking into the windows of another dwelling. Nobody appeared to be bothered by the noise of children's play or the general 'busyness' of the central area.

Dwellings in the courtyard to the south **12** and west **3** of the estate did not back onto communal open areas and from interview data it seemed that these families specifically chose these areas of the estate in order not to suffer loss of their privacy, which they feared from the communal open spaces. These families appeared to be very happy with the situation and did not feel left out of things; they had keys to the central courtyard and tended to make good use of them both for children's play and short-cutting to other areas of the estate or the shops. Householders with dwellings which did not back onto the open space, however, felt that the design of the estate would have been improved if all houses shared directly in the amenity. But this would have cut down the element of choice which allowed some families to opt out of communal life if they wished to do so.

Some nuisance had been caused in the central area by dogs which were allegedly allowed to run free and unsupervised around the estate. This was against the rules of the society, which required tenants to keep their pets under control in the central areas.

Cars and children

Cars entering the estate mix with pedestrians in the access roads where there is adequate space for vehicles turning **17**. These areas also tend to be used by older children for play which requires hard surfaces. There appears to be little danger to these children as cars entering the estate are slowed down by the general road layout pattern and in fact, cars are more likely to suffer damage from a hard kicked football than children from cars. Because houses have direct street frontage some residents have been annoyed by children kicking balls against the house walls.

Tenants

It is interesting to speculate why so many architects and planners chose to live at Southfield. The architects tended to be young, found the standard of housing in Edinburgh at a price which they can afford to be of poor design, and were very excited by the concepts incorporated into the design of Southfield. Most, however, hoped to buy large Victorian family houses or New Town Edinburgh flats in the future, and did not see themselves settling at Southfield as a permanent home. They were, however, enthusiastic about this venture and had told their friends about the

scheme, which tended to bring more architects into the society. Other tenants, however, felt architects and planners dominated the affairs of the society, expressed by the comment greeting the interviewer 'I do not know why you want to interview me—I am not an architect'. Residents were proud to point, out, however that the scheme had won a Saltire Society Award in 1967.

The administration of Southfield Housing Society

Southfield Housing Society was financed by money borrowed from the Scottish Development Department under Section 11 of the Housing (Scotland) Act 1962 over a period of sixty years.

At Southfield a member must buy an initial share in the society and is then required to pay a deposit on the house of his choice. This deposit is returnable when the tenant leaves the house, subject to deductions of any monies owing to the society for rent, heating, repairs etc. Initial rents were found to be based on too low a capital expenditure, and have had to be adjusted. Co-owners at Southfield claim income tax relief individually, and an attempt to introduce the option mortgage system was rejected at a meeting of shareholders. On leaving the society, members receive in addition to the return of their deposit, a payment based on their length of stay and the current value of their dwelling.

Management

Included in the rent is a management fee which was initially administered by the society. This fee covered administrative costs, insurance, loss of rent through houses istrative costs, insurance, loss of rent through houses remaining empty, maintenance, the wages of a resident caretaker and the provision of gardening and maintenance equipment. In the middle of 1970 the management of the society was transferred to a firm of property valuers and surveyors, and although residents have regretted this move to turn the management over to a professional agent who does not share their involvement in the estate it is generally thought that they may benefit from experienced professional service.

Residents interviewed reported that there appeared to be a lack of communication between the householders and the society, and because of this rumours about rent increases and other changes had been rife for quite a period. It would seem that for the co-ownership system to work efficiently and for residents to have a say in the management of their affairs, a good two-way system of communication must be established.

The caretaker

The Southfield Housing Society are fortunate to have a resident caretaker on the estate. The caretaker is responsible for the smooth running of the district heating system and for the general maintenance of the communal open spaces on the estate. Residents see the caretaker very much as a key figure on the estate and to many he is their main source of contact with the society.

Summary

Southfield estate appears to provide an attractive modern environment especially suitable for families with young children. It is probable however, with the high level of turnover on the estate, that wear and tear and maintenance problems could create an expense in the future. There is also a general feeling that although this is a friendly estate and social contacts are easy to make, the population is not permanent and that people do not really

13

15

17

13 *A successful barbecue was held in the open space in the summer of 1970*
14 *Visitors from other estates prefer their more conventional dwellings and stockade-type garden fences, supposing that Southfield residents suffer from lack of privacy. But in fact there have been virtually no complaints, and Southfield residents claim they enjoy high degree of privacy*
15 *Terrace on Craigmount Avenue North, shown in drawings G-L*
16 *Same terrace after safety rail was added to comply with city by-laws at request of city engineer*
17 *Parking for visitors' cars is on grass seeded perforated concrete block paving*

14

16

put down their roots in the estate. This general feeling probably leads newcomers to be less permanent than they might otherwise have intended. With increasing costs and higher rents this type of housing may not in the future attract long stay tenants because the spiralling increase in house values, particularly in urban areas, ensures that most owner occupiers of newer houses are compensated for high interest rates on mortgages by the appreciation in the value of their property.

SUMMARY

Ground floor area: 5 396 m² (58 083 sq ft).

Total floor area: 11 258 m² (121 180 sq ft).

Type of contract: Fixed price, all trades, Scottish Conditions 1954.

Tender date: August 1965.

Work began: October 1965.

Work finished (houses taken over): August 1967–September 1968).

Tender price of foundation, superstructure, installation and finishes including drainage to collecting manhole: £473 570.

Tender price of external works and ancillary buildings including drainage beyond collecting manhole: £54 434.

Total: £528 004.

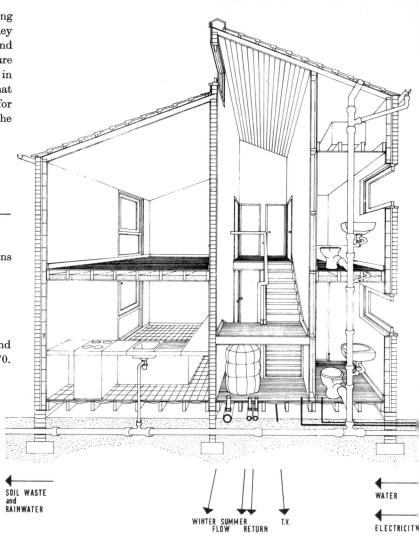

SOIL WASTE and RAINWATER

WINTER FLOW SUMMER RETURN T.V.

WATER

ELECTRICITY

13 Co-ownership Housing at Baron's Down, Lewes

designed by	Phippen/Randall & Parkes	*Barons Down was built in a*
associate in charge	R. T. Harris	*nine month period using the*
staff	D. O'Connor	*Quikbild system. This is a*
	S. Jonas	*good example of the*
quantity surveyor	Seymour Robinson &	*accelerating output of*
	Associates	*housing from the sources of*
consultants		*finance available for cost rent*
structural engineer	Anthony Hunt & Associates	*and co-ownership societies*
main contractor	Jewell (Building &	*working through the*
	Civil Engineering) Ltd	*Housing Corporation*

South facing terraces on lower slopes. These houses are approached from the north side, with no direct access onto the perimeter road. Privacy for living rooms is achieved by substantial screen walling. A footpath connects the lateral paths.

INTRODUCTION

The team of clients and consultants which promoted and developed this scheme was at work before the Housing Corporation was established and its experience as the 'Crawley Co-Partnership' was a help when it adopted the method of finance and procedures later designed by the corporation. The major difference, and the advantage which lay in these procedures, was that the source of all finance was one long term 100 per cent mortgage, overcoming the need for expensive short term bridging loans to the scheme's sponsors, followed by separate mortgages to each co-owner. The advantage to the co-owner was that he did not have to qualify for mortgage himself. Repayment and the accruing assets of the scheme were also fairly divided between the individuals and the society. Thus for the first time in this sort of housing the 'at cost' advantages could be enjoyed over the years by all participants, not only by the lucky few who occupied the scheme at first—and who by selling their share in the society could cash in on part of the increase in market value of the property.

Co-operative housing means that for the first time the architect of a total housing environment has clients who are closely identified with the residents themselves. Some of the people intending to live there can actually make their preferences known; they may be only a nucleus, with the remaining members still to be found, but client participation can influence the design and will continue thereafter; schemes are likely to develop and change during their lifetime and when they do it will be merely the separate dwellings and private spaces which become 'personalised', but the total environment under the control of the co-owners—with the help preferably of the architect who designed the scheme in the first place.

The present—and future—needs of a relatively small group of people therefore have to be analysed. The range of dwelling types must make for a balanced community and permit change and movement within it as people's needs or incomes increase or decrease. A sense of community has to be engendered by the relationship of buildings with common areas: by providing sitting out places for adults and meeting places for children; spaces which can be planted and tended by those living close by; common facilities—either built-in at the outset or anticipated in the future—such as laundries, club rooms, nursery schools, workshops for hobbies and so on.

Above all, the aim of the housing architect, which is to make a total design of which the dwellings are an important constituent part but not the whole, can be taken for granted and his ideas can be made available to a new class of people who neither qualify for a council house nor can afford to buy land and commission an architect themselves.

CLIENT'S REQUIREMENTS

The budget for this scheme was determined from advice given by the district valuer—and from marketing studies—that the top rental to be worked to should be under £7 a week for a three-bedroom five-person house and garage. This rental had to cover all service charges, maintaining funds and so on, but excluding rates. In effect the then current rate of interest made this rent equivalent to an all-in cost for the house of under £5 000. The site itself was expensive, being on a fine south-facing slope close to

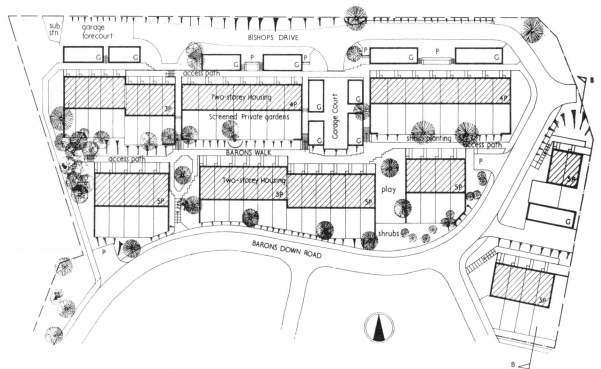

Site plan 1:1152. P *parking*, G *garage. Bishops Drive is a service road included in the contract sum

Type plans for three-, four- and five-person houses ($\frac{1}{16}$in = 1ft, = 1:192). B *bin store, delivery hatch and meter cupboard,* C *cupboard,* H *heater,* L *linen,* ST *store*

the town. The construction cost element in the total cost would therefore need to be low.

At the same time the houses were to be to full Parker Morris standards for space, services and equipment. And, in spite of the relatively modest budget, the society hoped for a good landscaping provision, a low cost, overburnt stock brick and other features which would set the estate apart from the local house builders' product.

The accommodation required by the society was to be in the form of five-person houses and four-person houses for family occupancy plus a smaller number of three-person dwellings to suit retired couples. The small units could be in flats but houses would be preferred. The final numbers were to be left to the architects but the cost of the land made it essential for the density of 150 bed spaces per hectare (60 per acre), established by an existing planning approval, to be held to. If it could be improved upon, so much the better.

SITE

The site of approximately 1·40 hectares (3½ acres) is west of Lewes immediately south of the main Lewes-Brighton Road. It was originally part of the garden of the Bishop of Lewes and was covered with mature trees, many of which remain. Besides the trees its most distinctive feature is a gradient of 1 in 9 to the south giving magnificent views over the downs from all parts.

Adjoining development was in hand below the site and the serpentine line of Barons Down Road, providing the boundary and terminating as a cul-de-sac within the site, was established.

An unusual feature of the site was a 0·9 m (3 ft) average depth of top soil overlying the chalk. This could not be built on and the difficulty could be overcome only by a combination of stripping, terracing, and deep foundation trenches.

PLANNING

A planning approval existed when the society obtained the site. The approval drawing showed forty-seven units, some in flats, set mostly against the contours and with their access between the blocks from the perimeter road at the south. The architects felt that the concept of houses served by cul-de-sac roads could not be employed without giving up the excellent views and the south orientation which were the main assets of the site. They found that more accommodation could be comfortably fitted in—without the need for flats—by cutting terraces along the contours and setting on them rows of fairly narrow fronted houses with all main rooms facing south on the private side.

Vehicle access could now be kept to the perimeter, with all garages and most parking spaces located at the top end of the site. Thus the person arriving by car would not penetrate the development. His garage would still be close to hand but out of sight and the garage building itself would give protection to the footpath serving the upper terraces. Since the garages were on level ground and incorporated off-the-peg structures with brick cladding this element in the cost plan was kept comfortably low.

Pedestrian movement within the site naturally follows contours along the terraces or drops down from one level to the next. The flow of movement through the site and away to the south controls block spacing which in turn allows some levelled and paved courts, some shared gardens and some tree planting to be disposed in strategic positions. The cross-section drawing through the site shows that the main lateral paths lie at the foot of banks. Thus the private sides of the houses, on the higher level, are out of sight and not disturbed by the noise of children. The natural enclosure of these paths, the use which is made of existing trees and new planting along the paths, and the spaces which they

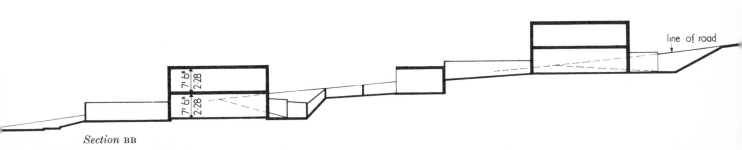

Section BB

1

2

1 *Approach to site from south. Breaks between terraces give pedestrian access to development*

3

make on plan provide one of the major interests in the scheme.

In a modern low cost housing scheme the architect is rarely in a position to work out his house plans from scratch; he is merely left to choose a plan which meets the conditions he is set. The architects did, in fact, work up their own plans in this instance and the choice was governed by the most economical and suitable frontages and by consideration of privacy, quietness and orientation. The smallest houses, at frontages of 3·81 m (12 ft 6 in) and 5·486 m (18 ft), could have all three rooms facing south on the private side. The larger houses, on 4·472 m (15 ft) frontages, must have their second and third bedrooms on the approach side. Thus the top end of the site, nearest to the garages, is used for the single-aspect dwellings; the lower and quieter slopes for the larger dwellings. This arrangement also has the advantage that families with most young children are given the easiest access to shops and other facilities off the site. The plan form itself gives little opportunity for the private open spaces which are a feature of most of the architects'

other work. However, the private gardens in this scheme are lavishly screened, making an important contribution to the total design.

The cost of an elaborate treatment of paths, paved open spaces, external walling and planting was appreciated and accounted for early in the planning of the scheme and is unusually high for unsubsidised provincial housing estates. Compensatory savings were needed so that the total cost could be kept within the strict limits imposed.

House plans

The superstructure cost had to be kept down to around £28 per m² (£2.60 per sq ft) for the largest houses and £30.66 per m² (£2.85 per sq ft) for the smallest. Working from first principles the architects adopted simple rectangular shells in long straight terraces. They allowed themselves no steps or staggers, no variants to the three typical plans, no projections, porches, stores or pends.

The structural criteria were thereby limited to the economics of floor spans, roof spans, loadbearing external walls and

2 *View from south along pedestrian route which penetrates site. Houses and the upper terraces also obtain views across downs, over rooftops of lower terraces*

3 *Looking along central footpath from west end of site: five-person houses on right, garden walls of three-person houses on left.*

4 *Typical view within site showing variety of spaces and moods achieved along lateral access paths*

5 *Garages at left are positioned at a change in level and help to enclose footpath. Houses on right are four-person single-aspect types*

4

5

6

partitions. Strict application of these economic disciplines were followed when the floor plans were prepared.

The internal layout of the house shells is shown in the plans on p 151. Their main feature is the maximum penetration of sunlight into the depth of the relatively narrow houses. Open plans are nevertheless avoided by using solid room dividers.

The houses are larger than minimum Parker Morris standards. The living-room, kitchen, hall and main bedroom are heated, have an extremely full provision of cupboards, fittings, electrical points and so on, and are designed to give a high insulation value for both heat and sound.

There is an extensive use of glazing on the south side, incorporating aluminium sashes. Finishing materials are both practical and cheap: some use is made of purpose built joinery such as divider units, sliding partitions and Parana pine stairs. A comprehensive unit beside front doors gives meter cupboard, bin storage and delivery hatches, accessible from both outside and inside.

House construction

After investigating alternative methods the architects decided that the Quikbild system would give greatest economy, speed, flexibility and control over quality.

This firm is normally geared to providing local authorities with houses from a standard range, to be built by associated contracting companies. It was nevertheless prepared to supply and erect whichever of its components the architects considered best value for money.

The following parts were made up to suit the house plans:
1 cross and end walls, including plasterboard linings and insulation;
2 front and rear cladding panels, including timber window and door frames and external doors;
3 first floor construction and finish;
4 roof construction including ply decking and insulating board;
5 loadbearing partitions including door linings and plasterboard finish to one side;
6 plumbing core including soil stack, waste and service connections.

(The other main elements, supplied by different firms, were aluminium vertical sliding and louvre windows, asphalt roof covering, internal doors, ground floor coverings, ceiling finishes, the balance of plasterboard linings to loadbearing partitions, non-loadbearing partitions, electrical installa-

6, **7** *Spine footpath through centre. A garage group penetrates scheme at one point, breaking line of white painted fencing*

8, **9**, **10** *Interior views of a five-person house. Kitchen is at centre of plan and can serve either living-room or dining end of kitchen. House is only 4·369m (14ft 4in) wide but plan provides a generous living-room. Heating unit can be seen at centre of picture*

9 *Kitchen, looking towards living-room. All fitments except cooker and washing machine are standard provision for all houses in scheme*

10 *Private garden beyond living-room is typical for all houses. Pitched roofs of private development opposite unfortunately curtail southerly vision over the downs. Houses on upper slopes have better views, because flat roofs are used within the scheme*

7

8

9

10

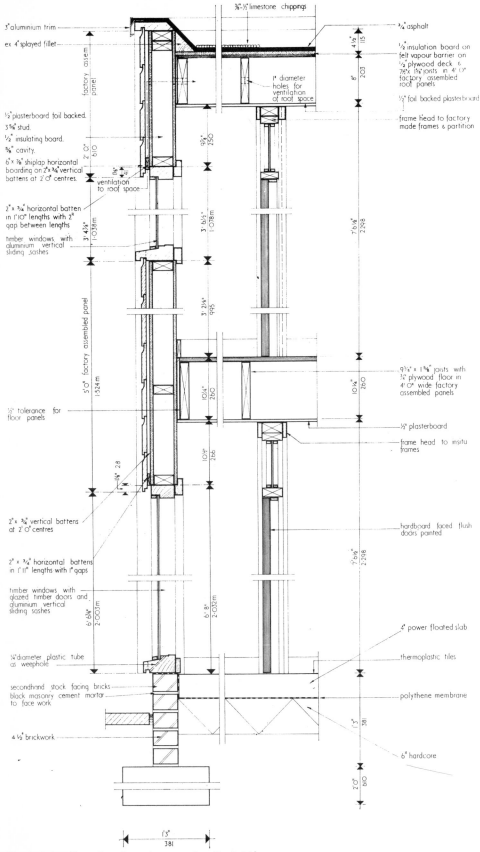

3" aluminium trim

ex 4" splayed fillet

factory assem. panel

½" plasterboard foil backed.

3 ⅝" stud.

½" insulating board.

⅝" cavity.

6" x ⅞" shiplap horizontal boarding on 2"x ¾" vertical battens at 2' O" centres.

2' O" 610

ventilation to roof space

2" x ¾" horizontal batten in 1'10" lengths with 2" gap between lengths

timber windows with aluminium vertical sliding sashes

3' 4⅞" 1·038m

5' O" factory assembled panel 1·524m

½" tolerance for floor panels

1⅛" 28

2" x ¾" vertical battens at 2' O" centres

2" x ¾" horizontal battens in 1'11" lengths with 1" gaps

timber windows with glazed timber doors and aluminium vertical sliding sashes

6'6⅝" 2·003m

¼" diameter plastic tube as weephole

secondhand stock facing bricks black masonry cement mortar to face work

4 ½" brickwork

⅜"-½" limestone chippings

¾" asphalt

4 ½" 115

8" 203

½" insulation board on felt vapour barrier on ½" plywood deck & 7½"x 1⅝" joists in 4' O" factory assembled roof panels

½" foil backed plasterboard

frame head to factory made frames & partition

1" diameter holes for ventilation of roof space

9⅝" 250

3' 6½" 1·078m

7'6½" 2·298

3' 2⅛" 995

10¼" 260

10¼" 260

9⅝" x 1⅝" joists with ¾" plywood floor in 4' O" wide factory assembled panels

½" plasterboard

frame head to insitu frames

hardboard faced flush doors painted

10¼" 266

6' 8" 2·032m

7'6½" 2·298

4" power floated slab

thermoplastic tiles

polythene membrane

1' 3" 381

6" hardcore

2' O" 610

Typical detail section through external wall (1:16)

1'3" 381

tions, sanitary and kitchen fittings, staircases, glazing and decorations).

Internal loadbearing partitions were supplied with only one face finished, for ease of handling and placing into position and to allow all services to be installed within the thickness of the partitions.

Quikbild acted as nominated subcontractors, and the main contractor for all other works was selected by competitive tenders based on bills of quantities.

The procedure was a success in that the cost limits were maintained while the job was left entirely in the hands of the architects. As a bonus to the scheme the contract was completed within nine months—the first houses being occupied six months after the start. With a rate of interest on the mortgage at the then mortgage option rate of 5 per cent, it must be appreciated that each month saved on a house costing £5 000 was equivalent to about £32 in capital expenditure.

APPRAISAL

From a study of the design and the essential cost targets, and from a day spent meeting occupiers and inspecting the estate, it certainly appears that the scheme has succeeded. Indeed an effective test of success, in a competitive housing market, is that fifty-one co-owners were not difficult for the sponsoring society to find. There also seem to be signs that social contacts have formed themselves quickly, and members willing to participate in management of the schemes have come forward.

In appearance the scheme is appealing and surprisingly varied considering the extreme simplicity of both layout and building. The variety stems from the way the steep site has been exploited. The houses themselves are a white and neutral element against the sky; they do not dominate the scene. The brickwork in the scheme. however is rich in colour and texture: blue, black and red. It is used in a con-

taining role and as paving. It contains the terraces at the gable ends and projects to screen the gardens; it contains traditionally built garages, banks of earth and flights of steps. It is a dominant element between the rows of white houses and, with the modelling of the site gives the scheme all its interest.

From inside the houses the major interest is also the natural scene. The external walls at ground level are all glass, and bedrooms are glazed from wall to wall above sill height The views across open country are fine and all the advantages of a south-facing slope are enjoyed. Yet another aspect of value for money can be mentioned here: the warmth of the sun is captured and central heating is not required, even in January, so long as the sky is clear.

The internal layout of each house type also appears to work well. One particularly notices that well equipped and compact houses require very little movable furniture so that rooms in use remain airy and spacious. There also appears to be a tendency for tiled floors not to be carpeted, a factor which should be impressed upon the builder when he is putting the finish on his floor slabs. Floor to ceiling glazing brings out every blemish!

The architects make the basic assumption that privacy and private land are at the highest premium; public spaces play their part only in providing an attractive approach and intimate spaces for a chat with a neighbour on the way home. The play area was completed subsequently.

SUMMARY (TOTAL DEVELOPMENT)

Ground floor area: three person: 34·22 m² (368 sq ft).
four-person: 40·36 m² (434 sq ft).
five-person: 44·64 m² (480 sq ft).

Total floor area: three-person: 68·45 m² (736 sq ft).
four-person: 80·72 m² (868 sq ft).
five-person: 89·28 m² (960 sq ft).

Type of contract: RIBA private edition with quantities 1963 fixed price.

Tender date: September 1967.

Work began: January 1968.

Work finished: October 1968.

Final account price of foundation, superstructure, installation and finishes including drainage to collecting manhole: £133 763. Final account price of external works and ancillary buildings including drainage beyond collecting manhole: £42 382.

Total: £176 145.

14 Housing at Windsor

designed by	Mathews, Ryan & Simpson
partner in charge	Michael Ryan
project architect	Roy Latham
job architects	D. M. Potts
	P. E. Martin
	R. H. Hamilton
	J. R. Laine
quantity surveyors	Gardiner & Theobald
structural engineers	Ove Arup & Partners
electrical and mechanical engineers	G. H. Buckle & Partners
main contractor	Wates Construction

The Ward Royal Estate at Windsor is the first stage of a long term development planned for the town's central area. Its key position in an historic setting makes it of special importance, not least to local residents who have already made it the subject of some controversy; this is partly due to it being a 'cost rent' scheme, then a new departure for many local authorities

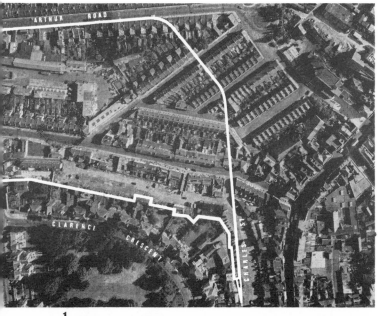

1

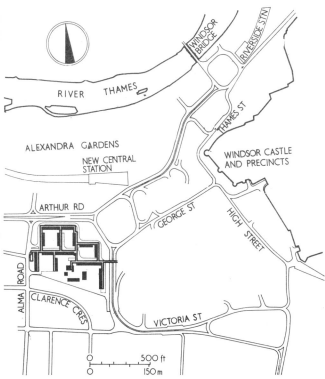

2

A *Town policy map (1:10 000) indicating planning proposals at the time of the building of Ward Royal, and showing its relationship to the town centre and castle*

1 *Aerial view before redevelopment, showing terrace housing, workshops and yards previously on site*

2 *Ward Royal from Windsor Castle round tower; station and St George's chapel at right*

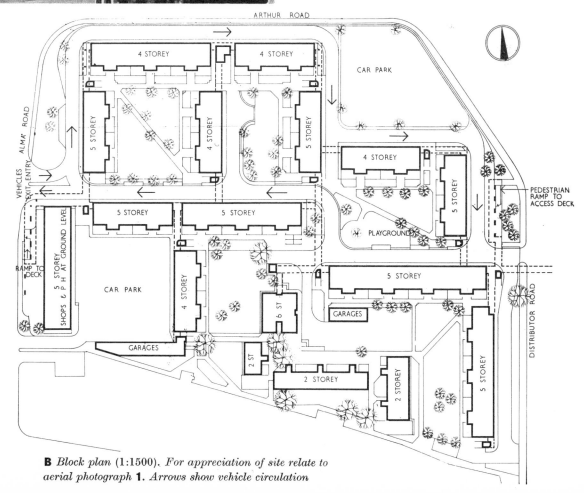

B *Block plan (1:1500). For appreciation of site relate to aerial photograph* **1**. *Arrows show vehicle circulation*

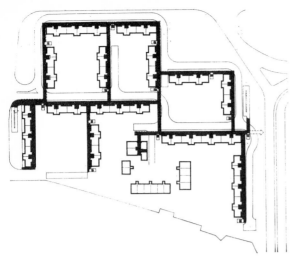

C *Block plan at second floor level* (1:3000) *showing plan of access deck (see* **E**)

CLIENT'S REQUIREMENTS, SITE, PLANNING

The Ward Royal Estate was part of the first phase of a central area redevelopment planned for the Royal Borough of Windsor. This plan involved demolition of condemned nineteenth century property, with subsequent redevelopment for housing.

The original requirement, later amended in detail, was for approximately 270 dwellings, including some forty-five flats for old people, six small neighbourhood shops, and one public house. Of these dwellings, 33 per cent were to have one bedroom, 50 per cent two bedrooms, and 17 per cent three bedrooms.

The local by-laws and the County Planning Authority made the following specifications: car parking for two cars per dwelling—one permanent, one casual; vehicular access to be restricted to Alma Road; residential dwelling to be 312 persons per hectare (125 ppa); all habitable rooms to be above flood level—approximately 76 cm (2 ft 6 in) above ground level.

The site of 3·16 hectares (7·8 acres) on flat ground close to the castle, is contained by Arthur Road to the north, Alma Road to the west, Clarence Crescent with its Regency houses to the south. A new distributor road was to be developed along the line of Arthur Road and along the eastern boundary of the site. Originally the site contained approximately 250 dwellings (housing 750 people), and approximately thirty shops and six public houses. These dwellings were mainly terrace type houses of late Victorian vintage.

Apart from the general problem of 'housing', particular care was to be paid in considering the relationship between the scheme and the town with its historical associations, from both inhabitants' and tourists' point of view. The aim was to open up the prospects of the castle and close off, as far as possible, those of the adjacent station and gas works.

The high standard of car parking and high cost of site (about £55 000 an acre) pointed to dual use of site by placing dwellings over cars. These considerations, with those of service roads and vehicles, led to the adoption of 'Buchanan principles'—vertical segregation of pedestrians from motor cars.

Problems of orientation, noise, topography, privacy and general social factors led to adoption of the 'court' principle —a formal court arrangement on the north side, with informally landscaped areas to the south, closing off views

of the station and gas works and forming a sound baffle between the main road and residential areas within the site. Shops and pub were placed along the western boundary to 'balance' the main shopping centre.

The old people's flats were planned as an integral part of the scheme, in the area to the south, adjacent to the houses of Clarence Crescent. Of the forty-five flats, twenty-one have been planned in a six-storey block with lift, this block being under the direct supervision of a warden; the remainder are nearby in two-storey pavilion blocks.

Although the size of the project was marginal for the choice of industrialised building it was early decided to take advantages of system techniques because of their shorter construction periods and, with the shortage of craftsman, their quality of finish. The technical solution was developed with Wates Ltd at an early stage in the design process.

APPRAISAL

At first sight this is an impressive looking scheme—a cool, smooth example of 'glossy' architecture and a distinctive landmark in a rather drab sector of the town. On closer acquaintance, however, it reveals social and functional problems in its design, which are particularly disappointing in view of the time and trouble which the council took in canvassing informed local opinion and in setting up a special housing subcommittee to try and ensure the best possible solution. Criticism of the design, therefore, must be matched with the high standards attempted.

Cost rent effects
The planning background was the cause of initial controversy. The council's implicit aim was to upgrade the neighbourhood's 'status' by replacing worn out houses of low income families with new dwellings for high income families—on a 'cost rent' basis. Original residents were offered first refusal of the new flats, but with rents up to £12 a week very few could afford to live there, the majority being obliged to move to estates on the outskirts of the town. This seems a misuse of government housing subsidies (the scheme had a normal government subsidy but was outside the council's usual rent pooling policy), since the people who benefitted least were the original residents. Many of them felt outsmarted by the council, which they regarded as being more concerned in presenting a good image to the world and attracting tourists than in their own real needs; it was only the lack of effective political representation that avoided a major dispute.

Given a cost rent scheme, however, it seems fair to ask whether tenants who pay a higher rent to the council actually get better value for their money. Certainly they do not get better than average local authority housing standards since the MHLG cost yardsticks still apply. Principally, the advantage is that people can avoid the housing waiting list and get a house quickly, if they can afford it, and also live on an estate with people of similar socio-economic status. In addition, it seems possible that better management and maintenance might be offered.

Management and maintenance
At Ward Royal, a resident estate manager is able to deal directly with tenants and the letting of flats. In spite of this, it is mainly on management/maintenance issues that tenants' grievances seem mainly to rest. There are complaints about the 'wrong sort' of tenants being allowed in—people who hold noisy parties, who do not control their children and who generally do not use the estate in a manner

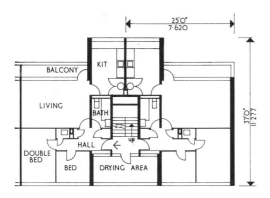

D *Five-storey block* ($\frac{1}{24}$ in = 1 ft, = 1:288). *Two bedroom flats at fourth floor (left) and third floor level (right)*

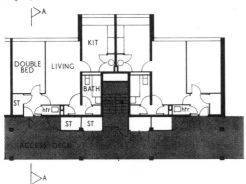

E *4/5-storey block* ($\frac{1}{24}$ in = 1 ft, 1:288). *One bedroom* ~~and~~ *flat at second floor level. Tinted area relates to block plan* **C**

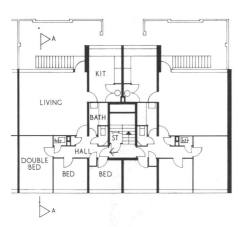

F *4/5 storey block* ($\frac{1}{24}$ in = 1 ft, = 1:288). *Three bedroom flat at first floor level, approached from access deck above*

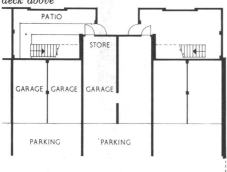

G *Five-storey block* ($\frac{1}{24}$ in = 1 ft, = 1:288) *Garages for flats over, with patio serving three-bedroom flat at first floor level*

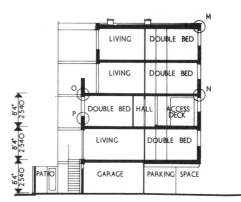

H *Five-storey block* ($\frac{1}{24}$ in = 1 ft, = 1:288). *Section* **AA** *Details* **M, N, O, P** *are on page* 169

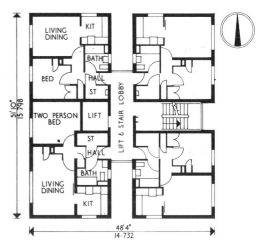

J *Six-storey block* ($\frac{1}{24}$ in = 1 ft, 1:288). *First to fifth floor plans. Warden-serviced one bedroom flats for old people*

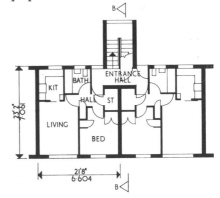

K *Two-storey block* ($\frac{1}{24}$ in = 1 ft, = 1:288). *Ground floor plan, one bedroom old person's flat. First floor plan is similar*

L *Section* **BB** *through two-storey block* ($\frac{1}{24}$ in = 1 ft, = 1:288)

3

3 *Approach view from Alma Road; five shops and a public house fit neatly under a strongly modelled façade*
4 *Typical compact internal courtyard. Soft landscaping*

is screened from access roads by high wall
5 *Selective photographs show that general image and appearance inside the scheme...*

appropriate to a 'private' residential development.

Over a year after completion of the site, it was these problems which seemed to dominate tenants' attitudes towards the scheme. The benefits, or otherwise, of the general concept of the scheme were not fully apparent to many tenants.

Special problems

Several aspects of the scheme will be of particular interest to designers.

First, there is the problem of fitting the scheme satisfactorily into its historic setting and achieving a high level of resident satisfaction with its general appearance; the importance of this in relation to overall satisfaction has been demonstrated in MHLG surveys.[1]

Second, how to reconcile a high provision for cars with acceptable levels of pedestrian safety and convenience.

Third, given a deck access solution where all dwellings are off the ground, there is the particular concern of how to achieve a satisfactory social environment for mothers and children at home.

Inevitably the use of industrialised building techniques here, as in other schemes, makes it easier to assess the

4

6

7

8

detailed quality of design, since the greater element of repetition makes any basic virtues and faults more apparent. It does seem, however, that the designers have been over-sensitive about repetition being a cause of monotony, and have introduced a degree of complication into the general pattern of design which has created fundamental problems of circulation and convenient use of spaces. With such an inherent defect, it seems not surprising that cost planning was a particular problem, the solving of which has probably meant less care being devoted to some of the detailed planning problems associated with a deck-access solution.

The setting

The Ward Royal estate at Windsor has a strong, assertive character in keeping with that of the old town. It is particularly distinctive in that it presents an image of a white-walled precinct which contrasts, perhaps rather too sharply, with the immediate surroundings of brown brick buildings **3**. Similarly, the massive scale which the estate presents when viewed from the north will be more appropriate when vistas to the castle are eventually opened up.

Along the southern boundary a piece of the site has been allocated to flats for older people.

Planning and spaces

The layout drawings show the extent to which the planning aims within the estate have been achieved; blocks have been arranged to create pedestrian courts screened from roads; a one-way traffic system provides car parking under buildings; there is segregation of pedestrians and vehicles, with a pedestrian deck at second floor level linking all blocks and giving direct access to the main shopping centre; all inhabitants have direct access to gardens without crossing roads.

The residential density of the final scheme is 247 persons per hectare (100·1 ppa), giving 279 dwellings (at 2·8 average household size), of which sixty-four have three bedrooms, 106 two bedrooms and sixty-four one bedroom; the remaining forty-five dwellings are old people's flats.

Height of blocks is restricted to three and four floors above garage level. The three-bedroom flats **F** are planned at first floor level with patios at ground floor; the one-bedroom flats at second floor **E** have direct access from the pedestrian deck; two-bedroom flats **D** are at third and fourth floor levels, with staircase access from the deck. Drying areas for the one- and two-bedroom units are planned at third floor level, facing either north or east.

In general the relationship between block height and size of court is well handled. Some courts on the northern side, however, seem crowded with spaces catering for a variety of activities, and this possibly detracts from any feeling of spaciousness. The flatness of the site is not relieved by any artificial changes in level and is rather emphasised by the constant height deck.

Spatial quality is helped by the variations in size of courts, but the effect is rather too subtle to give the impact and variety that seems to be needed. Basically the fault seems to be an overall pattern without an adequate focus. The six storey block seems little more than an incident within this pattern, and the adjacent lift tower (containing the

*can seem very satisfactory **6** In other situations **7** bald textures and light tones seem too severe. **8** Lift area reveals clumsy application of 'Buchanan principles' of pedestrian/vehicle segregation*

9

10

11

9, 12 (p 166) *Two and six-storey flats for older people. Ground floor tenants in tall block complain of children playing football on grass outside. No kickabout area is provided*
10 *Vehicle entry point at Alma Road; direction*
11 *Car parks for visitors are a long way from some of dwellings. Because of size and bleak appearance they might have had higher priority for screening*

only lift serving the deck), which might have served this purpose, seems poorly located. More specifically, an estate of this size and number of residents should surely have some kind of central space which either contained or linked up all communal facilities such as sitting areas and play spaces, and gave the overall pattern more cohesion. The present spaces are fragmented and too small to contain even a convenient kickabout space for children.

Traffic circulation
A great deal of space at ground level is taken up by wide one-way roads. These roads serve garages beneath each block, which means that the road system is largely determined by the pattern of blocks. It seems rather wilful to arrange blocks into a courtyard formation and then try to devise a one-way system to cope.

The result here is a tortuous route which meanders around the edge of the site and back down the middle, with culs-de-sac springing off to pick up stray blocks **B**. Culs-de-sac have to allow for two-way traffic, and two-way traffic is not normally expected at blind junctions with a one-way system; visitors in particular tend to drive carefully through the scheme.

Signposting to dwellings along the route is not provided other than a direction map at the entrance.

Also, one-way road systems on 'private' estates should not be too long. For people living near the entrance it seems unfair that they should go the long way round to get out when there is often so little traffic about. It was not surprising, therefore, to hear of at least one car accident on the first blind corner of this estate caused by someone tempted to cut back on the one-way system.

Parking
Casual parking generally is not conveniently located for access to dwellings. Large car parks here mean that many residents and visitors have a long walk to their destination, and invariably these areas are noisy, particularly at night, and do not present an entirely satisfactory appearance.

Useful parking could have been located in smaller groups near the foot of access stairs, thereby being as close to the dwelling as possible. Some residents (often those with two cars) and most visitors, indicate their feelings on this matter by parking in the carriageway closest to the stairs, and it is difficult to blame them.

A quick check on the total of ground space eaten up by roads, garages and parking shows it to be approximately 40 per cent of the site area. The reason is partly an uneconomic use of road space and partly the council's request for 200 per cent provision for cars. There is a strong argument for reducing the car provision in a central residential area such as this, where cars are used less because the shops and railway station are within easy walking distance; in addition, a separate economic rent for a garage, rather than an inclusive dwelling rent, would also effectively reduce the demand. The present parking spaces are under-used, and this provision might have been phased if only to allow more ground space for pedestrian use initially.

The deck system
The deck system **C** also has certain problems. A feeling that it is too high off the ground would be less worrying in a different situation. Certainly the number of dwellings and size of site seems large enough to justify it, and the system will be continuous with the future shopping centre. The inconvenience is particularly noticeable, for example, when people wish to cross safely from a northern court to a southern one.

In theory, pedestrians should climb stairs out of one court on to the deck and descend stairs into another. In reality, old people, children and pram pushers prefer to cross the site at ground level, negotiating the barriers and walking along the roadway. This is no great safety problem since refuges are provided for pedestrians in emergencies, but the roadway and blocks down the centre of the site have created a divisive element which might have been avoided. Long ramps are provided at each end of the deck system. There is only one lift **8** serving the deck, this seems hardly adequate for so many dwellings, and it is not easy to find. The designers would have preferred more lifts but they were ruled out on cost.

Signs, names, numbers
Signposting on the deck system is minimal, and people are expected to use their own initiative. The layout direction board at the entrance of the site is useful to people arriving by car but is well away from any part of the footpath system.
Names have been given to identify either courts or isolated blocks (and in one case a vehicle cul-de-sac), and while this seems the most sensible method if one is trying to give identity to the forms and spaces in the block pattern, the inherent inconsistency of the method is bound to cause confusion
In addition the deck system contains several culs-de-sac which seem rather long in relation to the compact nature of the continuous routes. This means that residents who live on them have less choice of routes and tend to be rather isolated from the main stream of pedestrian traffic. The latter point seems important in that opportunities for chance meetings with neighbours passing on the deck are reduced.

Social contact
The inherent advantage of a deck access system is not just that it enables safe and easy movement around a scheme but that, in channelling people past front doors, it does allow them more opportunity for chance social contact with neighbours. It seems a pity, therefore, that there are no windows which overlook the deck from adjacent dwellings. A small window from a through living-room in each of the flats at deck level would have allowed people to see and greet passing neighbours. If contact is not desired then a drawn curtain provides effective privacy (the MHLG scheme at Oldham is a good example of this principle). As it is, the windowless walls along the decks **13** give a feeling that residents are rather isolated from each other.
Residents living in flats which are reached by the stairs off the deck seem similarly isolated. The problem here seems mainly due to the rather cramped and poorly lit space provided for a staircase serving up to six dwellings and the impression is given that a cost saving has been made here which, in comparison with the money lavished on the deck system generally, does not seem a fair balance. A communal 'entrance hall' character might have been considered, which would have enabled a greater measure of mutual acknowledgment. Entrance areas in the two-storey flats show this character very convincingly.

Flat plans
The plan of the three-bedroom flat **F** shows how the front door is virtually in darkness and how all bedrooms are under the deck. In addition, it illustrates the interesting policy of bedrooms being small for sleeping, and living-rooms **15** large for leisure.

12

13

14

15

13 *Typical view along second floor deck. Recessed entrance area for one bedroom flat on left might have been better related to common stair entrance,*

*eg for prams Dining/kitchen **14** and living room **15** in three bedroom flat. Dining area seems inadequate for entertaining guests*

Furniture arrangements in the single bedrooms are tight, and thus double use of these spaces as an occasional play-room or study needs careful attention. The large living-room with its full height glazing is splendid, but the very small, high-walled patio makes an odd comparison, and the long staircase **18** into it adds to the doubt whether this space will be fully used. All flat plans have a standard arrangement of kitchens, which seem rather small for entertaining guests to a meal.

The plans generally, however, seem very satisfactory, judging from tenant reaction, and the slight anomalies are the result of working within the chosen structural discipline.

Structure and finishes
The structural system as finally modified to meet the MHLG cost yardsticks is precast concrete cross-walls at 5·486 m (18 ft) centres, with in situ concrete floors. The spandrel panels are precast concrete with external brick facings. All the large precast concrete panel cross-wall units were manufactured at a site factory.

Internal finishes are as far as possible kept 'dry'. Floor finish in the flats is vinyl sheet flooring, with felt insulation backing. Walls generally have wallpaper applied directly to the concrete; bathroom walls are finished in steam resistant paint. Ceilings are finished in paint. These finishes applied direct to the kind of structure used here will certainly not help to reduce the transmission of impact sound.

Kitchens and bathrooms are serviced from the central service duct adjacent to the staircase. The internal bathrooms have mechanical extract, and the space heating is by means of gas fired warm air units with ducts to the living-room, hall and bedrooms.

Externally, the elevations are clean and crisp. The pattern of window shapes, projecting bays and angular profiles all against a white background, form a highly satisfactory composition of light and shade. With textures there is much less variety; the exposed aggregate finish to concrete edge beams seems hardly an adequate contrast to the smooth, hard finishes presented by all the glass, concrete and bricks.

Similarly with colour. The general intention is to use the whiteness of the brickwork and concrete as a backdrop to bright splashes of colour in curtains and in the paintwork along the decks. In general these brightly coloured areas have little impact, owing to the overwhelming proportions of brickwork and concrete. The whiteness seems all pervading and permanent, and the efforts of tenants and external decoration to compete with it seem small and transitory by comparison. This seems a rather negative approach to designing a colour scheme, relying as it does on a fashion for brightly patterned curtains and trendy colours. If a brick with a richer colour and texture had been used, the feeling of austerity might have been avoided.

Landscaping
This imbalance in the pattern of colour and texture is, however, really apparent only at deck level and from outside the scheme. At ground level inside the courts the green grass and foliage of trees and shrubs have more effect and as the planting matures much of the background will be obscured. Considerable attention has been paid to providing climbing plants against walls, and shrub planting generally has been placed in large beds where it stands a better chance of flourishing without interference. Apart from a few isolated examples of plant beds being sited on the desire line for a footpath, their location is good and protective rails seem not to be needed.

It is welcome to see a high quality of soft landscaping in a housing scheme, and the money spent on planting and greenery in these courts is worthwhile, judging from the reaction of tenants. This landscaping brings with it additional problems of maintenance in these communal areas and, ideally, money needs to be allocated to allow extra maintenance care of planting, particularly in the first few crucial years.

Individual courts **4**, **5** have been generally well handled with simple details in pavings, railings, seats, lighting, and so on, although details involving manhole covers are not resolved very tidily. In particular there is a delightful children's playground **17** near the centre of the scheme where children and adults can meet. All these formal meeting places are secluded and sunny and are popular in the summer months for sitting out. It seems rather a pity that they do not all link up together in any cohesive pattern so as to enable children and adults to use the whole scheme at ground level more easily. This again would promote more informal social contact between people who are just passing through.

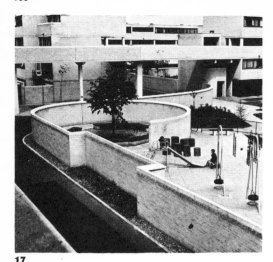

17

16

19 *Neat high walls around·patios seem incongruous in relation to size of spaces*
17 *Another example of priorities seeming out of balance; a delightful playspace/meeting place is not easily accessible, and therefore has limited usefulness*

16 *In small single bedrooms convenient furniture arrangements are not always possible*
18 *Staircase access from living room to patio*

18

19

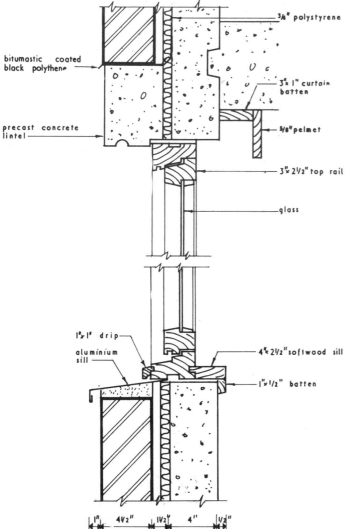

¾" asphalt on sheathing felt

2" lightweight insulation slab

vapour barrier on 8" concrete roof slab

timber firring

aluminium trim

M *Five-storey block, detail at roof* (1:16)

4½" facing brickwork

¾" cavity

¾" polystyrene

plastic skirting trunking felt backed vinyl

8" concrete slab

glass fibre

¼" asbestos

bitumastic coated black polythene

3"x 1½" tanalised softwood grounds

N *Five storey block, detail through access deck roof* (1:16)

¾" polystyrene

bitumastic coated black polythene

3"x 1" curtain batten

precast concrete lintel

⅝"pelmet

3"x 2½" top rail

glass

1"x 1" drip

aluminium sill

4"x 2½" softwood sill

1"x½" batten

1" 4½" 1½" 4" 1½"

O, P *Five-storey block, detail of horizontally pivoted window to living room of typical flat* (1:8)

SUMMARY

Ground floor area: 5 848 m² (62 952 sq ft).

Total floor area: 20 023 m² (215 523 sq ft).

Type of contract: Negotiated. Firm price.

Tender date: May 1967.

Work began: June 1967.

Work finished: June 1969.

Final account price of foundation, superstructure, installation and finishes including drainage to collecting manhole: £1 099 175 9s 9d.

Final account price of external works and ancillary buildings including drainage beyond collecting manhole: £181 281 8s 10d.

Total: £1 281 996 18s 7d Excluding certain items not applicable amounting to £23 411.

15 Welsh Village Housing at Cefn-coed-y-cymmer

This development at Cefn-coed-y-cymmer gives the lie to the facile assumption that any small local authority, which may be too remote from individual parish pumps to offer a genuine forum for public participation, lacks the capacity to perform its *functions adequately. The subject of this building study, an excellent example in itself of the successful exploitation of a difficult site, is only part of an urban renewal project which would reflect credit on an authority with twenty times the population*

designed by J. R. Gammon, H. O. Williams & Associates
job architect Alan Jones
quantity surveyor Scannell & Manby
main contractor Rees & Kirby Ltd

CLIENT'S REQUIREMENTS, SITE, PLANNING

The community of Cefn-coed-y-cymmer is situated in South Breconshire but adjacent to, and north of, Merthyr Tydfil in Glamorganshire. It is set on high ground with an unspoilt hinterland of the Breconshire National Park behind. Historians state that a community existed on the site in the Middle Bronze Age (1500-900 BC) and although development visible today has resulted from the Industrial Revolution, its roots are far deeper. Its rapid expansion took place during the development of the great Iron Belt, where the ingredients for the manufacture of iron and steel—iron ore, coal and limestone—were found in close proximity. The community grew up alongside the vast Cyfarthfa Iron-works. Although the now derelict works has been supplanted by new industries, many of the inhabitants have still been occupying substandard housing unworthy of their heritage.

The site

The then Vaynor and Penderyn council was aware of the socially destructive effects of large-scale slum clearance. It therefore resolved to undertake a phased programme of re-development and rehabilitation which would leave the community structure intact. An immediate difficulty arose from the way the village was hemmed in by topographical barriers, necessitating the provision of new housing within existing boundaries to initiate the programme. The only vacant site available was one with a very steep slope and deplorable ground conditions which varied between running sand, requiring piled foundations, and excavation in ironstone. There was compensation for this costly expedient in the fine southern aspect with its panoramic view of Cyfarthfa castle to the east, the river immediately in front and a magnificent viaduct to the west.

The site area is approximately 0·27 hectare (two thirds of an acre), with a narrow plateau along Pont-y-capel road dropping away suddenly to a 1:2½ fall to give about 10 m (35 ft) overall change in level; thence another plateau before the valley makes its final descent to the river.

Design aims

The first aim was to achieve a satisfactory solution to the development of steeply sloping sites. The whole of the architect's office undertook a study tour of housing in France and Switzerland, the latter particularly for its similar topography to Wales. At the same time the scheme had to be economically viable, which implied the use of a simple repetitive structure and the inclusion of as many dwellings as possible to share the abnormally high cost of site works.

Tenant satisfaction was considered of prime importance. This meant that each dwelling had to enjoy the maximum possible benefit provided by the lovely views, and the sunshine obtained on the southern slope with, of course, the proper relationship room to room within each dwelling. On another level the aim was to create almost a cave dwelling, with its suggested warmth, easy defence and security—easy to be part of the community or to opt out.

Finally, the development must fit in with its site and the existing village architecture to the enhancement of both. The dwellings had to be of small scale, with each self defined, having something of the excitement and surprise one gets when walking through Cefn-coed, with the view constantly changing, suddenly opening out into magnificent views of the surrounding countryside, then closing up again. The dwellings had to try to capture something of the adaptation to the environment of the existing dwellings, similar to the two storey houses fronting Pont-y-capel road,

which become three and four storeys as they step down the slope, and also the charming 'odd' shaped dwellings at junctions and bends in the roads.

Scheme design

The thirty-four dwellings, which range in size from two to five person flats, are designed to Parker Morris standards and centrally heated—50 per cent by gas and 50 per cent by electricity. They are contained in two separate blocks, one of three storeys along Pont-y-capel road, the other a five storey stepped block partially built into the hillside to the south.

The three storey block contains fourteen dwellings with all the ancillary stores serving these dwellings contained in a podium. The stepped block contains twenty dwellings in four upper storeys, while the lowest contains garages and various stores. This block takes its form from the side of the hill into which the lowest three storeys have been set, each backing 2·130 m (7 ft) over the storey below, thus providing every dwelling with a terrace across the full width of its frontage. As the lower storeys are built into the hillside, all have been designed as single aspect dwellings facing south.

In order to avoid expensive tanking against the retained ground, covered walkways have been formed between the hillside and the blank rear face of the dwellings. These walkways, apart from providing access to the lower dwellings directly from ground level, also serve as ducts carrying all the drainage and services for the block.

The two blocks are linked by three footbridges which cross over a central open area separating them. This open area is free of vehicular traffic and can be used as a 'toddlers' play space. The bridges continue on the north side as walkways, which pass through the three storey block out on to the roadway at the top of the site. At their southern end the bridges terminate in staircase towers which connect all floors of the stepped block and provide access to the garages and stores at the lower ground level. It is possible therefore to walk off the level of the road serving the development, pass through the higher level block and have access to the top floor of the five storey block without having to climb any stairs. Thus only ten flats in the upper two floors of the three storey block are in fact above pavement level. The mixed accommodation enables some of the smaller units to house old people, who will thus be integrated into the population of approximately ninety-six persons.

One design factor little met with elsewhere is the serious incursion of sheep into buildings. Sheep are freely left to roam in the village, with the obvious results, so that fencing and gates have to be provided at strategic points to keep them out. It was at first difficult to convince tenants that the walkways and bridges were in fact equivalent to normal pavements, and not enclosed corridors as in multi-storied flats.

The construction is traditional, with brick cross walls, in-situ concrete floors, roofs, bridges, walkways and flower boxes. The whole built off concrete cross beams, supported on concrete piles. Windows are in timber, and the brick is a light grey silicate brick. The whole visual effect was to complement the natural grey and black stone outcrops seen in the Brecon Beacons near the site. No attempt has been made to 'garden' the site, but careful thought was given to a really natural setting for the building, with trees, grass, shrubs, etc, planted as though the building came afterwards.

The building of the scheme involved many difficulties, including the successful tenderer going into liquidation

172

during the early stages of the work, necessitating re-negotiation of the contract.

APPRAISAL

Bliss was it in that dawn to be alive . . .

Poetic exaggeration, perhaps, but not a gross over-statement of the emotional response among many architects in the early nineteen sixties to what promised to be the first revolution in housing design since the *Ville Radieuse*. Ideals of the early pre-war years had turned sour among the bleak acres of eclectic modernism and cut price *unités d'habitation* shorn of the community facilities central to the original concept. Mixed development, an eminently British compromise, had already by 1959 been subjected to stringent criticism[1] by the architects of Roehampton, its most successful example.

During the fifties, with Team 10 acting as a primary catalyst, several different strands in the concept of mass housing were being explored simultaneously. Their formal manifestations—'street deck', 'casbah', 'ziggurat', 'cluster' —all had one common feature; the desire to re-create in modern terms the social homogeneity lost when the traditional street was abandoned.

The 1964 Preview issue of *The Architectural Review*, giving for the first time pride of place to housing, encapsulated the formal component of the new movement as 'the rediscovery of the third dimension in housing design. Whatever Le Corbusier may have said about the plan being "the

generator" the fact remains that the section is the crucial representational device when it comes to demonstrating the kind of environment that a building has to offer . . . All the outstanding designs in this issue are conspicuous in some way for their sectional organisation . . .' The emphasis on formal values was unfortunate in that it suggested a new architectural gimmickry. In reality the movement, greatly influenced by informed criticism from outside the profession, was based on considerations (however obscurely expressed) of a total social organisation.

The dawn, like Wordsworth's, proved false. Within weeks of the election of a new government, housing minister Crossman warned architects to 'cut out the frills'—an ominous message in a context where architects were un-accustomed to affording 'frills' in any case. Then followed the Housing Cost Yardstick. To be fair, had this account-ants' device been based on a realistic assessment of building costs in the first place and been subject to the regular reviews promised, it might have fulfilled the high minded intentions expressed in the ministry circular which accom-panied its announcement. Possibly it improved housing standards among the worst local authorities. But its effect on the evolution of ideas was disastrous. Public offices, instead of learning from past mistakes were forced to repeat them. The cut-back in the housing programme hit hardest the small private architects' firms among whom were the pioneers of the new movement. As one example (there are others), the authors of the competition winning scheme chosen as frontispiece in the preview quoted, have in eight

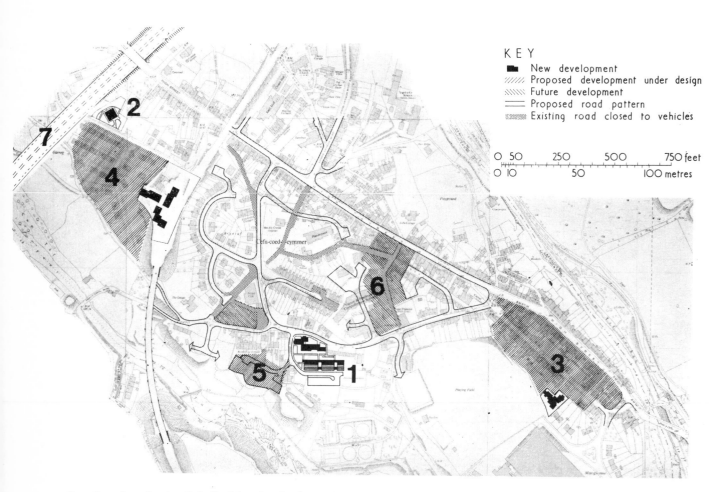

KEY
New development
Proposed development under design
Future development
Proposed road pattern
Existing road closed to vehicles

Location plan showing Cefn Isaf housing development (the subject of this building study) 1 in context of phased village renewal. 2 council offices; 3 Field Street area; 4 Maes-y-garreg area subsequently completed; 5 Wern Road area (not proceeded with); 6 proposed shopping and community centre (not proceeded with); 7 new Heads of the Valleys road

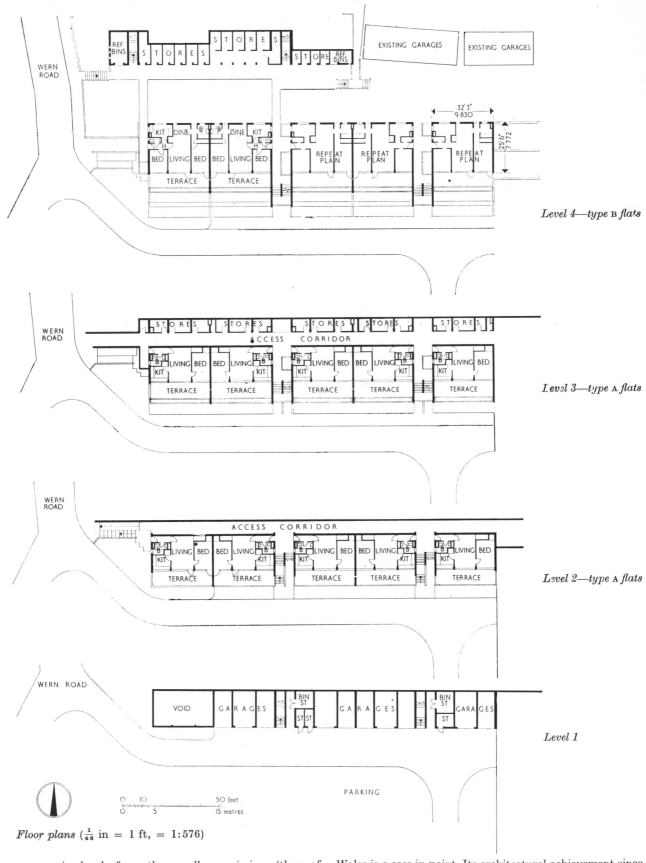

Level 4—type B flats

Level 3—type A flats

Level 2—type A flats

Level 1

PARKING

Floor plans ($\frac{1}{48}$ in = 1 ft, = 1:576)

years received only four other small commissions (three of them from one London borough).

A geographical shift in the creative use of design talent was an unforseen consequence. Previously the innovators had come from the housing authorities of London, a few big cities and the new town corporations. The first two were particularly hard hit by yardstick controls; whereas development areas and other regions where building costs were relatively depressed tended to be favoured. South-

Wales is a case in point. Its architectural achievement since the nineteenth century and until quite recently has been unremarkable; now the situation appears to be changing. As far as local authorities are concerned the region enjoys an important advantage in falling under the jurisdiction of the Welsh Office instead of the DOE. Its regional architects are very conscious of the need to improve standards and, though subject to the same financial constraints, are more inclined to use their margin of discretion in favour of a promising scheme than are their opposite numbers in

Whitehall, who suffer the constant anxiety of creating embarrassing precedent. At the same time they discreetly persuade local authorities (most, being much smaller than their English counterparts, have no architects on their staff) to employ private consultants. There has been the odd disaster; but also other instances, of which the collaboration between the then Vaynor and Penderyn rural district and the Swansea firm of Gammon, Williams & Associates promises to be an exceptional example, where a really creative partnership has resulted.

Cefn Isaf housing, impressive on its own account, is only one part of a larger project for restructuring the village of Cefn-coed-y-cymmer (see map p 172), the third settlement of any size within the rural district. For its small population

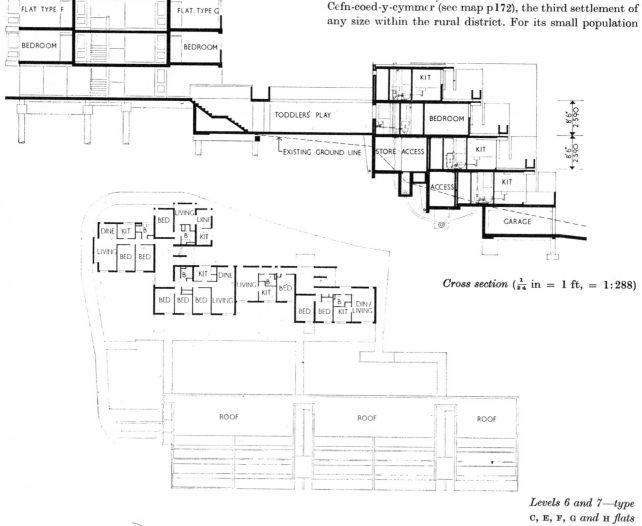

Cross section ($\frac{1}{24}$ in = 1 ft, = 1:288)

Levels 6 and 7—type C, E, F, G *and* H *flats*

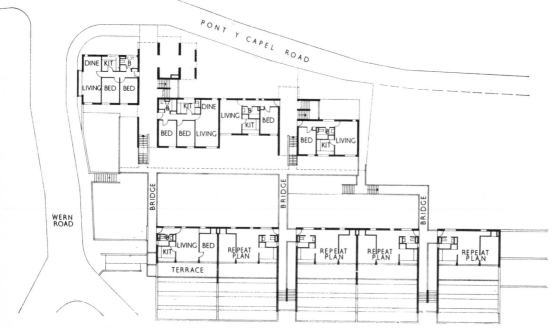

Level 5—type A, C, D *and* E *flats*

1

2

1 *New council offices nearing completion*
2 *Top of Field Street. The pub is to remain in new scheme*
3 *Bottom of Field Street. Building which closes view on right was to be rehabilitated*

3

(less than 7000; the new council offices **1**, by the same architects, are a reflection of the intimate scale on which the local authority operated, the council had an impressive post war housing record. But in Cefn particularly there remains a sizable residue of housing which must be classed as 'unfit' by even the most tolerant standards **2 to 4**. With a gross density of one person to every six acres it is ironic that the council should find itself in the same predicament as a central metropolitan borough with no spare land for expansion.

Hemmed in on three sides by the rivers *Taf Fawr* and *Taf Fechan* (the name of the village means 'the woody ridge by the confluence of the waters') and on the north by the spectacular new Heads of the Valleys road, the only alternative to nibbling into the Breconshire National Park beyond the road cutting was to build within developed boundaries on difficult sites. After Cefn Isaf was to come the adjacent Wern Road development containing larger family units, but· this was dropped because of ground conditions. Together with 'windfall' land from the railway closure, their completion was planned to allow the clearance of the worst area of Field Street, for which the architects have prepared a sensitive scheme of rehabilitation and redevelopment (see sketches **4a** and **5a**); this has since got under way, and the final phase of the plan includes a new pedestrian shopping and community centre designed to draw commerce off the heavily trafficked A470 between Brecon and Merthyr Tydfil.

This 'pendulum' process of implementing a housing pro· gramme, often inevitable in cities, must be rare in rural areas—it needs so much less effort, to say nothing of capital cost, to knock up a few housing estates on virgin perimeter land. But in following their consultant architects' advice, Vaynor and Penderyn council have achieved something which, though not apparent in the account books, this heritage-conscious land may remember them for—a much improved village without social disruption.

While emphasising the practical difficulties of the Cefn Isaf site the architects stressed its opportunities. Their *élan* in exploiting the challenge leaves little doubt which consideration carried more weight.

The building has an air of having been designed with enthusiasm, and it may not be entirely fanciful to suggest that the architects' pleasure is communicated to the occupants. Their willingness to admit borrowing ideas is refreshing. Once a perfectly respectable practice, such an admission (except by an architectural knight beguiling his audience with historical analogies), is too often avoided in today's obsessive striving for originality. Evidence of their

4

4a

5

8

5a

6

7

4 *Part of Field Street as it was and* **4a** *as proposed from approximately same viewpoint*

5 *Turning off Field Street as it was (High Street in background) and* **5a** *as proposed, from same viewpoint*

6 *West along Pont-y-capel road, block* A. *Large windows on returns light stairs to ten flats which do not have direct access from pavement level*

7 *Detail from opposite direction showing how bays of type* F *flats project over pavement to form closure. Way through to west link bridge under*

8 *Panoramic view from south-west showing relationship of block* A *to block* B *and of access levels to natural ground slope*

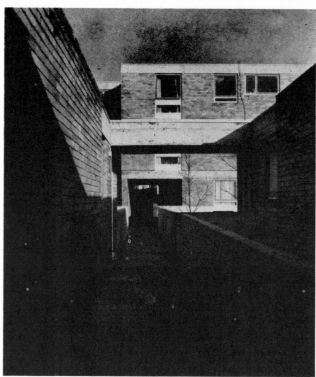

9

10

9 *Eastern stair whose six half-flights cover the total height differential across the site*
10 *From level 5, bridge from block B passes through block A to join Pont-y-capel road*

Swiss studies is clear[2]. The dominant motif of those great concrete flowerboxes **20** echoes a theme from Camberwell's Bonamy Street[3]. But if originality may be defined as an appropriate reinterpretation of an idea in a new context, this is an original scheme.

A somewhat disturbing feature of the design is the disparity of its two parts. Block A, on the upper plateau, is coolly styled in traditional brick, concrete and timber detailing which seen in isolation might be anywhere. Only when one moves in close or walks through **7, 15**, does it really become part of its environment. Block B in contrast, articulated not only by its stepped section but also by aggressive stair towers and rugged concrete projections, catches the local dialect at once. This stylistic dichotomy (only apparent from Wern Road **8**) cannot be bridged by weakly detailed and badly executed concrete walkways, although it has in time been masked by the trees planted in the enclosure optimistically labelled 'toddlers' play space'.

Another unsatisfactory feature of the overall design is the eastern end of block B, where the strong directional axes of the covered walkways **16** peter out into a bank of ankle-deep mud. One understands the architects' desire to leave the landscape as they found it, but the walkways demand some formal resolution. A row of temporary prefabricated garages on what should logically be the north-east corner of the site has contributed to the layout problem—that is the price of Welsh democracy.

Circulation

The access system provides a skeleton for the whole scheme. By exploiting natural site levels a three dimensional circulation grid has been formed so that every flat except those on the upper floors of block A can be approached by at least two different routes—a practical convenience which lends social cohesion to the parts.

Access to block A dwellings, a conventional grouping of two or three flats per floor around a common stair, is remarkable only for the generous space allotted to well lit landings—permitting their use for unplanned activities like drying clothes. The circulation pattern acquires an extra dimension in block B where corridors and bridges allow access to every flat at its own ground level **8, 10, 15**. The two enclosed walkways **16** are somewhat forbidding with only two intermediate sources of natural light in their

11 Block A with communal terrace at level 5
12 Large living room to four-person type B flat in block B. It has partial dual aspect into central play area. The five-person type in block A is similar but with full height window in north wall. Perversely, there is no opening in the wall behind the pianoforte which could give direct access between kitchen and dining area. Both these plans with single undifferentiated living space, do not strictly conform to Parker Morris recommendations

54·860 m (180 ft) length. Location of front doors on the stair landings emphasises the 'back alley' character of the corridors. Herein is a significant departure from a social tradition whereby the street, on to which dwellings *front*, is the natural focus of community life.

This flexible circulation system means that, with one exception, servicing six levels of living accommodation without a lift raises no serious problems. The exception is refuse collection. Two refuse bin stores are provided in the base of each block and it was presumably intended that tenants should carry down their own or that someone should be responsible for collecting daily. Predictably, neither happens, and almost every front door sports a large obstructive dustbin outside. Collection by hand trolley would have been simple and it seems a pity that no provision was made for paper sack containers.

The flats

An abnormal distribution of dwelling sizes (twenty-one two-person, two three-person, nine four-person and two five-person flats) suggests a high proportion of elderly people. A design criticism which should be noted, though not perhaps laboured in a rural situation, is that eight of the thirteen family dwellings are in block A without any private outdoor space. There is also some ambiguity about the terrace with planting tubs **11**. Though designed as part of the communal area, tenants overlooking it on that level feel a proprietary interest which could prove a built-in cause of friction.

The flat plans provide pleasantly proportioned and convenient spaces, without the painful contortions sometimes occurring where there is a dominant conceptual basis for the layout. They were, of course, designed before Parker Morris standards became mandatory in 1968 but after the publication of *Homes for today and tomorrow*, so it is reasonable to assess them in the light of that report. All plans seem short of internal storage, though external stores are generous. Particularly noticeable is the lack of pram space in all family dwellings: a damp, remote store is no substitute. Even the larger flats have a dining/living room instead of the usually preferred dining/kitchen. Though the arrangement does result in a splendidly large room, it also means only one living area. Perversely, there is no direct connection between kitchen and dining area though, in every case, the two rooms adjoin **12**. The four-person flat type B gets into trouble—living room separating the two bedrooms—through having to follow the unequal bay spacing of the two-person A types above and below. The smaller flats are harder to fault. Type F is an ingenious solution to a north aspect: cantilevered projections ensure adequate sunlight and a good view of the doings of Pont-y-capel road **6, 7**. But it is the residents of block B who are the privileged ones with their view across the valley, superb private balconies **18**, and enormous flower boxes the produce from which ranges from radishes to exotic creepers.

Construction and services

Construction is traditional brick cross walls and in-situ concrete with timber frames. Internal walls and block partitions are wet plastered. Roofs are felted on screeds laid to fall. Good heat and sound insulation is achieved by cavity party walls, floating timber floors on glass fibre quilt and laminated polyurethane ceiling panels. The architects tend to apologise for the quality of finishes—contractual difficulties resulting from the bankruptcy of the original contractor have made quality control difficult. The fairfaced concrete is a particular disappointment to them (our photographs, taken between rainstorms, emphasise its defects). But the character of the design is strong enough to wear minor defects, and a certain roughness is more appropriate to the situation than a slicker product. Plumbing and drainage have been rationally designed as shown in section (though one questions the need to have taken the rainwater from the private terraces down inside the building, with the result shown in **17**). As an experiment

13

13 *From level 4, viaduct framed by block A and western bridge. Recent rain exaggerates poor quality of concrete work*
14 *Western walkway through block A to Pont-y-capel road. Exemplary use of finest materials, somewhat marred by poor workmanship*
15 *Western profile of block B shows how each floor has direct access to pavement level. Right, fine view down valley towards Cyfarthia castle*
16 *Moving in from 15 to a dark access corridor. Steel gates (with perverse braces!) added to keep sheep out*
17 *View across living room to bedroom in type A flat, block B. Window wall extends across full frontage of this single aspect type. Clumsy duct casing to rwp from terraces above is uncharacteristic of services elsewhere*

15

16

17

18

19

20

18 *Typical 9.140 m × 2.130 m (30 ft × 7 ft) private terrace in block B. Even in mid-January on a sunny day the solar heat gained through the window wall is considerable. In summer the overhang*

tempers midday sun. Flower boxes well used. Proprietary whirligig clothes dryers, provided by the council, create their own mobile sculpture **19** *Conversation slit between adjacent terraces.*

Tenants are offered the option of a blocking panel but none has been so far requested. In Wales conversation is an art valued above privacy **20** *Tiers of flowerboxes, reminiscent of the*

Bonamy Street in Camberwell, but executed with more finesse

half the dwellings are heated by gas and half by electricity. When visited for appraisal, with several degrees of frost outside, the flats were certainly warm, though the temperature was boosted by solar gain. Perhaps an old lady complaining of cold feet—like the council clerk who suggested the heating system in his new offices was defective, despite his wall thermometer reading 15·6°c—was the victim of poor circulation.

Conclusions

The limited opportunity for assessment suggested user satisfaction was high. There was praise for the convenience and comfort at Cefn Isaf and no hankering after 'the old place', often found among those forcibly uprooted. The Brecon foothills in midwinter are no place for a survey in depth, however. Ultimately one must rely on a well developed sixth sense of people's reaction to their environment. Judgment will be subjective and partly conditioned by opinions expressed at the beginning of this appraisal. But Cefn Isaf did seem a housing scheme which achieved the architects' design aims and also some of the promise which six years ago seemed near to more widespread attainment. When the whole socio-political basis of public authority housing was being questioned, it was fascinating to observe the relationship between architect and tenant. Most architects who have worked for a large housing authority know that personal contact with his real *client* is, if not impossible, firmly discouraged—proper channels exist. In Cefn, where everyone knows everybody, matters are arranged differently. If somebody wants a defect remedied or a

clothes dryer provided then Mr Gammon or Mr Jones just have to be caught when next on site. Of course the request may be just as pointless as an unsigned requisition mislaid in a 'pending tray', but one suspects not. Without making any general assumptions from particular hypotheses it might be worth questioning whether perhaps the cherished ideal of tenant control is more likely to be achieved by smaller rather than larger housing authorities, whose organisational structure could be sufficiently informal to leave architect and user unentangled in bureaucratic coils.

SUMMARY

Total floor area: 2 793 m² (30 061 sq ft).
Type of contract: Fixed price.
Tender date: February 1966.
Work began: May 1966. (Terminated April 1967. Restarted November 1967.)
Work finished: May/June 1969.
Multi-storey dwellings.
Net habitable floor area: 1 848 m² (19 890 sq ft).
Gross floor area: 2 793 m² (30 061 sq ft).
Price of foundations, superstructure, installation and finishes including drainage to collecting manhole: £151 466.
Price of external works and ancillary buildings including drainage beyond collecting manhole: £14 379.
Total: £165 845:

16 Housing Estate at The Lanes, Rotherham

The Lanes at Rotherham which gained a Ministry of Housing and Local Government award in 1970 is a local authority low rise medium density scheme. The range of house types are all planned with patios, some of them terraced, and the interest of the scheme is in how this basic criterion has influenced detail planning, the layout and the overall success of the project

for	Rotherham County Borough Council (borough planning officer J. Winter)
architect and engineer	Gillinson Barnett & Partners
partner in charge	M. C. Dakin
architectural team	W. J. Dawson
	P. R. Greenwood
	L. Brown
quantity survevor	Henry Vale & Sons
main contractor	Frank Haslam Milan

16 Housing Estate at The Lanes, Rotherham

A *Site plan: 1 one-bedroom single-storey houses, 2 two-bedroom single-storey houses, 3 three-bedroom houses, 4 two-bedroom stepped patio houses*

CLIENT'S REQUIREMENTS, SITE, PLANNING

The site, approx $2\frac{1}{2}$ km ($1\frac{1}{2}$ miles) from Rotherham town centre and surrounded by pre- and post-war semi-detached houses, was mainly virgin land falling from west to east. Trial holes indicated layers of brown and grey clay overlying clay shale at an average depth of 2·1 m (7 ft) with indications of coal outcrops in places.

The brief called for a mixed development of smaller units for older persons and four- and five-person family units, the older persons' dwellings to be arranged in small clusters throughout the scheme. Ground or level access was to be provided to as many dwellings as possible.

From a perimeter link road short culs-de-sac penetrate the housing area, serving integral garage units and the central area. Dwelling groups are arranged in a fairly rigid pattern along the contours and are stepped down the site, the balanced cut and fill arrangement providing direct access from ground level to all units in two-storey blocks. The pedestrian network avoids vehicular routes, linking all sections of the site with adjacent bus services and converging on the central square.

All dwelling types are L-shaped on plan, and single-storey house and house units are generally paired. Stacked units are grouped in several ways horizontally and vertically in two, three and four storeys, and all dwellings have private patios or gardens with aspects ranging from south-east to south-west. Central heating in excess of Parker Morris standards is provided by individual gas-fired ducted warm air systems which also provide water heating.

Construction is basically loadbearing brickwork and blockwork on concrete strip foundations. Suspended floors are precast concrete with an insulation sandwich and flat roofs are of timber construction. Monopitch roofs consist of trussed rafters, felt, battens and concrete tiles and tile hanging. Walls are dry-lined throughout internally.

The area of the site is 4·97 hectares (12·28 acres), and 230 dwellings accommodate 834 people at a density of 169 persons per hectare (68·4 ppa). The number of dwellings per hectare is 47 (19 per acre). There are 180 car spaces with provision for more in the future. The 230 dwellings comprise 52 two-person, one-bedroom single-storey houses, 45 four-person, two-bedroom single-storey houses, 18 five-person, three-bedroom houses and 115 four-person, two-bedroom stacked dwellings in two-, three- and four-storey blocks. There are also a meeting room, estate office and two shops.

APPRAISAL

Rotherham's house building activity since the war has provided a large amount of three-bedroom family accommodation on vast council estates to the north and south-east. Later phases of redevelopment have subsequently got under way with a view to seeing that the balance is restored by the provision for smaller households. The council also decided to strike a better balance between private and public housing by assigning more sites for private development.

Having decided on these general policies, Rotherham can learn an important lesson for the future from one of its own schemes—The Lanes. This lesson has to do with size and scale of proposed developments. The Lanes consists of 230

184

1

2

3

1 *Cul-de-sac off perimeter road*
2 *Footpaths between terraces mostly follow contours. Curiously, external lighting is not mounted on walls apparently because of*

lack of co-operation between housing and lighting departments. Architects were not to blame
3 *Main changes of level occur where flats are banked one above the other*

flats and houses in the centre of an earlier, very large scheme of semi-detached houses. Quite apart from providing, in the same area, a greater choice of house size, the scheme transforms the older estate simply by being very different from it and by being about the right size.

The degree of repetition within any one design is crucial in avoiding monotony—bane of all large scale housing schemes, whether public or private. The Lanes succeeds in

providing sufficient variety to sustain visual interest over the whole site with very limited means. At this density it would be difficult to achieve this degree of success if the scheme were larger, without also extending the range of house plans. The lesson for Rotherham's planners is that, in general, any one scheme should rarely be much bigger than The Lanes if it is to have the identity of place so important to its inhabitants. If, for site reasons, larger schemes are commissioned, these questions of size, scale and sense of place should be uppermost in the designer's mind when determining the overall plan's structure.

Nature of access for pedestrians and vehicles is usually the strongest determinant of the development's scale. At The Lanes cars are kept mainly to the perimeter and penetrate the area to a limited extent only by short culs-de-sac **1**. General pace of movement within the scheme is therefore very slow and the slight shifts of alignment of building forms are telling in the footpath vistas. The main lines of building are rigorously horizontal along the contours of the sloping site and all the stepping is concentrated in the cross section of certain terraces so that views and movement along the contour footpath **2** are given maximum contrast with views and movements up and down the slopes **3, 4**. This highly organised disposition of buildings on the ground contrasts in turn with the sea of semi-detached houses surrounding The Lanes, each pair set at its own ground level along a road system moving more or less diagonally against the slopes of the undulating ground.

Car parking and access
The plan provided 108 garages for 230 flats and houses, of which 48 could be built later as separate garage blocks according to demand, which in the event has not materialised, since people prefer to park in the open· free of charge, rather than rent a garage. Of the rest 45 are lock-up garages and 15 are open car ports next to the front doors of the flats **5**, so that none of the garages in the scheme is as useful as a garage can be when it is adjacent to the flat and lockable. The car port arrangement is the most convenient and is cheaper to rent than a lock-up garage.

One cul-de-sac gives access to the pair of shops in the small pedestrian square at the scheme's centre **6**, but extra parking space has not been allowed for. The part of the road nearest the shops is narrow and delivery vans parked there block access to garages outside the flats. It would have been better to provide a small parking area near to the shops, even at the expense of the pedestrian area in the square. This could have been done without interrupting pedestrian routes.

Minor irritations are also caused by refuse disposal men to the tenants whose flats open off the cul-de-sac. Generally each house or flat has access at ground level and dustbins are emptied by workers using the footpath system. Of the flats 17 are reached via a deck or raised footpath connected to ground level at each end and at the centre by ramps **7**. Although the architects agreed with the cleansing department that dustbins at the upper level would be carried down the ramps to be emptied, some collectors find it easier to drop the refuse from the deck to the road below.

Children's play and private open space
Because of the predominance of small flats, the number of children living in this area is relatively small. No specific children's play area is provided **8**, although the original design for the square outside the shops included a small play mound. This attracted children from other areas too and, as a result of the noise, local residents prevailed on the housing committee to have the mound removed. The lack of a planned children's play area is probably not at all serious in this kind of layout where the footpath system lends itself to a whole range of play activity. Small children have the private patios or enclosed gardens in which to play at home.

These patios generate the whole plan and, despite their small size, provide a major amenity to every house and flat. They vary in character considerably from a garden on the ground **13**, through which the house is approached, to a more sheltered and private arrangement where the house is entered from a footpath on the side away from the garden.

4

5

4 *View out of estate*
5 *Car port with front door and store under cover. Lock up garages are adjacent*

7

6

In many cases pairs of such gardens share a low fence and thereby lose their privacy. Incompatible neighbours could suffer in such circumstances. The most successful patios are those upper ones **12** in the two-, three- and four-storey blocks where greater privacy is ensured and the view from the patio lengthened. They are also more sheltered than the others, being enclosed on three sides without a break.

The patios are open to the east and receive sunlight from east and south. This is not the ideal orientation; a slope to the west would have been a more favourable site on which to develop the theme of this layout.

House plans

The particular character of The Lanes is established by the limited range of house types; single-storey houses for two or four persons **K**, **L**, two-storey family houses for five

6 *Even with limited means, variety is achieved in marked contrast to earlier housing*

7 *Square at core of plan where shops are sited*
8 *No purpose-designed play area is provided, but*

children find layout of The Lanes adaptable to their use
9 *Ramp serving upper level*

footpath rises from central square near shops

10

11

10, 11 *Footpath system.*
Single ground finish would
have been more useful,
easier to maintain and
better looking
12, 13 *Patios vary from*
exposed corner of ground to
very private terrace in
stepped block of flats

12

13

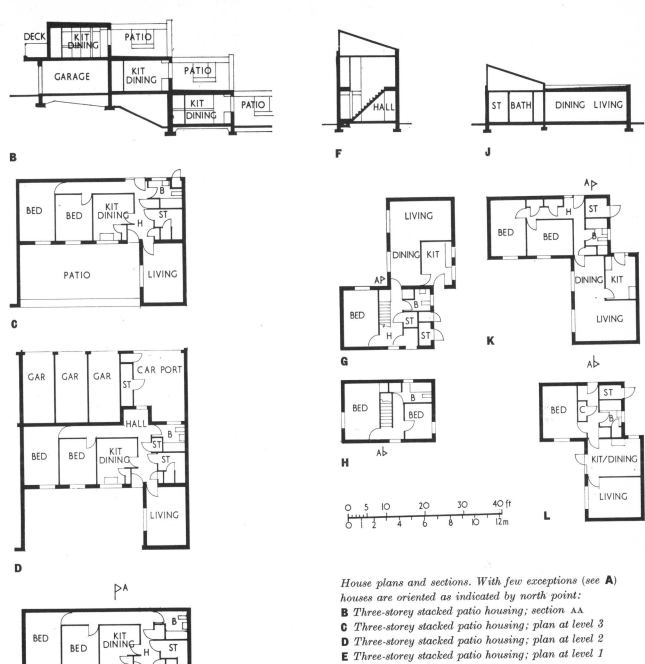

House plans and sections. With few exceptions (see **A**)
houses are oriented as indicated by north point:
B *Three-storey stacked patio housing; section* AA
C *Three-storey stacked patio housing; plan at level 3*
D *Three-storey stacked patio housing; plan at level 2*
E *Three-storey stacked patio housing; plan at level 1*
F *Three-bed/five-person house; section* AA
G *Three-bed/five-person house plan; ground floor*
H *Three-bed/five-person house plan; first floor*
J *Two-bed/four-person house; section* AA
K *Two-bed/four-person house; plan*
L *One-bed/two-person house; plan*

people **G**, **H**, and four-person flats in blocks with a stepped section **B**, **C**, **D**. All types are L-shaped in an attempt to enclose the garden or patio. The upper flats of the two-, three- and four-storey blocks do this effectively. The patio of the ground floor flat is really a small garden exposed to passers-by, although the wide range of tastes among householders could render this unimportant.

The other single-storey-house plans are hardly big enough to arrange around a patio successfully, although they are well over Parker Morris area standards. As a result, the houses have to be spread out to achieve an acceptable patio dimension and this has let the breezes in. More effective use of space inside and outside could probably have been achieved with oblong plans used chequer-board fashion, or in terraces with garden walls. It seems as if in the detailed formulation of the plans, the full usefulness of the patio has been sacrificed to preserve the house's L-shaped outline.

A number of minor criticisms can be levelled at the house plans and some of the details. The two- and four-person houses have useful outside stores **14** for garden tools, lawn mowers, deck chairs, bedding out plants, muddy boots and other items for garden use. The siting of this is inconvenient, being off the indeterminate space at the side of the house away from the garden. It would be better located next to the patio. Tenants of the patio flats could also use such a store and some of them lack one in which to keep the refuse bin. They do not have either if they are at ground level. Each house and flat has adequate storage off the hall, but none in the bedrooms except for one of the bedrooms of the five-person house.

Interiors
It is a pity that the single-storey houses were not planned with the living areas in the arm of the L which faces the

street and patio. This would have given the kitchen and living room east/west orientation and a view on to the street. The architects recognised this need to have a window facing the street for the disabled and elderly, and introduced a projecting bay window in the bedroom at a later stage.

The dining/kitchen of the stacked flats is separated from hall and passage by a glazed screen **15** which extends from floor to ceiling. This takes away potentially useful wall space in both kitchen and hall and would be better as a solid screen up to 1·524 m (5 ft) high with glazing above.

Some tenants find the warm air controls at high level difficult to reach **16** and the form of heating is not entirely satisfactory, particularly for elderly and incapacitated people who find it either too expensive or inadequate. The housing department has therefore had to consider other forms of heating for future schemes, and improvement of that of The Lanes.

The choice of windows is rather odd for this type of development. With the exception of the upper floor of the larger family houses, all the windows can be cleaned easily from the outside, yet a pivoting reversible window has been used, equipped with a stay catch awkward to release, particularly in the kitchen where it has to be reached over the sink. Apart from these details, the quality of the windows and ironmongery is generally good, and the use of stain rather than paint on window frames seems to be liked by most people.

Landscaping

In a close fitting environment such as this it is imperative that ground surfaces receive the same study and are designed with the same care as the buildings themselves. There is a shortage of ramps up the slopes **18** and some of the junctions of materials on the ground could be better managed **17**. It was a surprise to see that external lighting was not mounted on the walls. This was not the architect's fault; it depended on whether the housing or lighting department should pay running costs and the unimaginative attitude of the lighting department.

The use of an arbitrary mixture of pitched roofs and flats will disturb some people, but it has the effect of varying the local skyline along the footpaths. It may be possible in future schemes to achieve this totally by the disposition of buildings on the ground combined with a fuller use of pitched roofs.

14 *Garden store is nearer neighbour's than tenant's garden*

15 *See-through kitchen wall*

16 *Some heating and ventilation controls are out of reach*

14

15

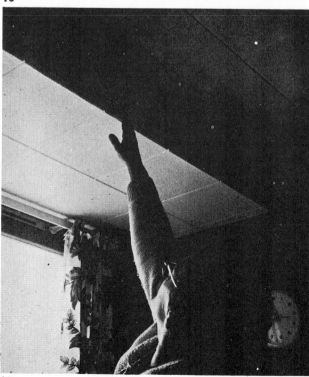

16

17

17 *Ground finishes and levels are not always well handled*

18 *One flight of steps would have been enough, the other could have been ramp*

It is because the basic idea of The Lanes is so good and the definition of the layout plan so very skilfully handled, that one's attention finally comes to these small points of detail which prevent the whole scheme from being of very high quality.

18

SUMMARY

Ground floor area: 14 042 m² (151 145 sq ft).
Total floor area: 15 945 m² (171 632 sq ft).
Type of contract: RIBA fixed price.
Tender date: July 1967.
Work began: October 1967.
Work finished: May 1970.
Price of foundation, superstructure, installation and finishes including drainage to collecting manhole: £549 951.
Price of external works and ancillary buildings including drainage beyond collecting manhole: £129 054.
Total: £724 005.

17 Housing at Linden Grove, London SE 15

Linden Grove, Southwark, follows on from the competition-winning Bishopsfield housing, Harlow, by the same architects. It was commended in the 1971 Civic Trust awards, and also in the 1971 DOE *housing awards*

for	London Borough of Southwark
by	Neylan & Ungless
assistant architects	Robin Kornweibel
	David Barnett
	Anthony Horan
quantity surveyors	Davis, Belfield & Everest
structural engineer	Flint & Neill
main contractor	London Borough of Southwark building department.

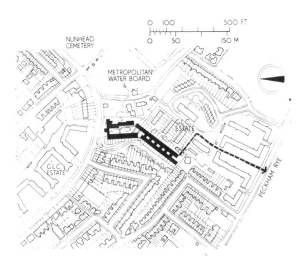

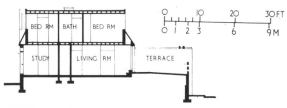

A Linden Grove site plan

CLIENT'S REQUIREMENTS, SITE, PLANNING

The site is in a 19th century area of Camberwell near
Peckham Rye. It is a long thin strip of land, just over one
hectare (2½ acres), lying off Linden Grove and surrounded
by the gardens of neighbouring houses, except for one end
fronting on to the road. It contained some good mature
trees, mostly around the edges, and there was a fall of up
to 1:10 across the narrow dimension with a gentler slope
down the length of the site.

The brief asked for approximately 60 dwellings—about 40 of
them for families and 20 of them in the form of small flats
arranged to form an old people's community with shared
common rooms and a warden's flat. The completed scheme,
accommodating 242 people at a density of 240 persons per
hectare (96 ppa), provides the family dwellings in 41
houses, varying in capacity from one to seven people. They
are two- or three-storeys high and each has a private garden
or large terrace. The old people's flats—10 single and 10
double—are arranged together in one block with their communal rooms and shared bathrooms, while the warden's
flat bridges the space between this block and the adjoining
houses.

There is parking or garaging for 40 cars and space for
more, if required, and a service and garage road runs down
one side of the site roughly parallel with the line of buildings.
It is on the lower side of the site and below the level of the
houses, so that it has been possible to provide most of the
car-parking in bays cut under the terrace gardens of some
of the houses.

The narrowness of the site and the position of the trees
suggested a linear development down the centre: a paved
walk runs the length of the site flanked by houses opening
directly off it. The walk changes in level as the ground rises
and falls and it varies in width with the shape of the site,
widening into a small square near the entrance from Linden
Grove and contracting at the other end to 3·7 m (12 ft),
bridged in places by the upper floors. The walk was designed
in the hope that eventually it would be possible to provide a
link through a neighbouring estate to nearby Peckham Rye.
Planning of the houses varies according to their position:
those flanking the walk at its narrow point are designed
with their main rooms looking outwards over their gardens
and trees, but high-level roof lights are also introduced on the
walk side to bring cross-lighting and sunlight into the living
rooms. The houses flanking the square are more open in
character with some windows overlooking it, but sized and
positioned to avoid intrusion from outside.

The old people's flats are arranged in a block on one side
of the square with a private garden for the old people behind
it. They are planned on two floors on one side of a corridor
and look over the square at its widest and most animated

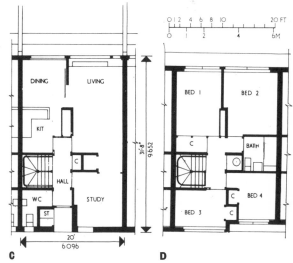

B *Linden Grove, location plan. Dotted line shows pedestrian route proposed but not implemented. Nearest shops and bus stop are at bottom of Linden Grove to north-west*

C *Block 2: ground floor plan. Cooker is in corner to left of worktop*
D *Block 2: first floor plan*

E *Block 2: section*

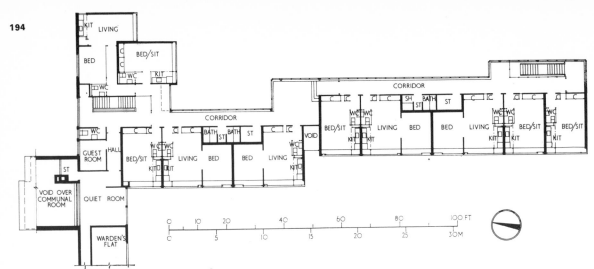

F *Sheltered housing block: first floor plan*

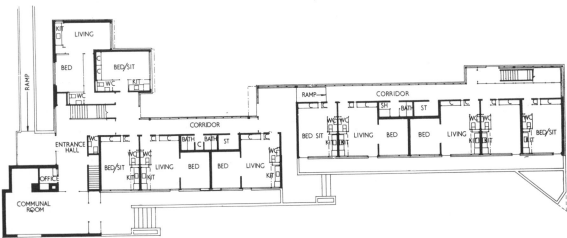

G *Sheltered housing block: ground floor plan*

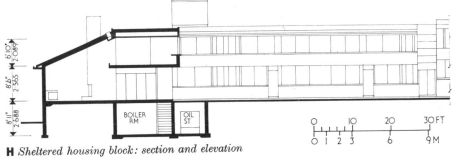

H *Sheltered housing block: section and elevation*

J *Block 2 and sheltered housing: perspective section
showing entrance square and warden's flat bridging over*

point; the corridor, which is staggered to provide casual sitting corners along it, looks over the quiet garden. Windows, which can be curtained and which have deep reveals, have been introduced in the walls between living rooms and corridor to give the option of a view of the garden and some of the common space of the building.

Construction is conventional: brick cross-walls with timber floors to the houses and concrete floors to the old people's flats. External finishes have been chosen to reduce maintenance and at the same time to provide a flexible skin to the sometimes complicated form of the building. Up to the first floor level, vandal height, the walls are generally cavity brickwork with an insulating block inner skin. Above that height, they are of insulating block hung with asbestos cement slates. The spandrels between the aluminium sliding windows are clad with corrugated aluminium sheeting, while fascias, parapets and so on are clad with purpose-made sheet aluminium units.

The houses are heated by gas-fired, ducted warm air heaters housed in a central unit in each house. The old people's flats are heated by a radiator system with oil-fired boilers which also provide hot water.

The scheme was designed in 1964-65 and work started on site after several hold-ups in March 1967.

K *Block 1: second floor plan*

L *Block 1: first floor plan*

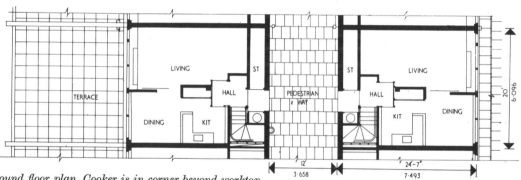

M *Block 1: ground floor plan. Cooker is in corner beyond worktop*

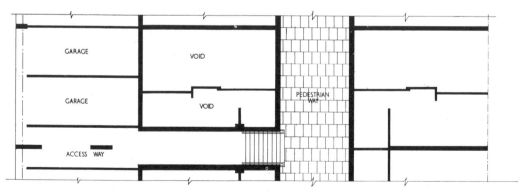

N *Block 1: garage level plan with steps up to pedestrian way at ground floor level*

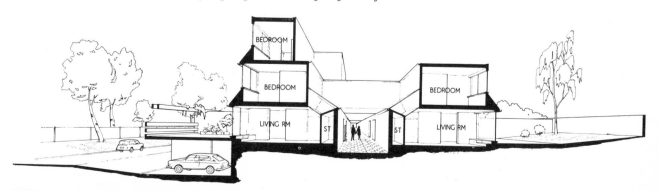

O *Block 1: perspective section facing north-east*

APPRAISAL

Linden Grove is the second housing scheme by Neylan & Ungless. It is not as unique as was its competition-winning predecessor, Bishopsfield at Harlow, but with a third project at the Emmanuel Church site, also in Southwark, it demonstrates an unusual concern with housing problems and social interactions within a community, and also with architectural aesthetic objectives so often emasculated by yardstick graphs.

Each of the three sites is different: Bishopsfield is magnificently located on a hillside facing south **P**, isolated by its own formal excellence from neighbouring Harlow developments; Linden Grove is part way down a slope crowned by Nunhead cemetery woodland, a narrow splinter across the bias of the hill, 19th century terraces to the south, pre-war LCC housing to the north and mixed post-war GLC housing dividing the cemetery from Peckham Rye to the south and south-west **B**; Emmanuel Church site, pincered between the Southern railway viaduct and Walworth Road, is overlooked by Southwark's 18-storey Mansion Street development completed in 1964. This poses problems of scale and privacy in addition to noise. The density of Harlow is 175 persons per hectare (70 ppa), Linden Grove has 240 persons per hectare (96 ppa) and Emmanuel Church site has 350 persons per hectare (141 ppa).

Five main concerns
The architects had five main concerns in conjunction with aesthetics: first, at both Linden Grove and Harlow, as Neylan says, 'to respond more explicitly to site conditions than is fashionable with most modern buildings'; second a concern with individual privacy and identification between individual and dwelling; third, a desire to reduce the distinction between housing and flats, giving both similar amenities; fourth, the generation of a sense of place and community within the larger urban pattern; and finally, pedestrian and visual lines of movement.

Within brief and density constraints, the architect's approach, although increasingly limited by yardstick, is fresh and constantly evolving. Hypotheses are tested and often re-used in different ways. Thus, though similar means are used to achieve a high degree of privacy in Bishopsfield and Linden Grove, dwellings in the former look inward and in the latter outward: the reason for this is the architects' response to differing site conditions.

The top floor patio is a device identical to Bishopsfield and Emmanuel Church site **Q**, giving similar amenity to a house while achieving maximum sunlight and privacy. The attempt to unify open and covered spaces in each dwelling is common to all three projects. The architectural vernacular of Emmanuel Church site borrows much from Bishopsfield **P**, **R**. That at Linden Grove is an attempt to find more flexible ways of building.

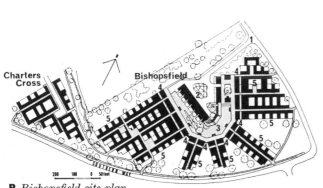

P *Bishopsfield site plan*

Key
1 Approach to site
2 Visitors' parking
3 Pedestrian platform, garaging under
4 Ring of 4-storey flats
5 Patio houses

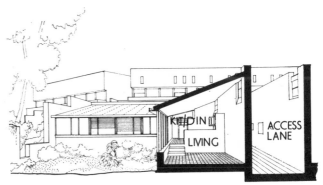

R *Diagrammatic perspective showing typical Bishopsfield courtyard house: bedroom windows also face into court*

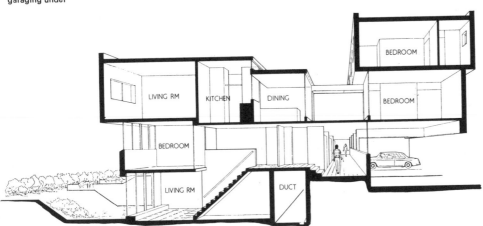

Q *Emmanuel Church site section through north block parallel to Mansion Street: roof level patio over pedestrian way achieves maximum privacy and sunlight*

1

2

3

Bishopsfield

Although this appraisal is concerned with Linden Grove, it is important to consider its Harlow progenitor. Bishops-field hill is an exciting site **1**. Approached from the north **5**, the hilltop forms the nub of the scheme, providing economi-cal access to car-parking below the terraces that rise in steps to blocks of one- and two-person flats enclosing a flexible public space. This natural theatre has already been used by a vigorous tenants' association for a carnival **3**. This semi-circle forms an inviting and stimulating fulcrum from which the majority of housing units fan like fingers from a palm down the hillside. Green wedges seen through breaks in the upper ring cunningly relate to open views of land-scape and countryside beyond, while separating blocks of courtyard housing. Inversely, each high, narrow lane approach to these frames distant housing areas and invokes memories of more ancient towns. These blind lanes are punctuated by entrance doors and small kitchen windows **2** to family houses planned round walled open courts **R**.

Smaller public courts open from the lanes, subtle focuses amending view and direction. The pedestrian is offered the delight of a choice of routes from A to B. Even in the generally neglected concrete netherworld of car-parking, the unexpected vista, twist and turn excite interest and

1 Bishopsfield from south: typical lane access to courtyard housing leads to garage area with steps up to northern entrance terraces; windows in north block direct eye to radiating lanes
2 Typical lane at Bishopsfield: slope exploited to provide double-volume living rooms lit by windows at high level. Dining/kitchen is half level up with narrow view to lane
3 Carnival time at Bishopsfield (photo: Harlow Citizen)

identification. The solution—economic in terms of land use assigned to access and service—allows pedestrians' interests to predominate. The architectural clarity of this concentric

4

5

design is nowhere more apparent than from hills to the south where the potent rhythm of dark slate roofs and sturdy brick walls contrasts with surrounding less incisive, more conventional housing layouts.

Planning, social and design objectives

All three projects demonstrate the architects' skill in synthesising planning with social and design objectives. At Linden Grove not all planning objectives have been realised owing to the omission of an important pedestrian connection with Peckham Rye via the adjoining GLC estate **B**. This is critical in relation to the sheltered housing; shops and buses at Nunhead and Peckham are a long walk. Faded local shops and a bus stop are at the bottom of Linden Grove, but a shopping-laden climb up the hill is a daunting prospect.

The proposed link was a more level short-cut to Peckham Rye, and for children it avoided crossing two main roads. The design is deliberately linear **A**—a pedestrian street narrowing from the small square near the entrance to a partially covered walk between the bend and the southern boundary, and it is irritating to be funnelled along its length to an irrational full-stop. The buildings on the

bend of Linden Grove are domestic in character like the terraces further down the hill. The bend is exploited to turn cars and pedestrians into the western service road and core (again comparable to Bishopsfield and equally economical in land use terms). In the Harlow pattern visitor-parking is immediately obvious close to the turn-in, that for tenants almost hidden. At Linden Grove both visitor-parking and service road below are hidden from the western terrace elevated on a high grassy bank. The main pedestrian entrance is under a bridge below the warden's flat, screened to the north-east by the pitched roof of the projecting common room **6**. Visual unity is sustained by the blank slate face to the flat and slate flank and roofing to the common room, designed to allow the sheltered housing to be welded unobtrusively with the rest of the scheme **9**.

The design gives privacy for old people facing the walk and provides an entrance from the road specifically related to their accommodation and communal rooms; also secondary entrances from inside the walk and the eastern secluded garden. The ramped approach to the old people's block slips protectively across the face of the building, skilfully evocative of its sheltered nature, although inconveniently higher up the slope **10**. The entrance platform is shaded by a carefully-conserved tree—an object lesson in

6

7

8

tree preservation close to buildings, a foil to controlled detailing, a visual link with the cemetery beyond and a favourite summer sitting-place overlooking the road.

Steps and bends

Both housing blocks exploit the slopes: the outward-looking character of the dwellings to the west is appreciated by tenants. The bend and contours of the site **7** are manipulated deftly to unite different block forms and act as a cross-roads. Shallow steps lead down, contracting through a narrow entrance to service road and garages **11**. Others in reverse process pass between laundry and sheltered housing to open into the garden behind the latter **22**. From this raised viewpoint old people can observe comings and goings in summer and watch toddlers in one of their favourite play areas.

As at Bishopsfield **8**, steps and ramps are used to advantage to direct gently, focus views and contrive an interesting floorscape. In addition they emphasise the enclosure of this fulcrum which dominates the strong directional emphasis and serves to pull a good deal of play towards this end of the blocks **12**. Colour here also plays a subtle role as the tone of steps and paving picks up that of the darker Crowborough bricks with cohesive effect.

4 *Emmanuel Church site, south block. Access to individual front doors is by stairs. Note refuse cupboards below canopy, aluminium sliding windows similar to Linden Grove*
5 *Northern hilltop entrance to Bishopsfield for cars and pedestrians, garaging below stepped terrace. Brick vernacular, scale, rhythm of east block facade repeated at Emmanuel Church site*

6 *Linden Grove grassy bank directs pedestrians into core of scheme below bridge of warden's flat and gives privacy to western gardens. Note viewing window from projecting common room*
7 *Attractive floorscape steps and pavings unite blocks, accentuate domestic scale and enclosure; steps up to garden on right*
8 *Paving, Bishopsfield: skilful ramp detail*

9

10

11

Beyond this point the walk narrows between the two- and three-storey block—not open as the Bishopsfield lanes, but partially-covered by bridging bathrooms at first-floor level **14**. This deals with light angle restrictions which otherwise would preclude a linear solution **0**. The interest of upward views contrasted with intervals of dark and light, although formally skilful and intellectually stimulating in an abstract sense, is not appreciated by tenants who feel this is unpleasantly oppressive, disliking the blind walls with no outlook **15**.

Glazed front doors would have given welcome light to halls and partly compensated for the sense of isolation felt by occupants of east-facing dwellings with no ground floor outlook beyond the boundary of their sloping gardens. The length of this block combined with the absence of views out to the walk create the least satisfactory aspects of the scheme **0**. Here a balance is lost; introversion, mitigated at Bishopsfield by views to lanes, has become restrictive.

All dwellings have attractive outlooks from living rooms to gardens or spacious patios **13**. The kitchen/dining room, which seems rather small for large families, is standard throughout and connected by a sliding door to the living rooms. In the larger dwellings an extra study/bedroom or living room is connected by a sliding door with the living room. This, in addition to doors from hall and dining area, creates a space awkward to furnish. The cooker adjacent to narrow shelves poses cleaning problems and is potentially dangerous **17**. Ventilated food cupboards are an unfortunate omission. Stairs with winders **16**—always controversial—are visually exciting but difficult and expensive to decorate —a factor which worries tenants.

As at Bishopsfield, well-designed storage space is used where possible as a sound barrier between bedrooms. Similarly

lighting is considered carefully. Rooflights add interest and unexpected shafts of sunlight, a subtle and attractive feature reminiscent of Bishopfield housing. Full-height sliding widows open from living and dining to gardens. Irritatingly, steps up are provided only from living rooms. Tenants in the linked housing block complain of dark halls in addition to murky entrance porches.

Sliding windows at first floor level are criticised universally as being too wide for cleaning from inside the building, an oversight admitted by the architects and rectified in Emmanuel Church site. The building profile adds interest and distinguishes the scheme from most council housing. But with the lack of gutters robust enough to support ladders, it exacerbates window-cleaning difficulties **18**. Apparently a diminishing band in Peckham, cleaners are further frightened by the need to carry ladders through impeccable interiors where in one case even the dog was tinted lavender to match the decor.

For security reasons several tenants would have preferred lock-up garages rather than open bays below patios **18**, but as garaging is virtually hidden from Linden Grove and overlooked from gardens opposite there has been less trouble than expected. The housing manager, who was initially critical, later became satisfied.

With the exception of aluminium cladding panels, about the weathering of which doubts were expressed, the appearance is restrained and attractive. Detailing is efficient, controlled and of a high standard. The materials, including dark slates, darkish bricks and aluminium, are generally cohesive. The block profile, although partially derivative from light angle legislation **12**, is highly individual and three-dimensionally directional, as illustrated by the section through the link block **0**. The diminishing height of windows

12

14

13

on east and west elevations **13**, reminiscent of Georgian façades, has the same result—imprinting an immediately effective scale despite the totally different vernacular.

Vandalism and play

The two-storey dwellings **9**, **12** facing the sheltered housing accommodate the largest families (six and seven persons). There are more than 40 children living here which with those inevitably attracted from the rest of the scheme plus intruders from the LCC estate opposite, creates, as confirmed by tenants, caretaker, warden and social workers, undue noise and nuisance on occasions. The decision to give this busy outlook to the elderly is reasonable, especially as the advanced age of many limits movement. Double-glazing their flats would also effectively seal them from all but visual contact in winter.

It was perhaps a mistake to house so many families with young children in this zone. Vandalism is not generally initiated by children living in this scheme, but by those from less privileged estates in the neighbourhood. This is common to the majority of new housing in similar locations, a constant headache to housing management and a problem not appreciated sufficiently by architects. At Linden Grove old people have been upset by abuse while other tenants, delighted on arrival with planted flowerboxes **12**, **15** have

found that plants and replacements quickly vanish. Extensive glazing at the entrance to the sheltered housing is an obvious and expensive target. Despite these attacks, the estate has suffered less than most others in the borough—a factor attributed by the housing manager to tenants' interest and pride in it.

Residents have recently formed an association, mostly to voice complaints related to unsatisfactory play provision, but also to organise activities for themselves and the elderly for whom they feel concern and responsibility. Thus, as at Bishopsfield, a strong community sense is developing, assisted by rehousing of previous neighbours *en-bloc*, a wise policy often ignored owing to organisational complications. Play provision is worrying. Toddlers are catered for, but the caretaker's plans to add a roundabout near the junction between blocks has not been achieved because of objections that it would attract older loiterers in the evening. The seven to eleven year olds who love riding bicycles along the walk are forbidden to since an accident at Southwark's Acorn Estate involving two children and a cycle caused extraction of considerable damages from the council. So children cycle in the service road—which worries parents—and play football on the only grassed area across the service road and edging the main road.

This all too familiar situation reflects shortage of play space

15

16

17

15 *Walk funnels between blocks below bridging bathrooms. Note railings to fire escape gallery and toplight to ground floor living rooms*
16 *Stairs with winders spatially exciting, but difficult to decorate as stair well is high*
17 *Standard kitchen: cooker position is restricted and narrow shelves are potential hazard*
12 *Cross-road: enclosure is favourite play area. Note*

railings to swing on (resultant noise irritates (adults) and flower boxes in danger of vandalism
13 *Pleasant western outlook: robust concrete rails and fascia unify lower elevation and contrast with refined detailing of dwelling facades*
14 *Overhead bathrooms shadow individual entrance porches with store and refuse off to side: stairs to garage below*

in the borough, but would be improved if the link to Peckham Rye existed. As parents point out, bored children quickly become vandals. Study of the economics of vandalism—the hard facts of replacement costs—might be a salutary method of convincing the authorities of the folly of yardstick limits. Sadly the architects confirm that another Linden Grove could not be built in later financial climates. Bishopsfield would appear even more Utopian.

Privacy

In a handbook, *Living in Bishopsfield and Charters Cross*, produced by the tenants' association, the introduction states, 'meeting your neighbours casually is made difficult by the high degree of privacy which is incorporated in the design of most of the dwellings: a positive effort must be made to meet other residents'. Unfortunately it is the depressed, elderly and shy, those most in need of human contacts who will not make this effort. Thus in this form of development, responsibility, clearly recognised by some Bishopsfield tenants, is placed on the community to ensure that isolation does not occur. For the robust the opportunity to live family life undisturbed or overlooked is freedom and relief.

204

18

19

A study of courtyard housing in Dundee used by Edinburgh University Architecture Research Unit to check and compare results with the earlier Prestonpans investigation (see p. 21) confirms the view that this housing form is popular because of the degree of privacy and consequent individual freedom provided. However, the Prestonpans study concluded that housebound, inactive or disabled tenants, without outgoing natures, would suffer unless also provided with a lively outlook.

The Dundee study additionally indicated that courtyard housing gave too much privacy to a minority neither inactive or immobile. Here a group of middle-aged housewives with no wish for close relationships with neighbours needed opportunities to see the world go by. Significantly this reaction is paralleled in Linden Grove which, unlike Bishopsfield, has many dwellings with no windows on to public circulation space, an omission deeply felt by tenants, especially a middle-aged couple facing retirement. As discussion with these and other residents showed, the active 55 to 70 age group faces special problems of adjustment which appear to be little considered in design and, more essentially, house allocation and management. 'Granny flats' linked to a number of Bishopsfield dwellings on the southern periphery are a welcome attempt to overcome one aspect of this problem.

Sheltered housing

The brief for sheltered housing at Linden Grove accorded with 1958 and subsequent MHLG directives to local authorities.[1] The flats were not intended for the very fit but for more-frail old people who could maintain, with occasional support, advice and help from a resident warden, an independent existence in security and companionship. Local authorities were advised that on social grounds such schemes should accommodate 50 per cent fit and 50 per cent frail to alleviate the warden's burden.

In actuality many schemes have, as here, a population almost 100 per cent frail. Thus 29 elderly people, mostly

20

about 78 or 80 years old, live in five double- and five single-flats on each of two floors, sharing three baths and a shower at each level.

The local authority housing department is responsible for sheltered housing and the allocation of accommodation, although a percentage of tenants were nominated by the Social Services department. It was unfortunate that the Social Services department did not have more influence on the allocation of flats. A number of very frail and disabled people are accommodated unsuitably at first floor level, and thus affected by the parsimony of DOE refusal to sanction finance for a lift in this type of two-storey accommodation. This is regrettable as clearance programmes and shortage of suitable accommodation mean that only the most frail and needy obtain places; also inevitably tenants will grow older.

Additionally it is unfortunate that bathroom accommodation has to be shared. The less elderly, especially married people, dislike the idea of sharing while the elderly, either because help is difficult to arrange or from personal choice, prefer to wash down in their rooms. Bathrooms are cramped and claustrophobic, making bathing difficult for those needing assistance or confined to wheelchairs. Showers are unpopular; at Linden Grove the old people are nervous of them.

21

22

23

18 *Sliding windows difficult to clean at higher levels. Note controlled detailing, successful scale. Some tenants would prefer Garage doors have been provided*
19 *Wide window sill forms bedroom-study area at Bishopsfield*
20 *Two-person flat: blind divides kitchen and living area. Cupboard is too high*
and curtains blow across cooker
21 *Common room, gallery at high level. Doors below to Limes Walk and square*
22 *Secluded garden pleasant but has no seats, and access for wheelchairs is difficult*
23 *Sitting alcove, a popular feature, allows accidental meetings overlooking garden. Stairs to ground floor at right*

Sitting alcoves formed where direction changes in corridors are more popular than the sitting room as there is the possibility of incidental contact in addition to sunny quiet views **23**. Sheltered housing within the Linden Grove community has encouraged concern from the tenants and singular initiative from the caretaker with regard to elderly people's entertainment and well-being. It is unquestionably a satisfactory means of housing the elderly.

Conclusions
The constant theme at Bishopsfield, Linden Grove and Emmanuel Church Street is concern with the individual, his freedom, the richness of his environment and its contribution to community development. This is why the work of Neylan & Ungless is so exceptional and significant. One hopes that DOE financial controls will not further restrict their devotion and initiative.

Both single- and double-flats are equipped with kitchenettes divided from the living rooms by blinds. In both cases the cooker is close to the sliding window, and tenants, especially on the lower floor where there is no wide sill, complain of curtains blowing inwards across the cooker **20**. Sliding windows are criticised by young and old as ventilation control is inexact; draughts are not controlled easily and rain blows in through the lower part of even a slightly open window. Wide window sills at first floor level, a device utilised in bedrooms at Bishopsfield **19** and successfully repeated in the common room, act as desk, table and display shelf and are very popular. Sliding doors between bed and living rooms in two-person flats are heavy and stiff—too much for a frail person.

Refuse cupboards at low level between living rooms and access corridor are heartily disliked because of the bending necessary to reach them, and because they attract small boys, creating a security problem if left unbolted. In practice refuse is collected by the caretaker.

The communal area **21** is used by the elderly and also occasionally by the tenants' association.

SUMMARY: Blocks 1 and 2

Ground floor area: 1805 m² (19 433 sq ft).
Total floor area: 3 803 m² (40 934 sq ft)
Type of contract: negotiated tender, fixed price bill of quantities.
Tender date: December 1966.
Work began: March 1967.
Work finished: practical completion October 1970.
Price of foundation, superstructure, installation and finishes including drainage to collecting manhole: £197 464.
Price of external works and ancillary buildings including drainage beyond collecting manhole: £16 286.
Total: £213 750.

18 Housing Estate, at The Brow, Runcorn

This housing estate represents a deliberate reversal of the now well-established Radburn principles of housing layout whereby pedestrians and vehicles are carefully separated. Here both people and cars use the access roads, which are ingeniously devised so that drivers respect the priority of pedestrians. Houses are informally arranged, the planting is allowed to grow wild, and no garages are provided

designed by	Runcorn Development Corporation architect's department
chief architect and planning officer	R. L. E. Harrison (in succession to F. Lloyd Roche)
principal architect; housing	P. Riley
principal architect, landscape	R. N. E. Higson
housing group staff	J. H. Smith
	P. Fauset
	T. J. Jenkins
	D. Chettleburgh
	D. Ritson
quantity surveyor	John Danksen & Purdie
chief engineer	J. Mercer
principal site development engineer	E. Jenkins
main contractor	Unit Construction

CLIENT'S REQUIREMENTS, SITE, PLANNING

The Brow was the first housing scheme to be produced entirely within the Runcorn office and was preceded only by the Halton Brook Estate where Midland Housing Consortium houses were used in a typical 'Radburn' layout. In planning terms the Brow forms a section of the Halton community which is now completed with the development of the adjoining Castlefields estate. However, it was decided at brief stage that the Brow site should be developed separately because of its immediate visual relationship with the older part of Halton village which it directly adjoins.

The housing is situated on the steep westerly slope of Halton Hill, dominated by the ruins of the Norman castle and having extensive views to the west over the Mersey estuary. The selection and consistency of external materials for colour and texture was a high priority in the design process, since it was felt imperative to produce a solution in harmony with the weathered brick and sandstone of the old village and the outcropping rock of Halton Hill. In terms of layout, the Brow departs from the strict interpretation of the Radburn principle as seen at Halton Brook, and is based on the acceptance of a high degree of penetration into housing areas by the vehicle and a sharing of certain areas by both pedestrian and vehicle. This produced an approach to the design of roads, culs de sac and parking courts, which by careful control of alignment, width and detail is intended to produce an acceptance by the motorist that once the housing areas are entered the interests of pedestrians are paramount.

The culs de sac serve private parking courts around which the houses are grouped. Traffic speeds and the character of the culs de sac are controlled by using minimum width roads—3·12 m (10 ft 3 in) wide with lay-bys for passing, and by the introduction of curves using granite setts for road edging. Earth shaping and planting are used to provide privacy in gardens and play a large part in producing a desirable residential environment.

The rapid transit bus route runs through the site and all the houses are within five minutes' walking distance of the bus stop, which is located adjacent to the local centre consisting of thirty-five flats, primary school, public house and shop. The houses on either side of the rapid transit route are connected by footpaths which converge on an underpass at the local centre.

The site covers 10·7 hectares (26·5 acres) and contains a total of 356 dwellings (excluding the thirty-five flats at the local centre designed by Anthony Grimshaw) at an average density of 126 persons per hectare (51 persons per acre). Parker Morris standards are maintained in the houses and the construction is of load bearing brickwork with monopitched roof clad in concrete slates.

The first phase of the estate, constructed between November 1967 and November 1970 was planned to be 290 dwelling units, subsequently varied to 292. The second phase,

A *Site plan (1:5000). Halton Brow estate is inside thick broken line. Phase 1 of 292 houses is to west and south-east of centre, phase 2 of 64 houses is to north-east around the Clough. Layout of group of houses in north-west corner (tinted area) is shown in greater detail in* **B**. *Houses in Holly Bank Road and Halton Brow (at top) are assortment*

of prewar and early postwar council houses and spec housing. New access roads and busway route involved some demolition. School at Tanhouse is by Cheshire County Council, adjoining flats are by Anthony Grimshaw

B *Plan of group of houses showing pattern of peripheral road, access roads, parking culs-de-sac and foot-paths ($\frac{1}{128}$ in = 1ft = 1:1536). Private gardens are shown tinted*

commenced in June 1969, comprised sixty-four units. The distribution by dwelling size is as follows:

	Phase 1	Phase 2
Seven person two-storey	16	—
Six person two-storey	52	16
Five person two-storey	173	39
Five person one-storey	34	6
Two person one-storey	17	3
	292	64

APPRAISAL

The problems of housing design in England are generally related to the difficulties of overcoming a straitjacket of model street by-laws, local highway authority prejudices and doctrinaire rules of thumb applied by local planning officers. Time and again the potential for experiment has been shown to be present within the context of the organisation created by the new town development corporations or private speculative groups working on a leasehold basis. Within a new creative institutional organisation, it has been shown that delight, intimacy and human environment can be created. At Halton Brow a housing group of great freshness, charm and delightful scale has been created, showing that the uniform dead-hand of standard road design need not dominate housing layout design.

A fresh experimental approach
New Town development corporations must attract to their staffs the more pioneering spirits among professional designers—those hoping for a fresh experimental approach where job teams can implement new ideas. This factor seems to be dominant in the Runcorn New Town team in that the organisation is devised with the specific object of constructing the new town to a programme. The departmental jealousies usually associated with large local authorities, the divided financing arrangements which must be operated by local authorities, are reflected in the quality of what can be achieved on the ground. In Runcorn the chief officers meet every morning, and inter-professional teams are formed to handle projects. It is in this design team and pioneering spirit that professional dogmas are loosened up and where the ideas of the highway engineer, the architect, the landscape architect, social worker and quantity surveyors begin to integrate towards the achievement of common objectives. It is within this kind of context that the Brow housing scheme was designed.

1

Runcorn New Town master plan was produced on the basis of a major public transport system reducing the need for the use of private cars. If this approach is to be successful there ought to be some reflection of this policy in the design of the housing areas. The influence of the busway is already seen in the residential areas in the physical layout and the arrangement of the footpath systems.

The master plan

The Runcorn master plan was published in 1966 and prepared by Arthur Ling & Associates. The plan proposed a town structure based on a grouping of communities each with a local centre. The size of the communities, proposed at 8000 population each, is determined by the economics of the provision of social facilities in relation to population, acceptable walking distances to the local centres and the rapid transit stops in these centres.

Since the existing town of Runcorn with a population of some 27 000 was within the designated area, the diagrammatic concept of group communities had to be bent to fit local influence on the ground. This fact, together with the phasing aims of building the new communities nearest to the town centre first, led to the earliest residential areas being built to the north and west of the village of Halton, adjacent to the new town centre site.

Halton Brook, the Brow and Castlefields residential areas of which only the latter conforms to the master plan's community definition, now turn to old Runcorn for shops and amenities, apart from the local centre or temporary facilities. They will much more readily turn to the new town centre when this is opened in 1971 and the rapid transit system links them to it.

These three residential areas had special problems characteristic of new town development in Runcorn in that they needed initially to have these strong links with the old town centre and subsequently be re-orientated to the new town centre. They also had to cope with the problems that arose when growing numbers of residents had to await the provision of planned services and facilities such as schools, shops and churches.

Of the three areas, the Brow is unique in being neither physically tied into the existing residential areas of old Runcorn, as is the case with Halton Brook, nor being ultimately of community size and structure like Castlefields.

1 *Vernacular character of Brow estate contrasted with rectilinear pattern of* *Halton Brook estate behind. River Mersey is at top of picture, Widnes on far side*

3

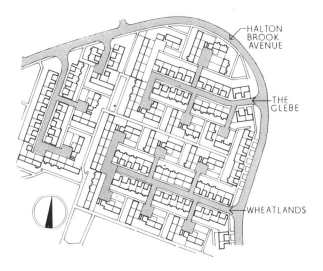

HALTON
BROOK
AVENUE

THE
GLEBE

WHEATLANDS

Vehicles and pedestrians

The experience of design, construction and the use of the Halton Brook estate **C** had led to the view on the part of the architects and the engineer that the rigid segregation and almost diagrammatic Radburn approach in this design provided neither satisfactory pedestrian/vehicular segregation nor a satisfactory housing environment. The dual access arrangements combined with the large numbers of garages and enclosed private garden space to each house, presented an intensely urban development with very little public usable incidental space.

Arising from this experience it was felt that a degree of pedestrian/vehicular segregation could be achieved by providing separate pedestrian paths which would merge

C *Part of Halton Brook estate (1:3750) vehicle routes tinted. Layout is conventional Radburn, with peripheral approach road, cul-de-sac access roads for vehicles, segregated pedestrian routes. For nearly all dwelling units garages are within curtilage*

2 *Vehicle access roads are narrow and curved to slow car drivers, allow pedestrians to move about unhazarded. Concrete kerbs are omitted*

from vocabulary; edgings are granite setts
3 *Pedestrian paths merge into shared vehicular courts and access culs-de-sac*

into shared vehicular courts and access culs-de-sac, and that the speed of vehicular movement could be controlled and reduced to a level commensurate with pedestrian safety by reducing roads to a width of 3·12 m (10 ft 3 in) and consciously introducing curves **A, B**. The circulation pattern therefore offers alternative routes for pedestrians, some entirely separate from the vehicle access ways and sometimes crossing them as well as accepting pedestrians on the vehicle access ways **2, 3**. A road from Halton Brow runs round the western edge of the site between the residential area and the line of the north/south expressway. This peripheral road serves culs-de-sac to the lower half of the site west of the rapid transit route. The upper part of the site is served by culs-de-sac from Halton Brow and an existing road leading from Halton village.

The footpath system therefore leads down from the existing Halton village to the Tanhouse local centre and rapid transit stop and up from the western half of the site to the centre also.

The intention to include shared routes within a housing layout immediately posed numerous design problems which had to be overcome by fresh design thinking and a degree of detailed involvement not associated with the conventional road-with-footpath frontage access layout. Immediately questions of the location of public utility services must be raised, questions of abandoning the comfortable framework offered by model street by-laws and really detailed thinking about how to achieve privacy without isolation and a pleasant non-stereotype relationship of house group to house group.

In trying to overcome the difficulties presented by these factors the design team in the Runcorn Development Corporation have been eminently successful. On entering the culs-de-sac the driver has a sense of being tolerated only and not being present as of right. The closeness of the buildings and the curvilinear roads reduce speed to a minimum and he feels it would be a gross discourtesy to blow the horn at a pedestrian sharing the same route. This principle of sharing the circulation route is the basis behind the whole success of the scheme.

The development corporation staff have carried out tests on the Brow peripheral road and average speeds of 33·6 kph (20·9 mph) were achieved as compared with 40·5 kph (25·2 mph) at Halton Brook. In the cul-de-sac speeds of 21·9 and 29·9 kph (13·6 and 18·6 mph) respectively were recorded, which seems to indicate that the design of the roads in the Brow is successfully performing as was intended.

Vernacular appearance

The decision was taken at an early stage to attempt to create a vernacular appearance in the Brow housing and that the keynote of the character should be conformity with the general appearance and feeling of Halton village. To achieve this a mono-pitch roof structure was chosen, clad with stone coloured sand faced concrete slates, walls of sand faced brown brickwork with black mortar and black stained timber windows. The variety of levels imposed by the sloping site, combined with the possibility of switching the roof pitch to suit various circumstances, has led to a most satisfying sense of individual grouping and village-like character **5, 6**. As a result, picturesque groupings and views (almost each one being an entirely successful composition) have been achieved without, one feels, conscious detailed design.

In detail the expression is sculptural if a little forced, and the houses do not have the relaxed conviction of vernacular detailing. The vertical plane of the fully slated mono-pitch

4

4 *Alternative pedestrian paths are separate from motorised vehicle ways*
5, 6 *Variety of levels and*

roof lines give satisfying sense of individual group and village character
(*See page 212*)

5

roof lines up exactly with the face of the brickwork below, and this gives a clipped appearance. The black stained woodwork of the window frames helps to unify the wall surfaces and yet emphasises the openings as modelling. It is interesting that the windows are of moderate and manageable sizes as regards both curtaining and maintenance and give adequate light. The detail below the slates and over the window heads leaves some room for doubt as to weather-tightness and future maintenance costs **7**. The device of cladding the inset porch areas with uniform v-jointed soft board painted white gives striking emphasis and even gaiety to the entrance features **8**. Tenants, however, have found the brick floor surface of the porch unsatisfactory and several cardinal red polished and painted floors are to be seen, as are plastic 'gothic' ironmongery fixed to the doors.

Soft landscape setting

In contrast to the hard urban forms of Halton Brook with its conventional Radburn layout, all the enclosure of private space, screening of vehicular roads and car courts is achieved solely by the use of mounding and planting, with materials of the kind found in wild landscape and semi-wild hedgerows. Generally, private gardens are formed not by screen fencing, but by providing a bank of earth heavily planted to form a natural barrier between public and private spaces. Thus the design provides at the earliest possible stage a soft landscape setting which helps the visual maturity of the scheme.

Considering the roads and footpaths, gardens and play areas together with the houses as total landscape, materials used conform to the vernacular feeling. Standard concrete kerbs have been omitted from the vocabulary and all road and footpath edgings are carried out in inclined granite setts, while the road surface is to the UDC standard requirement in black mastic asphalt with a grey aggregate. Footpath edgings consist merely of creosoted timbers and

7 *Window head details may cause maintenance troubles*
8 *White-painted V-joint softwood cladding inside porch gives emphasis and gaiety to entrance feature*
9 *Modelling of ground helps conceal parked cars*
10 *Landscaping in early areas achieved maturity surprisingly early*

11 *Architects attempted to retain natural pond. A playground was substituted when residents complained of shallow-depth water hazards, but this led to demands from residents to remove a source of noise*

will eventually be softened by over-spreading plant growth. Footpaths to the front entrance doors are carried out in the same brick as the walling to the houses. Extensive modelling of the ground helps to conceal groups of parked cars **9** and provide spatial division from one court to the next. In the first completed areas the landscape has achieved, in fourteen months, a surprising maturity **10**.

The enclosures to the private gardens **13** were not always must have been worried that their offspring could disappear into the nearby construction sites or road works. The costs of approximately £80 to £90 per dwelling for soft landscaping were relatively high, but with the maturing of the estate the economics of this seemingly romantic approach has a chance to prove itself in low maintenance costs.

7   8

Play areas

The majority of play areas **12** are of a scale suitable for toddlers or pre-school children, although they are generally tucked away at or between gable ends. They are not adequate, because the children can wander off since they are out of sight and older children soon lose interest and move off. Some of the difficulties of catering for residents accustomed to an urban setting in a major city were revealed when the design team attempted to retain a natural pond in the central open space of the first phase **11**. While most attractively treated with vertical log edging and retained in very shallow depth, the residents' complaints made it necessary to fill in the pond. The resulting level space surrounded by a ridge mound made an ideal play area for older children equipped with some conventional playground rocking boats, etc. However, the new source of noise then imposed on the residents led to demands to remove the playground. This is a great pity, but typical of the problems housing authorities must face. Surely participation and democratic involvement would be a means of avoiding this kind of negative solution brought about as a result perhaps of a vocal minority.

9

Parking

While the brief intended that garage groups should be constructed to serve the Brow area, none of these have yet been erected and it is clear that only with the most disastrous visual intrusion could these be included within the car courts. The consequent problems of parking cars where there is no alternative location for the owner to store his vehicle have led to vehicles being towed away because they are not licensed or are in a state in which they cannot be driven.

Internal planning

The three house types, two-storey five person, single-storey five person, and single-storey two person, are designed to meet mandatory standards with the exception of the heating installation. In this case gas fires are provided to serve living rooms and dining kitchens only. Economical square plan forms are used for the five person two-storey houses **G** and two person one-storey **E**. Some people felt that the pram store is needed as a general store; the pram must then be kept in the dining area. The arrangements whereby the meters are accessible from the exterior for reading (grouped with the refuse sack store beneath in the entrance porch) works well. While the easy access to the garden is appreciated by residents the possibilities of do-it-yourself canoe building, creative woodwork or stripping down the motorbike are decidedly limited. The kitchen units and divider between kitchen and dining area **15** are finished in beech faced plywood and after only a few months' use tend to look tatty. Sitting rooms and bedrooms **14** are small but efficiently planned.

10

11

12 *Toddlers play areas are tucked away. Older children lost interest, and preferred the more vigorous challenge of new town building sites*
13 *Children can disappear from private gardens*

A progressive achievement

It is refreshing to see the doctrinaire approach to planning for man and motor in residential areas being abandoned. The recognition of the fact that pedestrians and vehicles must mix in the areas close to the home and the effort of designing for safety to meet this fact is the real progressive achievement of this design. So many dual access Radburn layouts cannot work because children will insist on using all the estate for play, including the car courts, and because access is more often direct on the vehicular side.

Anyone dealing with the problem of designing housing areas, who understands that the boundaries of the design constraints lie where legislation and rules-of-thumb abut political institutions and local authority administrative procedures, will applaud the achievement represented by the Brow estate.

It is clear that while a measure of the maestro is necessary in order to experiment, the touch must be tempered by the humility which knows and designs for more humble standards of life and aspiration than those of the designer.

SUMMARY

Ground floor area: 45·52 m² (490 sq ft).
Total floor area: 91·04 m² (980 sq ft).
Type of contract: RIBA local authority, fixed price with quantities.
Tender date: April 1969.
Work began: June 1969.
Work finished: mid 1971
Price of foundation, superstructure, installation and finishes including drainage to collecting manhole: £2 712.
Price of external works and ancillary buildings including drainage beyond collecting manhole: £168.
Total: £2 875.

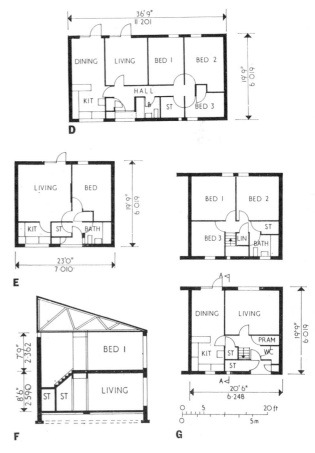

14

D *Plan, single-storey five person unit* (1:250)
E *Plan, single-storey two person unit* (1:250)
F *Section* AA (1:230)
G *First floor and ground floor plans, five person unit* (1:250)

14 *Sitting room and child's bedroom as furnished for show house*
15 *Divider units between kitchen and dining area looked smart for show house, but now look tatty*

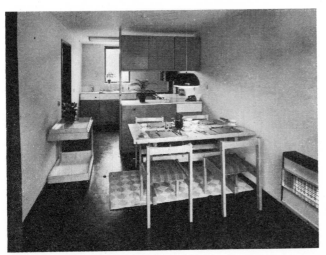

15

19 Housing and Old People's Home at Burghley Road, London NW5

This housing scheme is an instructive example of some of the problems which London boroughs encounter on difficult sites. It is a composite project, comprising cluster blocks, tower and terrace housing, with an old people's home in the centre; cohesion is achieved by a limited range of materials

for	London Borough of Camden
by	Department of Architecture, London Borough of Camden
director of architecture	S. A. G. Cook
deputy director	P. Clapham
project architect	John Green
group architect	Michael Wilson
assistant architects	Martin Hendy
	Michael Smith
assistants	Brian Wyett, Clyde Gougah, Trevor Davidson, Henry Ridley, Adam Heppenstall
quantity surveyor	Monk & Dunstone
services engineer	London Borough of Camden Department of Architecture Service Group
structural engineers	Ove Arup & Partners
	J. Lancaster
landscape architect	David Lee
main contractor	London Borough of Camden Building Department

CLIENT'S REQUIREMENTS, SITE, PLANNING

The site is situated in the triangle of land bounded by Highgate Road to the west, Fortess Road to the east and the Midland Region Railway to the north. On the west, College Lane, a pedestrian footpath, connects to the north past Grove Terrace to Parliament Hill Fields. Two railway properties are situated between College Lane and the site, housing a model railway club and a social club. To the east of the site, the Acland Burghley School is situated. To the south of the site in Lady Somerset Road and Burghley Road there are three-storey terrace houses, many of which are in multi-occupation.

Site and overall planning requirements

The site, known locally as 'The Alps', has a varied history. It was developed by the railway company as a site for a generating station and hostel for railway engine crews. Later the generating station was converted to the Harbar Bar Works, and the site itself was used as a depository for soil excavated in the construction of the Hampstead—South Tottenham branch line. It has unique character in an urban area, with views over large areas of Gospel Oak and Hampstead and it also forms a convenient link for children who cross the site on school journeys.

The site was developed for housing purposes accommodating 165 dwellings and 172 car-parking spaces, a 60-bed old people's home, maintenance depot and play and community centre at 247 people per hectare (100 ppa).

The grass site is 2·55 hectares (6·3 acres), comprising 0·32 hectares (0·78 acres) for old people's home, 0·05 hectares (0·12 acres) for the children's play area, and 2·18 hectares (5·40 acres) for housing.

Entry of vehicles from Ingestre Road is acceptable as primary access to the site. Vehicular access from Little Green Street is for emergency use only.

The site is an undulating area with trees and vegetation. The scheme has been designed in low-rise blocks (three and four storeys) with one eight-storey block on the northern part of the site next to the railway. Accommodation to be provided included 37 two-room flats, 90 three-room flats, 28 a play centre, maintenance depot and car-parking for 172 cars (112 under cover).

Vehicular access is from Ingestre Road and runs parallel to the railway at the north end of the site. Cul-de-sac access roads lead to the low-rise housing blocks and pedestrian ways are designed throughout the area with access via Little Green Street to Highgate Road.

APPRAISAL

Kentish Town, in which Burghley Road is situated is characterised by the scale and consistency of the 19th century system of terraces and streets. Although the fabric of the houses remains permanent they are capable of a subtle expression of changing occupancy, through the decay and renewal of their exterior finish. Variations of social class or ethnic group take place cell by cell to give richness and variety within the uniform scale and organisation of the whole pattern.

Public housing is being introduced into large clearings in this system, and in contrast to the 19th century builders the

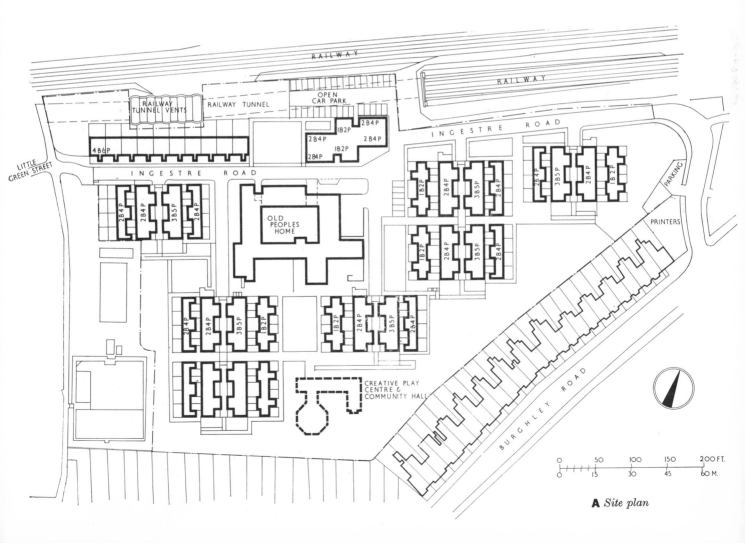

A Site plan

architects of the new schemes have not arrived at a consensus about the appropriate form of housing. Consequently each new estate is like a fragment of an ideal city set apart as a social and aesthetic oasis and disconnected from the remains of the 19th century context.

The housing at Burghley Road has the quality of an unprecedented solution to a specific problem—a new invention. The first impression is dramatic and unforeseen after the humdrum brick and stucco of the surrounding Victorian streets. Hidden behind existing houses the scheme comes suddenly into view revealing the successive silhouettes of cluster blocks and the tower (photo p 216). The effect of the clusters is castle-like rather than domestic: 'Like fortresses, you could defend them against an army,' to quote one of the children there. This exciting but forbidding character is confirmed by the dark russet bricks in black mortar, which unify the whole scheme. Even the window frames are painted brown.

Site planning and density

Admittedly the site does not invite integration with the surrounding area. Previously allotments and railway land, it is isolated by the railway along the north side and falls precipitously towards back gardens of Lady Somerset Road and Burleigh Road to the south. With no frontage on to a through road and vehicular access limited to one end, it is a back land. Even so the particular way in which the site is developed makes few concessions to the surroundings. The

1 *Hill has been levelled and cut into series of interlocking plateaux on which buildings stand*
2 *Main vehicular access*

road is used as play street by children. Entrances to terrace houses are protected by glazed porches

1

2

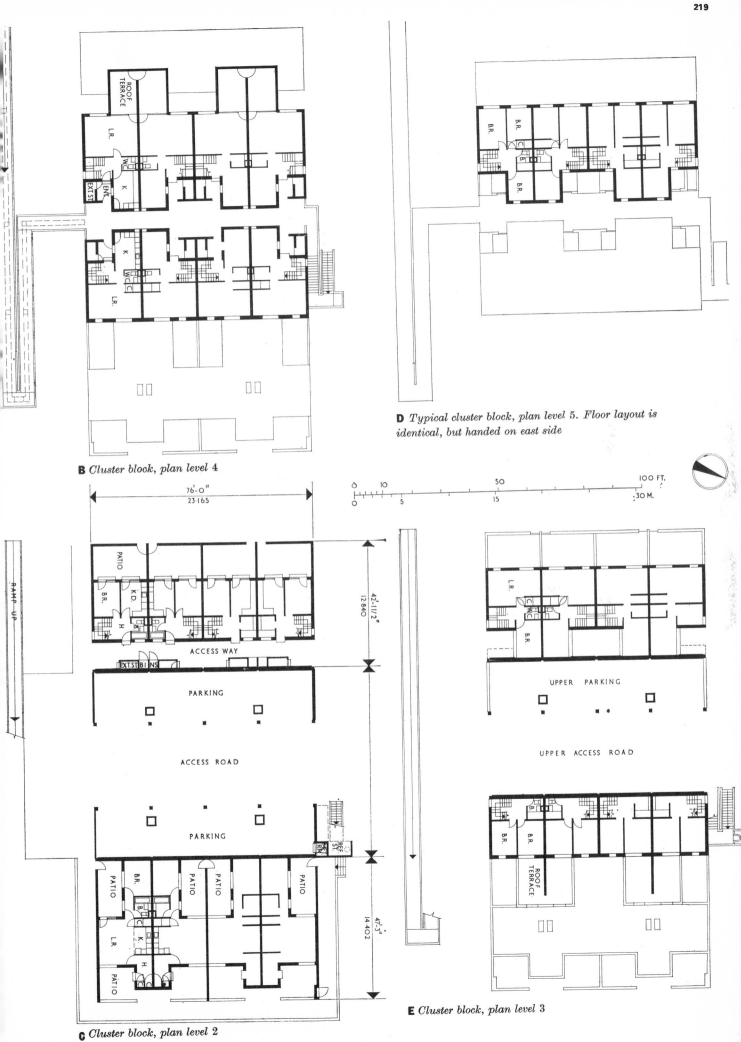

D *Typical cluster block, plan level 5. Floor layout is identical, but handed on east side*

B *Cluster block, plan level 4*

C *Cluster block, plan level 2*

E *Cluster block, plan level 3*

220

3

4

F *Cluster block, cross-section*

GROUND BEAMS FOR PILES

B.R. L.R. ENT ACCESS ENT L.R. B.R. L.R. ACCESS PARKING ACCESS ROAD PARKING PATIO L.R. PATIO PATIO

5

3 *Parallel footpaths connect and align the cluster blocks. Illustration shows entry courts to two-person flats*
4, 7 *Steep fall of site means that walks suddenly drop into canyons of steps or become galleries overlooking sunken courts.*
5 *Cavernous vehicular spaces under the clusters are*

conspicuous
6, 8 *Ramps are exciting but expensive way of gaining access to upper units*
9, 10 *Street deck is enclosed on both sides by entrances to maisonettes through small yards. Detailing is robust and carefully considered*

8

9

10

cluster blocks, conceived as independent units to cope with the abrupt changes of level on the hill side, fit their own grid of north/south culs-de-sac and transverse pedestrian routes. In terms of figure and ground the blocks are positive and the spaces between residual. The consequence of the grid is a variety of fortuitously shaped areas at the edge of the site, which insulate the scheme from the world beyond its boundaries.

Road access, children's play
Road access was limited to the single entry from Ingestre Road; from this the main distributor is drawn in a line towards the other principal point of pedestrian access but this seems to be the only option given the gradient along the south edge. The drawback is that the terrace houses and tower are cut off from the rest of the scheme in which pedestrian segregation has been largely achieved. It was striking to see the whole width of the road **2** used as a pedestrian mall, particularly by young children who felt no compunction to stay on the pavements.

Generally the roads are enclosed as culs-de-sac within the cluster blocks, a system which would have been achieved throughout the site had not the old people's home been brought into the brief after the original site plans had been determined. As a result three clusters were displaced to expose lengths of road each side of the old people's home. Although the number of cars is limited, the effect is visually disrupting. Generally the spaces between buildings are conceived as level plateaux enhanced by carefully detailed paving. The two culs-de-sac intrude into this pedestrian scene with the borough engineer's aesthetic of cambered surfaces, black macadam and radiused curbs.

The steep changes of level of the site have been manipulated into a series of interlocking plateaux **1**, connected by ramps and steps, upon which the buildings stand and in effect much of the hill has been levelled and cut into a continuous substructure. As a result the series of parallel footpaths **3** which connect and align the cluster blocks offer a variety of experiences which might not be expected from the plan. Level walks drop suddenly into precipitous canyons of steps or become galleries overlooking sunken courts **4, 7**. Children enjoy this, for the changes of level around the buildings offer alternative routes for chasing on foot, roller skating and bicycling. It is possible that the fortuitous nature of the spaces around the buildings is inherently stimulating for children and the provision of play equipment in specific and rather obscure parts of the site seems almost superfluous.

Cluster blocks
The cluster blocks are the main constituent of the scheme; the other building types seem to be introduced expediently, the terrace houses take up the slot of space by the railway and the tower puts back, in a limited area, the accommodation displaced by the old people's home. Back-to-back stepped sections of this kind are a device for optimising the conditions of light and view between blocks as well as providing sheltered parking, enclosed street access instead of a gallery at second floor level, and patios for the upper units on the roofs of those below. Conceived as groups of 16 dwellings, which can be arranged in basically three kinds of section, the cluster blocks are intended to mediate between the need to adapt to different site gradients and to present the direct labour organisation, which built the scheme, with replicating construction. When considering the basic land use properties of clusters in relation to other building forms, this argument about site layout appears to be misconceived. What is startling about the cluster blocks and apparently perplexing to some of the residents is the huge scale of the

11 *Kitchen/dining room to upper level units of cluster block is rather small for five people*
12 *Single living room has to be play room as well*
13 *In spite of stepped section providing large areas of roof, private open space of upper units is limited to* *small enclosed yards*
14 *Six-person terrace houses have spacious living room subdivided by folding screen. Does this give sufficient acoustic privacy for a large family?*
15 *Areas of asphalt are exposed to view where roof is not used as terrace*

vehicular spaces which they contain **5**. Over the road the height of 4·42 m (14 ft 6 in) provides access for fire engines but this is continued over the car-parking on one side to allow the units above a view over those on the ground. These spaces admit more daylight than is usual in internal carparks but they are 'gloomy', to quote one of the residents, and their cavernous scale makes them too conspicuous for their modest function.

Access to the upper level
Access to the upper units in the clusters is by ramp or stair. Along the southern edge of the site the ramps overhang the falling ground and climb above the tree tops. The effect is elating on a fine day but must be bleak in rainy weather for a mother with two children and the week's shopping. The ramps **6, 8** are wonderful in a bloody-minded Corbusian way and an expensive attempt to improve the access to the upper units.

The milieu of the second floor street **9, 10** is sympathetic; it is superior to a single-sided access deck because of its enclosed feeling and sense of occupancy conveyed by the just perceptible sounds of radios, voices, and the clink of washing-up. The little entrance yards, which allow each family to express possession of their territory with planting, contribute in the same way. The details withstand scrutiny; the raked joints, boot lintels, brick sills and wooden gates give a robust and friendly impression. Between adjoining blocks the streets briefly and dramatically become bridges revealing penetrating views through the scheme or over the roof tops of Kentish Town.

Upper level units
In each cluster block variation the upper level units are the same, consisting of terraces of four- and five-person dwellings on each side of the access way. The kitchen conveniently overlooks the entrance yard for the supervision of young children, and the front door opens into a rather tight hall from which the stair leads to the bedrooms without intruding into the living area. There are limitations to this conventional arrangement. The kitchen **11** though intended for dining is rather small for five people and the sharing of the single living room by a family of five **12** precludes the pursuit of incompatible activities by different members.

As well as the entrance courts, enclosed roof terraces extend from the living areas of the five-person units and from one of the bedrooms of the four-person units. Potentially the whole roof area of the lower units might be used as a terrace for those above. Unfortunately, the cost of concrete slabs instead of timber joist construction has restricted the size of the open space **13** leaving a bleak area of asphalt **15** where the roof is unused. Advantage of this limitation has been taken for an aesthetic game. The terrace screen walls reflect the projecting kitchens and coincide with the walls of the bedrooms below, contributing to the overall effect of interlocking volumes upon which the appearance of the clusters depends. The heavy brick masses are carefully distinguished from the concrete frame which supports

11

12

14

13

15

16 *In tower most of flat doors on each landing face large central lift lobbies*   **17** *Tower is almost surrounded by road and hence by children playing*

them; the quality of construction is good and the general impression is that the buildings have been thoughtfully put together.

Combinations of two- and four-person units at ground level enable the clusters to adapt to different conditions. An unexpected characteristic of these units is that they are dual aspect relying on small and rather dark voids or patios for daylight. The four-person units combine a living room and bedroom on each floor but do not provide openings for these rooms to be used together. Access for pedestrians is top-lit by the alternating voids between the bedroom at first floor level. Sometimes the access way is below car level, but it is ironical that where the levels are the same, GLC Petroleum Acts require an intervening wall which obstructs direct entry from car to house.

The two-person units, planned as small patio houses, enable the cluster blocks to provide for two generations of a family. Entry is from outside through a projecting lobby which contributes to the visual theme of brick volumes. But again it could have been through the patio directly from the parking area if GLC regulations had allowed.

16

Terrace houses

Although next to the access road and exposed to the noise and visual intrusion of passing cars the six-person terraced houses do not have integral garages. The conventional two-storey arrangement gives a spacious 8·2 m × 3·7 m (25 ft × 12 ft) living room on the ground floor which can be divided with a folding screen **14**,

The glazed entrance porch which provides space for bins, meters and children's toys also satisfies the need for a sheltered threshold from which small children can make sorties into the world outside. The glazed roof and rough finishes also suggest how a cheap conservatory might provide more living space for children for the same cost as a conventional fully finished Parker Morris living room. After all children are the main users of houses.

Tower block

The architects feel that the form of the tower is justified socially because it accommodates only two-person units and four-person units with children over 15 years old. The large central lift lobbies **16** on to which most of the front doors of the flats face would seem to maximise the chances of people on each landing meeting each other.

The relation between the building and its site is unconvincing **17**. As well as being cut off by the access road, the tower overlooks car-parking to the north. These hard surfaces all round attract children whose shouting may irritate those residents who either have no children of their own or have children who have out-grown the noisy stage. The worst consequence of the site is that half the bedrooms face north towards the railway and are exposed regularly to the cacophony of goods trains.

Old people's home

One of the most important aspects of the old people's home is administrative rather than architectural. As elderly people are also accommodated in the ground-floor flats of the cluster blocks and in the tower, the old people's home represents a decisively different attitude to a proportion of

18

19

18 *Courtyard makes quiet centre for old people's home*
19 *Dining hall of home is exposed to view on south side. It may lack privacy but old people enjoy sitting outside entrance on fine days*

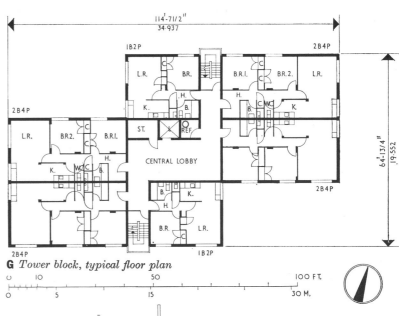

G *Tower block, typical floor plan*

H *Terrace of two-storey housing, first floor plan*
J *Terrace, ground floor plan*

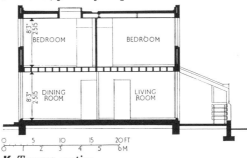

K *Terrace, section*

the elderly on the site. In this case the distinction may be justified. Those in the cluster blocks and tower are still capable of looking after themselves while those in the home, inevitably subject to the tidy-mindedness of the institution of which they are part are mostly physically handicapped. The architects have integrated the building into the estate by giving it a central position and a chunky form which relates it to the cluster blocks. With roads on three sides the outlook for much of the building is bleak and noisy but it may be that the bustle of people and cars is enjoyed by residents. For those who want peace there is the view on to the central courtyard **18**, and some get the best of both worlds in the rooms facing into the sunken courts adjoining one of the main pedestrian routes.

The dining hall, the communal focus of the home, is exposed intentionally in a public situation on the south side **19**. Its largely glazed volume contrasts with the small windows and castellated aspect of the rest of the building. It is difficult to know if this is a success. At first children stared in at the residents eating and the building seemed to offer inadequate privacy. On the other hand every resident is encouraged to come out from the privacy of his room into a semi-public world where he may meet old people from the flats and in

fine weather may be tempted to stay on the open entrance terrace facing south.

The home accepted DHSS practice in bringing all residents together for meals in one place and dispersing sitting rooms around the plan for small groups to meet casually. It deviated from DHSS in its scale—60 residents instead of the recommended 35. The number of residents and the centralised eating facility set the architects a problem which was inherently difficult to solve in terms of the current objective of small scale domesticity.

Perhaps inevitably, access to rooms on both floors is from a central corridor **20**, but this is alleviated where it becomes a gallery overlooking the central court and a bridge above the north-east entrance. The sitting rooms **21** introduce punctuations of light and subdivide the community into smaller groups.

Building form analysis
In conclusion an entirely different approach to the appraisal of Burghley Road will be considered briefly. Having discussed the detailed effects of the building as it has been designed, the choice of building type will be questioned in terms of a theoretical approach to building form.

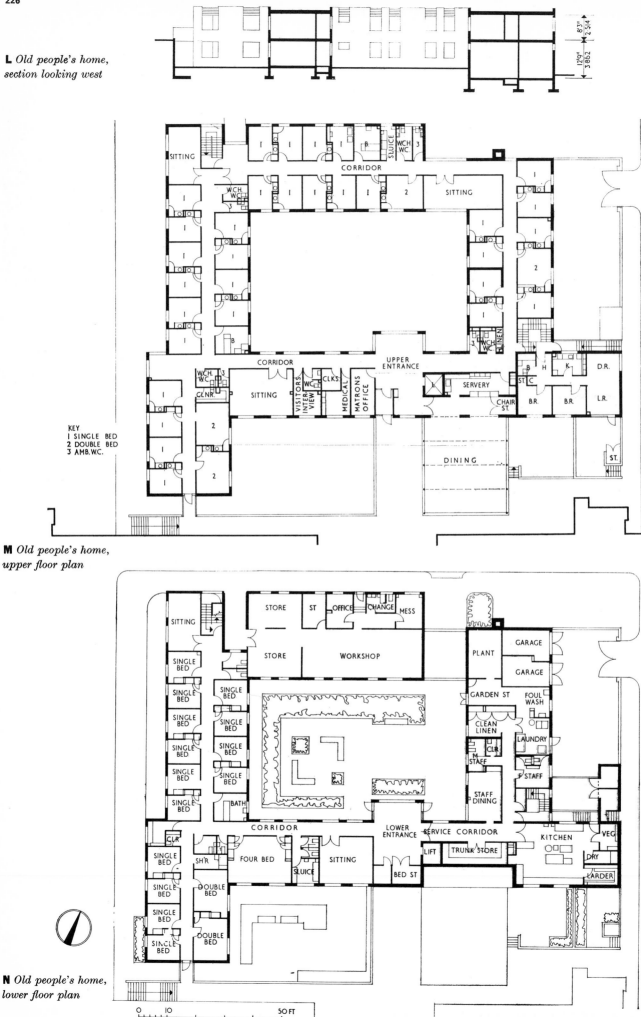

L *Old people's home,*
section looking west

8'3" 2.514
12'9" 3.862

M *Old people's home,*
upper floor plan

SITTING

CORRIDOR

B.
SLUICE
WCH. 3
WC.

WCH.
WC.

SITTING

2

SITTING

1

2

CORRIDOR

WCH. 3
WC.
CLNR.

SITTING

VISITORS
INTER-
VIEW

WC.
CLKS.

MEDICAL

MATRONS
OFFICE

UPPER
ENTRANCE

SERVERY

CHAIR
ST.

3
WCH
WC.

LINEN

ST.
C
B
H
K

B.R.

D.R.

B.R.

L.R.

2

2

KEY
1 SINGLE BED
2 DOUBLE BED
3 AMB.WC.

1

DINING

ST.

N *Old people's home,*
lower floor plan

SITTING

STORE
ST
OFFICE
CHANGE
MESS

SINGLE
BED

STORE

WORKSHOP

PLANT

GARAGE

GARAGE

SINGLE
BED

SINGLE
BED

SINGLE
BED

SINGLE
BED

SINGLE
BED

GARDEN ST

FOUL
WASH

SINGLE
BED

SINGLE
BED

CLEAN
LINEN

LAUNDRY

SINGLE
BED

SINGLE
BED

CLR

M
STAFF

F STAFF

SINGLE
BED

BATH

STAFF
DINING

CORRIDOR

LOWER
ENTRANCE

SERVICE CORRIDOR

KITCHEN

VEG

CLR

SINGLE
BED

SH'R

FOUR BED

SITTING

LIFT

TRUNK STORE

DRY

SINGLE
BED

DOUBLE
BED

SLUICE

BED ST

LARDER

SINGLE
BED

SINGLE
BED

DOUBLE
BED

0   10   50 FT
0   5
15 M

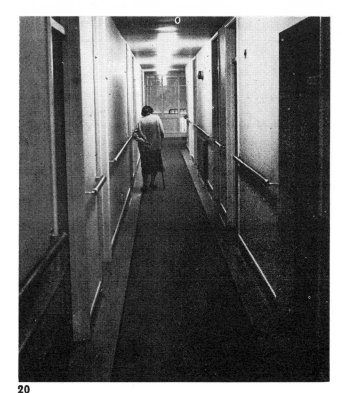

20

21

20 *Access to rooms in old people's home is from central corridor*
21 *Sitting rooms introduce light and space into circulation; area at south entrance particularly favoured*

This is not an abstract exercise without a basis in user requirements. Inevitably the criteria by which Burghley Road and other high-density schemes are judged tend to be those which can be fulfilled with terraced houses—pedestrian access at ground level, integral garages, private open space with earth for planting and direct access to public open space. These conditions can be met economically by buildings with a maximum of three storeys, so the relevant question to ask is whether there are alternatives to the clusters which can disperse the four-storey accommodation in low rise at the same density.

In a 1970 paper[1] for the Centre for Land Use and Built Form Studies, Lionel March has advanced a mathematical modelling technique for the study of built form to replace, with mathematical argument, what he sees as our 'well intentioned but wrongly conceived design rules'. Theorem 4.1 is vitally relevant to housing design and specifically to the solution at Burghley Road. It states: 'Comparing infinite arrays of rectangular built forms controlled by a given angle of obstruction, the floor space index of an array of continuous courts is always greater than that of an array of streets, which in turn, is always greater than that of an array of pavilions for any given number of storeys.' (See **O, P, Q**).

In other words, at Burghley Road, it is probable that linear forms, terraces and streets with the same distance between them as the clusters would achieve equal density with fewer storeys, while courts would achieve the density either with more space between buildings or lower buildings. It would be presumptuous to attempt to propose a resolved design alternative to the scheme built but **R** illustrates how a three-storey 3·66 m (12 ft) frontage terrace scheme, with slightly less space between blocks, can give the same accommodation with private gardens and integral garages for all family dwelling and three-storey walk-up two-person flats. Clearly the costs of adapting terraces to the changing

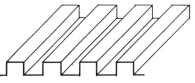

O *Array of streets*

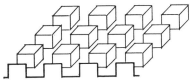

P *Array of pavilions*

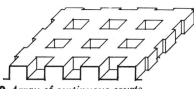

Q *Array of continuous courts*

site levels either with extensive fill or earth moving would be high, but it is unlikely that they would be higher than the concrete floors, concrete frame, dispersed drainage arrangement and peculiar foundation loading of the clusters.

Planning a continuous convoluted court form as in **S** can gain more space between buildings while maintaining the same density and corresponding more closely to the site contours.

Research into building form has a number of ramifications. It demands the attention of practising architects who should test the applicability of elementary models to the specific content of housing. It underlines the importance of making the right basic choice of form if the architect is not to spend his inventive energy unwittingly trying to compensate for the effects of a misconception.

As well as having quantitative advantages, street and court forms readily match the existing pattern of housing stock, which we no longer wish entirely to replace. In particular the development of site perimeters to gain density implies careful adaptation to the conditions around sites. Instead of being withdrawn and isolated on their own land, housing estates could be hardly distinguishable from the context into which they are inserted.

The final point concerns density. The traditional terrace adapted to incorporate garages can be built at densities up to about 247 people per hectare (100 ppa). From 247 to 370 pph evidence suggests that stacked arrangements are necessary, and although the cost yardstick increases it does not sustain the amenity offered by houses on the ground. Gardens and convenient access are denied and the private plot with its expression of family identity is replaced by some kind of megastructure which symbolises the unpopular intervention of government. Is it really worth building public housing much above 100 ppa?

SUMMARY: HOUSING

Ground floor area: 3042 m² (32 750 sq ft).
Total floor area (net): 11 497 m² (123 760 sq ft).
Total floor area (gross): 12 470 m² (134 230 sq ft).
Type of contract: Two stage, fixed price.
Tender date: September 1967 (groundworks); September 1968 (superstructures and external works).
Work began: February 1968.
Work finished: September 1971.
Price of foundation, superstructure, installation and finishes including drainage to collecting manhole: £759 140.
Price of external works and ancillary buildings including drainage beyond collecting manhole: £186 530.
Total: £945 670.

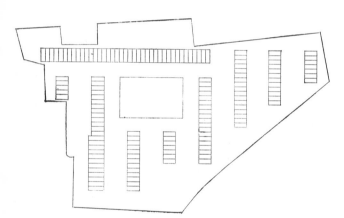

R *Burghley Road, hypothetical layout of accommodation with 168 dwellings, comprising 132 four-, five- or six-person terraced houses and 36 two-person three-storey walk-up flats in terrace*

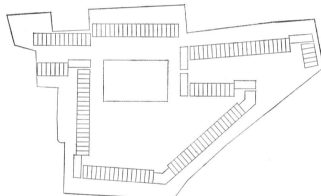

S *Burghley Road, hypothetical layout of accommodation with 172 dwellings, comprising 134 four-, five-, or six-person terraced houses and 38 two-person three-storey walk-up flats at corners*

20 Housing at Lillington Street, Westminster

1 *Stage 1 shortly after completion*

designed by	Darbourne & Darke
partners in charge	J. Darbourne & G. Darke
quantity surveyors	G. A. Hanscombe Partnership
structural consultant	Flint & Neill
mechanical consultants	
(heating)	Kennedy & Donkin
main contractor	
(stage 1)	Rush & Tompkins
main contractor	
(stage 2)	Kirk & Kirk

CLIENT'S REQUIREMENTS

This housing scheme, built for the Westminster City Council, was the subject of an open architectural competition in 1961. The winners were required to house 2 000 people on a site to the north west of Vauxhall Bridge in given proportions of dwellings of various sizes, ranging from four bedroom to bedsitting room units, together with an old people's hostel and communal amenities.

The winning scheme by Darbourne & Darke provides 777 dwellings at an overall density of 539 persons per hectare (218 ppa).

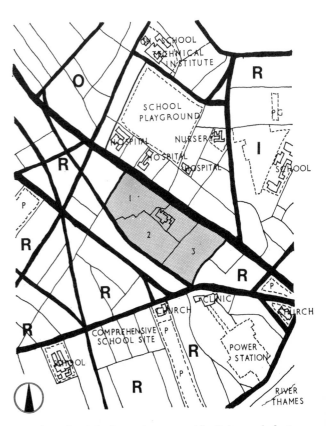

Location plan (site in tone), R = *residential,* I = *industry,* O = *office. Numerals indicate stages of construction*

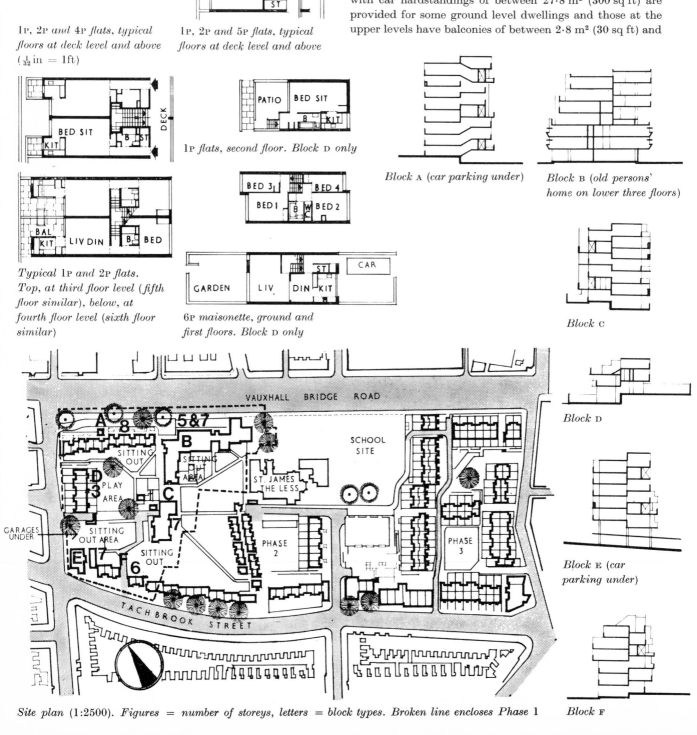

1P, 2P and 4P flats, typical floors at deck level and above ($\frac{1}{32}$ in = 1ft)

1P, 2P and 5P flats, typical floors at deck level and above

Typical 1P and 2P flats. Top, at third floor level (fifth floor similar), below, at fourth floor level (sixth floor similar)

1P flats, second floor. Block D only

6P maisonette, ground and first floors. Block D only

Block A (car parking under)

Block B (old persons' home on lower three floors)

Block C

Block D

Block E (car parking under)

Block F

Site plan (1:2500). Figures = number of storeys, letters = block types. Broken line encloses Phase 1

SITE AND PLANNING

The site, of four hectares ($9\frac{1}{2}$ acres) is in a closely built up central London residential area, relieved by green spaces in squares and gardens. It is enclosed by Vauxhall Bridge Road, Charlwood Street, Tachbrook Street and Rampayne Street, and is dominated by the 41·54 m (136 ft) spire of St James-the-Less Church and a school by G. E. Street, both of which had to be preserved.

The site was developed in three stages, each of them occupying about a third of the total area over a ten year period.

Stage 1 of the development consisted of 244 dwellings comprising 159 one- and two-person flats and 85 three- to seven-person flats and maisonettes in three-, six-, seven- and eight-storey deck access blocks. There is an old people's home and flats in the five- to seven-storey block.

Only 5 per cent of the dwellings are located and entered at ground level, compared with 36 per cent in phase 3. Gardens with car hardstandings of between 27·8 m² (300 sq ft) are provided for some ground level dwellings and those at the upper levels have balconies of between 2·8 m² (30 sq ft) and

3

2 *Upper level 'street' which has planted areas irrigated by roof drainage* **3** *Looking north along Charlwood Street*

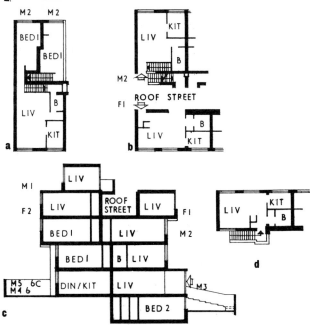

2.

a *Maisonette M2 at level below roof street, blocks H, L and M.*
b *Flat F1 and maisonette M2 at level of roof street, blocks H, L and M.* **c** *Section through blocks H and L ($\frac{1}{32}$ in = 1ft).*
d *Maisonette M1 at level above roof street, blocks H and L.*

6·7 m² (72 sq ft) or roof terraces of between 9·3 m² (100 sq ft) and 27·8 m² (300 sq ft).

The amount of open space (62·6 per cent) is large. This is accounted for mainly by the low area occupied by roads and by the use of underground car accommodation. By building close to the site perimeter it has been possible to concentrate the open space into large, well landscaped areas. Stage 3 of the development consisted of 289 dwellings comprising two-, three-, four-, five- and six-person households in mainly four- and five-storey blocks. The blocks consist of three-storey back-to-back crossover maisonettes at ground level with a central access deck at third floor level serving the small households.

This scheme is a completely medium rise solution at a very high density. It consists of four- and five-storey back-to-back crossover maisonettes at ground level with a central deck with lift access serving the smaller dwellings above.

Thirty-six per cent of all the dwellings are at ground level and so are all but four of the larger dwellings. All ground floor dwellings have enclosed private gardens of 300 sq ft but only seven of the upper dwellings have any private open space. Access generally is either at ground level or by lift to the third floor deck and then one flight of stairs up or down.

There is 58 per cent car provision—practically all in underground garages.

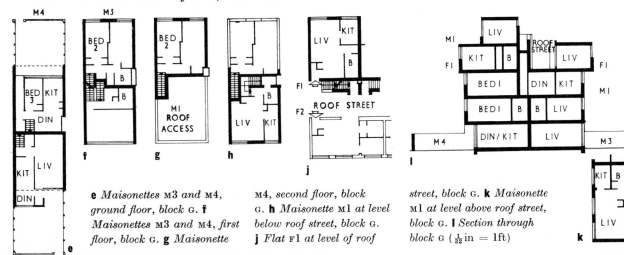

e *Maisonettes M3 and M4, ground floor, block G.* **f** *Maisonettes M3 and M4, first floor, block G.* **g** *Maisonette M4, second floor, block G.* **h** *Maisonette M1 at level below roof street, block G.* **j** *Flat F1 at level of roof street, block G.* **k** *Maisonette M1 at level above roof street, block G.* **l** *Section through block G ($\frac{1}{32}$ in = 1ft)*

4 *Looking north towards blocks C and B: Stage 2 just visible at right*

5 *Complexity shows up at junctions*

4.

APPRAISAL Stage 1

This scheme deserves criticism of the highest level. It is remarkable in that it shows a grasp of, and attempts to solve, the problems of high density urban housing. The buildings are used to create a large sheltered open green space which all dwellings overlook. It extends this green space by means of wide access decks lined with generous plant boxes right to the front door of most of the flats. It uses a complex section to maximise the use of the expensive access deck and to attempt to get sunlight into the depth of dwellings from two sides.

The split level section and the deliberate expression of elements such as access decks and private balconies have been exploited to create an interesting façade rather than the most economical building envelope. The entrances to many of the dwellings are comparatively dark, in some cases situated adjoining each other at right angles at the bottom of a flight of steps leading from the access deck. The larger dwellings are arranged on three levels with two levels between the kitchen and the entrance. Family dwellings have generous balconies, partly recessed, but no vision panel is provided to help link the dwelling to the outside and to discourage children from climbing.

The building, although slow to build and obviously expensive, reduces maintenance costs to a minimum and because of its structure has a long potential life.

There is an unfortunate disparity between the planning of the dwellings themselves and the excellence of the general environment and architectural concept, but the overall solution to a very high density housing problem is outstanding.

5

6 *View between courts from west*

6

APPRAISAL Stage 3

To look at it, you might suppose that the final stage of the four hectare (nine-and-a-half acre) Lillington Street housing scheme in Pimlico had suffered because of the ministry's cost yardstick and that it was therefore an inglorious tailpiece to an otherwise worthy competition winning design; but you would be wrong. The change in appearance is essentially due to a different dwelling arrangement allowing the provision of an amenity normally achieved only at much lower densities.

Gardens may be considered the right of every new-towner and the envy of every city dweller. Darbourne & Darke have achieved the seemingly impossible by providing a garden for every house—even if it is only a pocket-handkerchief 30 m² (320 sq ft)—and this at a density of 457 bsph (185 bspa) *without* the flats above.

The first three floors of all blocks in this stage are houses, with flats on top—instead of the complex arrangement of flats as in the earlier phases. The architects have tried to come to terms with the Victorian neighbourhood by reducing the overall height of the blocks, a fair amount of tile hanging (intended to be in sympathy with neighbouring slate mansards) and the use of vertical sash windows.

In section, stage 3 consists of two distinct elements. Family units form 40 per cent of the 284 total. Pairs of family units are interlocked in such a way that each has its own garden, surrounded by a high brick wall with the entrance through the garden. One house has its living room on the ground floor, while the other's living room is placed immediately above it, both facing in the most favourable direction. The 'favourable' garden is partly screened from the attentions of the living room above by a projecting entrance porch below.

The second of the elements is entirely separate and sits on top of the houses. It is based on a pedestrian roof street giving access to bed-sitter or one-bedroom flats either on the same level, or one floor up reached by external staircase, or

7

7 *Quality of landscaping is exceptional: ramped footpath serves also as emergency vehicle access*

234

8

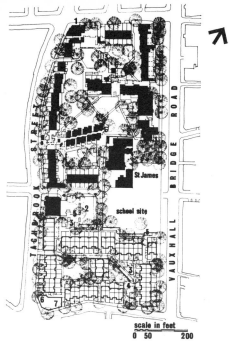

Key
1 Pub
2 Football pitch
3 Play area
4 Vehicle service
5 Underground parking
6 Surgery
7 Library

scale in feet
0 50 200

*Site plan: earlier stages shown
black, stage 3 in heavy outline*

9

10

8 *View from south-east service access*
9 *Roof street: access to maisonettes
with flats above. Arrangement is
intended to give feeling of individual
dwellings—particularly important if
flats are ever offered for sale to tenants*

10 *Stage 1 from internal court:
complex arrangement of flats above
rear of pub and boilerhouse*
11 *From below roof street bridge,
along north-west terrace. Flats 'in the
roof' reduce apparent height of blocks*

one floor down, interlocked with a family unit. The roof
street is reached by lifts and runs continuously between the
six blocks laid out as two squares. The total density is
618 bsph (250 bspa) for this stage.

The architects chose brick as a facing material for the entire
scheme. The colour of the brick may appear unfortunate and
it is a pity that a mature stock was not available as it would
have been more sympathetic to old Pimlico. Instead the
colour has been keyed to G. E. Street's church of St James-
the-Less, a somewhat tough and dismal memorial preserved
within the site.

The landscaping of this stage is very heartening. This item
is susceptible to last minute cost cutting, but in this case has
been 'preserved' by allocating various elements to different
sectors of the budget. Lavish use of transplanted trees, such
as Norway maple, wild cherry, birch, mountain ash and
hornbeam give the area an unexpected appearance of
maturity and are intended to grow to a height above roof
street level. It will be interesting to see how the efforts of
the mini-garden owners and roof-top dwellers soften the
angular building shapes in years to come.

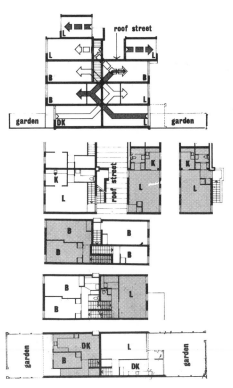

*Typical section, with floor plans,
showing system of interlocking units.
Access from roof street to two one-person
flats and two-person crossover
maisonette: from ground, to two
five-person houses*

21 Housing at The Barbican, City of London

at	The Barbican, City of London
designed by	Chamberlain, Powell & Bon (Barbican)
quantity surveyors	Davis, Belfield & Everest
structural engineers	Ove Arup & Partners
services engineers	G. H. Buckle & Partners
estate agency consultants	Goddard & Smith
main contractors	John Laing Construction Ltd
	Sir Robert McAlpine & Sons Ltd
	Myton Ltd
	Turriff Construction Ltd

(1:3428)

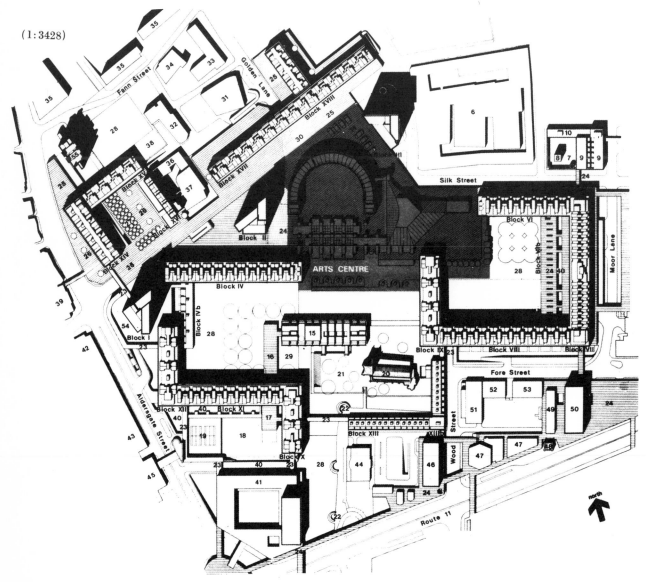

Plan showing Barbican developments: arts centre in tone

CLIENT'S REQUIREMENTS, SITE, PLANNING

Housing is the key to, and the *raison d'etre* of, the whole Barbican programme, the most ambitious attempt in Britain so far to bring people back into the heavily developed heart of a major commercial city centre.

Between 1851 and 1951 the resident population of the City of London dropped from about 125 000 to 5 000 and that of Cripplegate, the ward in which the Barbican lies, from some 14 000 to 48. By day the City was bustling with half a million commuting workers; by night it was a ghost town, a 'City of cats and caretakers'.[1] Here was an opportunity for providing some of these commuters with a home near their work, and it is to the credit of the City that they accepted as a matter of policy the recommendation of the then Minister of Housing, Duncan Sandys, that the Barbican area should become 'a genuine residential neighbourhood incorporating schools, shops, open spaces and other amenities, even if this means foregoing a more remunerative return on the land.'[2]

The Barbican contains 2 113 flats, let (at 1974 rents) from £840 p.a. upwards. The 15·2 ha (5 acre) site for the residential part of the Barbican development is bounded by Aldersgate Street to the west; London Wall, Wood Street and Fore Street to the south and Whitecross Street to the east and north-east; and by Red Lion Market, Cripplegate Institute and Fann Street to the north.

Commercial development surrounds the site on three sides while the northern edge of the site adjoins the subsidised housing of the City's Golden Lane Estate and the Peabody

1-5 Arts centre
6 Whitbreads brewery
7 Milton Court: GLC Fire Station—drill yard
8 Milton Court: GLC Fire Station—drill tower
9 Milton Court: maisonettes on top floor
10 Milton Court: Corporation of London offices
14 Electrical substation, London Electricity Board
15 City of London School for Girls
16 City of London School for Girls—preparatory school
17 City of London School for Girls—gymnasium
18 City of London School for Girls—lawn and informal play area
19 City of London School for Girls—tennis courts
20 St Giles Church
21 St Giles Court
22 Roman wall
23 Pedestrian bridge
24 Pedestrian podium at level 68.0
25 Pedestrian podium at level 77.0
26 Stairs to commercial area under podium
27 Tree tubs
28 Lawn
29 City of London School for Girls—lawn
30 Junction of Golden Lane and Beech Street (under podium)
31 Cripplegate Institute
32 GPO Training School
33 Police station
34 Jewin Methodist Chapel
35 Golden Lane Estate
36 Bridgewater House: offices
37 Murray House: offices
38 Bridgewater Square
39 Aldersgate and Barbican Underground Station
40 Mews
41 London Museum
42 London Salvage Depot
43 Bradbury Graetorex: offices
44 Barber Surgeons Hall
45 Multi-level car park
46 Lee House: offices
47 Podium shops
48 Saint Alphage Church (ruin)
49 Podium shops
50 Saint Alphage House: offices
51 Roman House: offices
52 Office block
53 Office block
54 Podium at level 59.0 with restaurant and shop
55 Students' hostel
Blocks I-XVIII are houses, flats, maisonettes, penthouses
and integral garage accommodation up to a maximum
of forty storeys high

1 *'Here is a town (which shall be nameless). Bombardments have spared us two little palaces (1) and a fragment of a royal road of Louis* XV *(2). In (3) are traces of the Roman occupation. In (4) a circulation centre which will be accentuated by diverting to it the vehicles now using the riverside road, so that this may be reserved as a pedestrian promenade. The heart of the town (5) will be reconstructed, but with certain new provisions; it will be forbidden to vehicles by chains of bollards as in (6). Vehicles are re-routed along (7) serving the cinemas, the cafés (8) and (9) and the blocks of flats furnished with common services (10). The heart of the town is thus reconstituted and intensified, but sheltered from disturbance.*
'A principle has triumphed: wherever bombs have done their work verdure flourishes, and upon the wide green spaces rise new buildings. Road alignments and their resulting interior courts are abolished. . . .'[3]

and Bunhill Fields estates. There is no easy access to any sizeable open spaces outside the site boundaries.

The site had been cleared of most buildings by the war, and activities contained in the few remaining buildings had to be accommodated elsewhere. The only structures to be retained are St Giles' Church and sections of the Roman Wall, which have been made a feature of the landscaping. Le Corbusier's description and sketch of 1946, **1**, could be adapted, without too much difficulty, to describe Chamberlin, Powell & Bon's Barbican development. For 'town' read 'part of a town' and for 'heart of the town' read 'arts centre'. Bombs flattened the Barbican site, **2** and **3**, destroying the wholesale warehousing that was no longer required when the pattern of distribution between manufacturer and retailer changed after the war.

2 *1939 Survey: built-up character of the Barbican site*
3 *1945 Survey: effect of bombing on the same site*

Because of the scarcity of building land in the City, maximum use of the site and high density were essential. It was also necessary to produce a scheme that would provide generous open space; a high standard of amenity and convenience; a pleasant, yet exciting environment and a definite sense of neighbourhood and 'belonging'.

The Barbican residential development incorporates 2 113 flats, maisonettes and terrace houses for up to 6 500 residents; a 200-room hostel for students and young City workers; new premises for the City of London School for Girls and the Guildhall School of Music and Drama; a theatre, a lending library, an art gallery, a concert hall and a studio cinema to serve residents of Greater London and its surroundings generally; shops, restaurants and pubs and a completely segregated system of elevated pedestrian walkways and terraces, with motor roads, service access bays and parking for 2 500 private cars located out of sight below pedestrian level. Children can play in the pedestrian areas and gardens so that there is no need for a special playground. A creche has been built which is temporarily used for administration.

Housing in concentrated in three towers each of over 40 storeys and in multi-storey terrace blocks grouped round squares, courts and gardens; in spite of the high residential density of 570 persons per hectare (230 per acre) there are 9·5 hectares (23 acres) of open space for amenity use, ie 1·5 ha (3·8 acres) per 1 000 inhabitants—more than double the area required by the planning permission. Apart from the 3·25 ha (8 acres) of lake and planting at ground level, most of the land has been 'used twice'—as pedestrian area or building and space over vehicle access and parking; as pedestrian ways or landscaped terraces over housing and the arts centre. Some 4·8 ha (12 acres) of new 'ground level' open space have been created by the elevated walk-ways

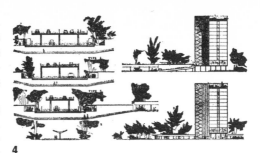

4

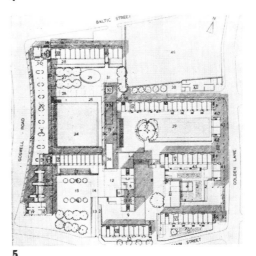

5

6

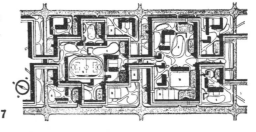

7

4 *Road sections from Le Corbusier's Ville Radieuse, 1930*
5 *Chamberlin, Powell & Bon's Golden Lane housing, 1953*
6 *Le Corbusier's 'City of Three Million', 1922: combination of point blocks and linear buildings*
7 Lotissements a redents *in Le Corbusier's Ville Radieuse, 1930*
8 *Chamberlin, Powell & Bon's first project for the Barbican, 1955, which consisted of four-storey housing around alternating private and public courts* **9**

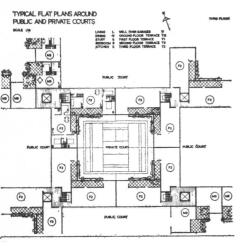

TYPICAL FLAT PLANS AROUND PUBLIC AND PRIVATE COURTS

8

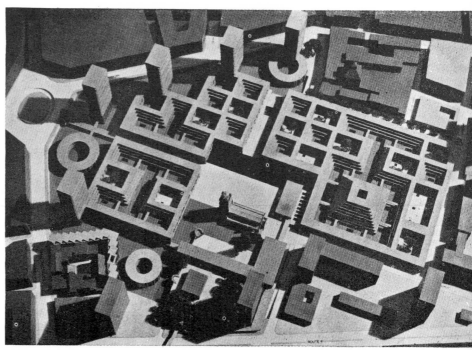

9

and podium terraces which form the main pedestrian level throughout the site. Space below the podium levels is used for housing, garages and 5·5 km of roads. Most of the arts centre—containing some 300 000 m³ (11 million cu ft) will be below podium level; the only parts of the centre which cannot be walked on are one of the two theatre fly towers and the art gallery.

In so far as the Barbican plan introduces a residential pocket into a predominantly commercial area it reflects the mood of the '50s which first sensed the impoverishment of urban life that would result from the rigid segregation of housing, offices, recreation, transportation etc. The Barbican itself, moreover, is much more than a residential centre. The earliest project (1955) included the Guildhall School of Music and Drama and a small theatre and concert hall. Later the City of London School for Girls was added and by 1968 the plans for a full-blown arts centre were approved which included a theatre for the Royal Shakespeare Company, a concert hall for the London Symphony Orchestra, a public library, an art gallery, a small cinema, restaurants, bars and shops. The school already makes a significant contribution to life at the Barbican in daytime when many residents are away at work, while the arts centre, when completed in 1977, should provide a powerful magnet for much of the City by day and for the whole of London by night.

The completion of the arts centre should also help to make the public pedestrian podium, now somewhat remote at two storeys above pavement level, more inviting, the main foyers of the theatre and concert hall being at pavement level and half-way between pavement and podium level. Because the ground rises to the north, the podium when completed will in fact have a lower and an upper level which will meet and overlap in the arts centre, the lower level providing direct access to the library, shopping arcade and a restaurant, the upper level to another restaurant. Like zoning, segregation of foot and wheeled traffic has its origins in prewar planning theory, though Le Corbusier in his Ville Radieuse project of 1930 insisted on the pedestrian's right to natural ground level and contact with nature, **4**. Cars are carried on an elevated roadway, while heavy traffic remains at ground level with underpasses for pedestrians. The immediate success of Chamberlin, Powell & Bon's earlier Golden Lane housing north of the Barbican site is due in no small measure to the easy way in which the pedestrian is taken in at pavement level (which is also shop level) and then down to the interior courts, **5**. But at the time the Barbican area was being designed, the then LCC and City planning authorities settled on elevated pedestrian walkways, some of which had already been planned in conjunction with the office development along London Wall on the southern boundary of the site. In any case elevated roadways even for local traffic, in a dense type of development like the Barbican, would generate an intolerable amount of noise; and it was noise which decided the architects to build over not only the underground railway but also Beech Street, a busy public road which bisected the site.

The difficulty of elevated walkways is the psychological one of persuading people up there. It has not been made any easier at the Barbican by the City's reluctance to provide escalators and by their own example along London Wall, where the lack of cover has made these windswept areas even less desirable than they might be. At least within the Barbican residential site it is possible to walk under cover all the way.

The success of this segregation must depend in the last resort on making the upper level extensive enough and with a quantity and variety of attractions sufficient to stop people using the roadside shops. If this sounds excessively authoritarian for present-day appetites, it must be said in defence that nothing could be worse than allowing a radical concept of this kind to remain half-digested. Here again the City have not helped matters by allowing new pavements at street level on the south side of London Wall.

In considering the built form which the Barbican finally took, two complementary influences must be taken into account. On the one hand there were Le Corbusier's prewar projects and certain precepts of the Modern Movement as a whole; on the other, growing dissatisfaction with the Modern Movement was making architects look increasingly at earlier historical models. In his City of Three Million Le Corbusier had proposed the combination of point blocks and linear buildings, **6** and, more specifically, *lotissements a redents* in his Ville Radieuse, **7**, where the smaller of the two set-backs is roughly the same size as one of the Barbican courts. The concept of flowing space, especially under buildings raised on stilts, and the interlocking of several volumes serving different functions, made possible by new forms of construction, also have their origin in the Modern Movement. At the Barbican the extensive water garden, which links the arts centre with the two courts and St Gile's church, forms an important unifying element. Equally, the way in which the volumes of the City of London School for Girls interlock with the housing block in the western court emphasises continuity as well as the mixed nature of the development.

At this point it becomes necessary to recall that the architects' first project of 1955, **8**, approached the design of the low buildings in a fundamentally different way to the one

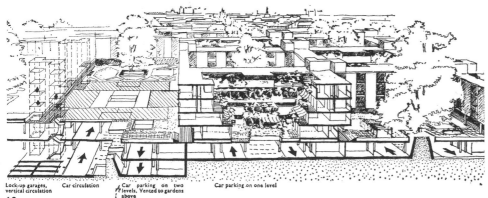

10 *Sectional perspective of the first Barbican project showing the stepped section on the private side and the low-level service roads*

11 *Albany, showing the covered access way and the closely spaced blocks of chambers*

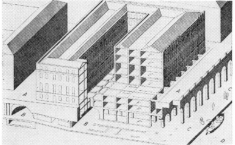

12

12 *The old Adelphi, from Bernoulli's 'Towns and the Land' showing superimposed road systems and their relation to the river*

13 *Chamberlin, Powell & Bon's second project for the Barbican, 1956*

14 *The old Adelphi terrace, showing podium treatment and traffic circulation on different levels*

15 *Carlton House Terrace: a terrace of residential accommodation rising from a podium*

16 *Le Corbusier demonstrating the likeness in scale and form between his* lotissements à redents *and some of Paris's historic squares* (53)

13

14

15

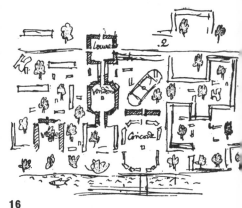

16

built, owing little to prewar planning theory and anticipating Sir Leslie Martin's studies in land use and built form of the late '50s. It arose principally out of the need for a density of some 750 persons to the hectare (300 to the acre) which together with profitable accommodation such as shops, restaurants and garages was considered necessary to make the project as a whole economically viable. It consisted of a chequerboard of four-storey housing around alternating private and public courts, **8**. For privacy and better light-angles the section on the private side was stepped, **9**, and low-level service roads, as in the present scheme, provided access to underground garages from which lifts connected directly with the flats above. The layout was conceived as a pedestrian precinct in which flats were approached under arcaded ways reminiscent of the Albany, **11**, or some of the chambers in the inns of court.

This project was rejected by the LCC on planning grounds because of its excessively high density and lack of clear open space. The second project of 1956, **13**, incorporated the northern part of the site between Beech Street and the Golden Lane estate, as well as two more schools, the City of London School (for boys) and the City of London School for Girls, the former being subsequently omitted. The main difference was in the housing, which now took a form that could provide fewer but larger areas of open space. The concept of three towers and of long terraces rising from a podium and enclosing lawns and water gardens has remained

unchanged during the subsequent modifications to the plan. As well as referring to the Hötorget development, then under construction in Stockholm, the architects drew deliberate historical parallels.[4] They singled out the old Adelphi as a complex example of multi-level crculation, **12 14**, and Carlton House Terrace as an example of a podium with terraces above, **15**. The size and scale of these older developments made them suitable as models, and it is interesting to recall that Le Corbusier had also attempted to demonstrate a likeness in scale and form between his own *lotissements a redents* and such historic areas in Paris as the Place Vendôme and the Louvre, **16**.

In the context of historical allusion and the growing interest in historic buildings, one should also recall that in their revised project of 1959, Chamberlin, Powell & Bon proposed and the City agreed to the re-erection of Bunning's Coal Exchange rotunda as the central space of the Guildhall School of Music, which was now separated from its drama department, **17**. This remarkable cast-iron structure would have given access, via its galleries, to the innumerable small rooms which constitute the bulk of the school's accommodation. Later, the City changed their minds because it was unsuitable, they felt, to incorporate an old Victorian structure in a new school, an argument which lacks all credibility in today's preservationist climate. However remarkable the first project for the Barbican may now seem, the larger scale and greater simplicity of the

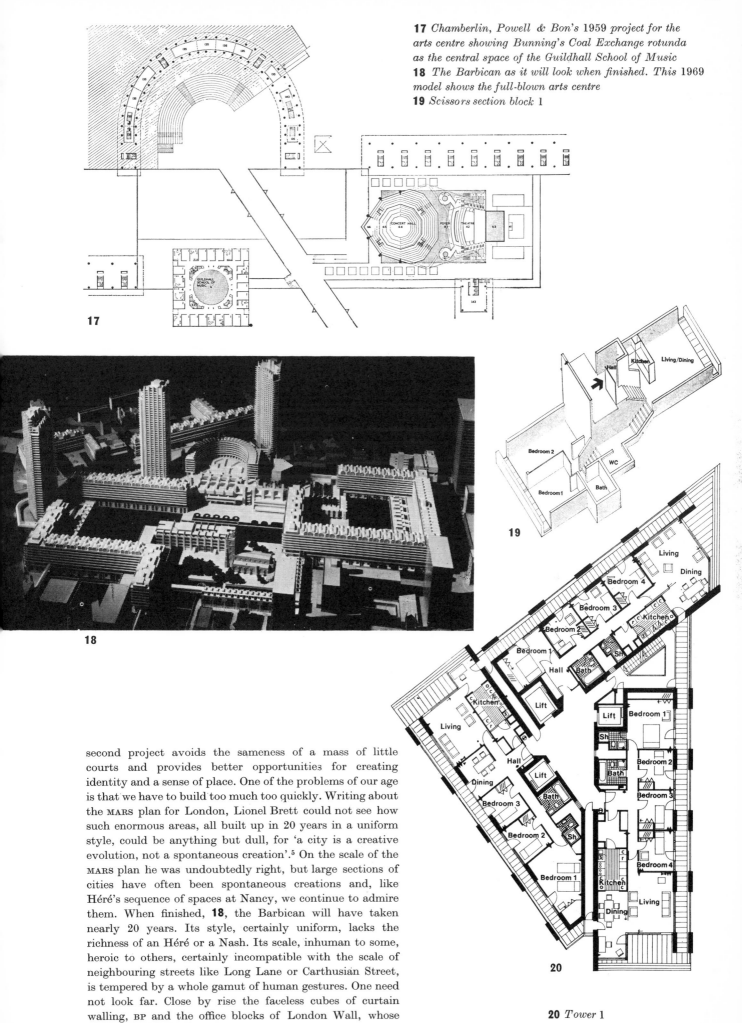

17 *Chamberlin, Powell & Bon's* 1959 *project for the arts centre showing Bunning's Coal Exchange rotunda as the central space of the Guildhall School of Music*
18 *The Barbican as it will look when finished. This* 1969 *model shows the full-blown arts centre*
19 *Scissors section block* 1

second project avoids the sameness of a mass of little courts and provides better opportunities for creating identity and a sense of place. One of the problems of our age is that we have to build too much too quickly. Writing about the MARS plan for London, Lionel Brett could not see how such enormous areas, all built up in 20 years in a uniform style, could be anything but dull, for 'a city is a creative evolution, not a spontaneous creation'.[5] On the scale of the MARS plan he was undoubtedly right, but large sections of cities have often been spontaneous creations and, like Héré's sequence of spaces at Nancy, we continue to admire them. When finished, **18**, the Barbican will have taken nearly 20 years. Its style, certainly uniform, lacks the richness of an Héré or a Nash. Its scale, inhuman to some, heroic to others, certainly incompatible with the scale of neighbouring streets like Long Lane or Carthusian Street, is tempered by a whole gamut of human gestures. One need not look far. Close by rise the faceless cubes of curtain walling, BP and the office blocks of London Wall, whose

20 *Tower* 1

Above podium

North-south terrace

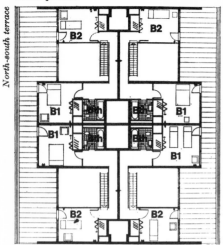

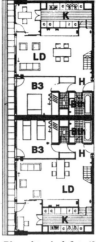

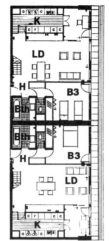

L	Living room
D	Dining room
LD	Living/Dining
B	Bedroom
Bth	Bathroom
K	Kitchen
S	Study
BSR	Bed Sitting room
DR	Dressing room
Lt	Lift

o	oven
h	hotplate
c	cupboards
r	refrigerator
w	waste disposal
s	sink

► single socket outlet
⊢ double socket outlet
► shaver
►◄ television
◆ telephone
▐ consumer unit
►◄ meters

Plan of typical penthouse maisonettes at roof level (7th floor above podium)

Plan of typical flats (1st-5th floors above podium); also of penthouses with internal stairs (6th and 7th floor above podium)

East-west terraces

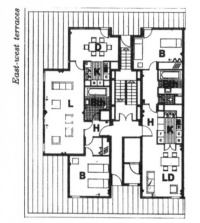

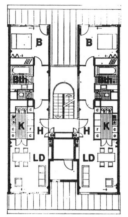

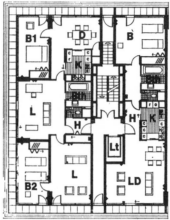

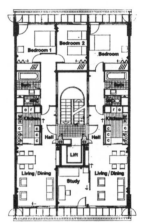

Plan of end flat at roof level (7th floor above podium)

Plan of typical flats at roof level (7th floor above podium)

Plan of end flat (1st-6th floors above podium)

Plan of typical flats (1st-6th floors above podium)

Podium level and below

East-west terraces

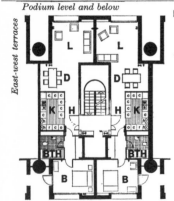

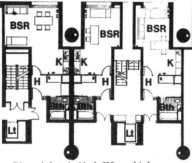

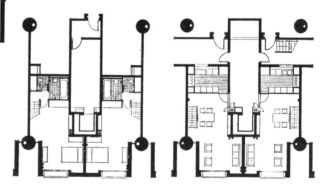

Plan of flats in block XI on first two levels below podium—living rooms face north into garden court (see 23 on p 245)

Plan of flats in block XI on third level below podium; flats have access from mews between the garages under the playground of the City of London School for Girls; each flat has its own car port on the mews side and access to the garden court on the opposite side through the narrow passage between the flats

Plan of two-storey maisonettes below podium in block VI, with car port and bedrooms at lower level, and living room at upper level accessibility either by lift from below or by open staircase in podium above

North-south terrace houses opposite east end of St Giles

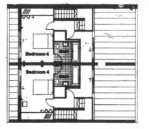

Plans of four-storey terrace houses with (from left to right) street level, level below podium, podium level and level above podium (note entrances at street and podium level)

244

22

21 *Block XVII seen from Golden Lane. In the front is the ramp which gives access to the podium. In the background is tower I. (See site plan)*

22 *A typical corner of a terrace block showing the pick-hammered concrete balcony fronts, the cantilevered balconies which surround the blocks and the barrel-vaulted penthouses. Fairfaced floor soffits are painted white.*

23 *The public podium of block XI looking towards Aldersgate Street. The top two levels under the podium are two-room flats and the bottom level is a one-room flat with a car port*

bulk constitutes a repeated assault on the eye. Barbican celebrates the skyline with penthouses of fanciful silhouette. Its slender towers, triangular on plan, have an elegance which is rare in modern architecture. Its podium may be one long sequence of unrelieved, hard surfaces, but from it one can look down at the gentle landscape of lawn and water gardens, and up at an infinite variety of plants softening the relentless horizontals of the pick-hammered concrete balcony fronts.

Although built for a middle-to-higher income group and therefore not comparable to council housing, the Barbican avoids balcony access and communal internal spaces, both forbidding in scale and brutal in finishes. Instead, access to flats is by closely spaced lift and staircase shafts. Where internal passages occur, as in the north-south blocks, a carpeted floor reminds one that moderately well-heeled tenants are in occupation. Regrettably the largest flats are in the towers, for the original brief did not anticipate as many families with children as have applied for accommodation. Regrettably, too, these flats are the least desirable, being single-aspect with all the rooms strung out along a corridor. Space standards generally seem low for the type of tenant the Barbican is intended to attract unless, as may often be the case, his flat is essentially a weekday *pied a terre* for a house in the country.

'If you would be known, and not know, vegetate in a village; if you would know, and not be known, live in a city.[6] Substitute 'suburb' for 'village' and Colton's words might well have been used by the City of London to lure back some of its lost population *and* voters. That they are coming back is evident from the speed with which the Barbican flats are let. But the success of the Barbican will not depend on its

23

success as housing. It will depend on its quality of pedestrian precinct and on its ability to attract large numbers of Londoners once the arts centre is finished. The principle of such radical segregation between cars and pedestrians is one that many planners would hesitate to follow today if they had the opportunity to design the Barbican all over again.

Yet even in its unfinished state, Barbican at week-ends, when the vast building site of the arts centre shuts down, is a haven of quiet. The completed Barbican may yet give us back a little of that 'city of refuge'[7] which Milton, who lies buried in St Giles's church, found in the London of his day and which the motor car is now increasingly denying us.

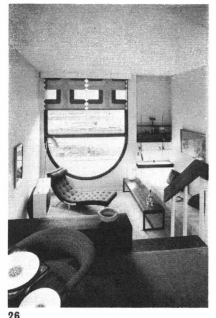

26

27

28

29

30

24 *In midsummer the sun strikes the north elevation of block VIII. As in all the terrace blocks in the south Barbican, the podium runs through at 21m above datum*

25 *From a balcony of block VIII looking down on to the stairs which lead to the garden and the water chute which supplies recirculated water to the pool. The rooflights serve the bathrooms, wcs and internal stairs of the under podium two storey houses of block VIIb*

26 *Typical two-level under-podium flat*

27 *Typical three-room flat in an east-west terrace block showing the open character of the design. On the right is the unusually wide passage forming the entrance hall as well as the link between the living and sleeping quarters*

28 *Typical bathroom showing wash basin and mirror with built-in cupboard set in matt-finished white glazed tiles*

29 *Entrance to the flats is from the public podium by means of frequent staircase and lift shafts. On the left is part of a service duct*

30 *Kitchen looking towards dining recess in typical north-south terrace flat*

Notes

Introduction: A Fast-Changing Decade

1 Jackson, Alan A, *Semi-Detached London*, George Allen & Unwin Ltd, London 1973

2 See DOE housing reports

3 Eversley, David, 'Problems of Social Planning in Inner London' in Donnison, David and Eversley, David (eds), *London: Urban Patterns, Problems and Policies*, Heinemann Ltd, London 1973

4 *Housing facts and figures*, GLC, London 1973

5 *Homes for Today and Tomorrow*, The Parker Morris Report, HMSO, London 1961

6 As published in *The Registered Housebuilders Handbook*, NHBRC, London 1969. Reprinted 1970

7 *Housing: The Way Ahead*, Report of the NALGO Housing Working Party, 1973

8 See Mallory, Keith and Ottar, Arvid, *Architecture of Aggression*, The Architectural Press Ltd, London 1973

9 In Jackson, Anthony, *The Politics of Architecture*, The Architectural Press Ltd, London 1970

10 See *The Architectural Review* November 1967

11 Ward, Colin (ed) *Vandalism*, The Architectural Press Ltd, London 1973

12 *The Architectural Review* November 1967

13 In *Building* 9 November 1973, pp 140-1

14 See Deeson, A F L (ed) *The Comprehensive Industrialised Building Systems Annual 1965*, House Publications, London 1964

15 See *Residential Areas Higher Densities*, Planning Bulletin no 2, HMSO 1962. Reprinted 1965

16 *Occasional Bulletins* published by the Nationwide Building Society, London

17 *Widening the Choice: The Next Steps in Housing*, HMSO, April 1973, Cmnd 5280

18 See Cullingworth, J B, *English Housing Trends*, Bell & Sons Ltd, London 1965

19 Attenburrow, J J, *Some impressions of the private sector of the housing market*, Current Paper 57/68, Building Research Establishment 1968

20 MacMurray, Trevor, 'Housing Policy: Home Ownership and Tomorrow's Environment,' *Housing Review*, March/April 1970

21 See Crawford, David and Dunbar, Mel, 'Straitjacket,' *The Architectural Review* October 1973. This article contains a detailed survey of the regulations which impinge on housing

22 *Local housing programmes*, Digest 154, Building Research Establishment, June 1973

23 See *Council Housing Purposes, Procedures and Priorities*, Ninth Report of the Housing Management Sub-Committee of the Central Housing Advisory Committee, HMSO 1969

24 'Local authority housing: a comparative study of the land use and built form of 110 schemes,' *The Architects' Journal* 1 August 1973

25 See Funnell, Martin and Werr, Patricia, 'Homes for Single Working People in Leicester,' *Housing* July 1973

26 See *Directory of Housing Society Schemes*, England Scotland and Wales and South East of England editions, The Housing Corporation 1973

27 Segal, Walter, 'Segal on courtyards,' *London Architect*, New Year Issue 1974

28 In *Building construction in connection with the Provision of Dwellings for the Working Classes*, Report of the Tudor Walters Committee, Cd 9191, HMSO 1918

29 *Community layouts in private housing*, National House Builders Registration Council 1970

30 'Local authority housing: a comparative study of the land use and built form of 110 schemes,' *The Architects' Journal* 1 August 1973

31 *Roads in Urban Areas*, HMSO 1966

32 *Second Report, Vehicle Manoeuvring Study*; *Third Report, Injury Accident Survey*, Housing Development Directorate 1974

33 Essex County Council County Planning Office, *Design Guide for Residential Areas*, Chelmsford 1973

34 *The Architects' Journal* 14 October 1970

35 Crawford, David and Dunbar, Mel, 'Straitjacket,' *The Architectural Review* October 1973

36 See Habraken, N J, *Supports: an Alternative to Mass Housing*, The Architectural Press Ltd, London 1972

37 See 'Habraken in Hackney,' *The Architects' Journal* 15 September 1971

38 *Housing Facts and Figures*, GLC 1973

39 Building Research Establishment, *Local housing programmes*, Digest 154 June 1973

1 Courtyard Housing at Dundee

1 Edinburgh University Architecture Research Unit, *Courtyard houses, Inchview, Prestonpans*, Edinburgh 1962

2 Edinburgh University Architecture Research Unit, *Privacy and courtyard housing*, Edinburgh 1966

3 Housing at Ravenscroft Road, West Ham

1 *Homes for Today and Tomorrow*, The Parker Morris Report, HMSO, London 1961
2 *Family Houses at West Ham*, Design Bulletin no 15, HMSO 1969

5 5M Housing at Gloucester Street, Sheffield

1 See *Designing a Low Rise Housing System*, Design Bulletin no 18, HMSO 1970
2 The results are published in *The Family at Home*, Design Bulletin no 17, HMSO 1969

9 Housing at St Mary's Redevelopment Area, Oldham

1 Design Bulletin no 19, HMSO 1970
2 *Moving out of a Slum*, Design Bulletin no 20, HMSO 1970; *New Housing in a Cleared Area*, Design Bulletin no 22, HMSO 1971
3 Design Bulletin no 21, HMSO 1970

10 Housing at Laindon, Basildon

1 *Cars in Housing 1*, Design Bulletin no 10, HMSO 1966
2 *Homes for Today and Tomorrow*, The Parker Morris Report, HMSO 1961
3 *Cars in Housing 1*, Design Bulletin no 10, HMSO 1966
4 *Safety in the home*, Design Bulletin no 13, HMSO 1962

11 Housing at Reporton Road, London SW6

1 *Old Houses into New Homes*, Cmnd 3602, HMSO

14 Housing at Windsor

1 See for example the article by John Noble and Barbara Adams in *The Architects' Journal* 11 September 1968

15 Welsh Village Housing at Cefn-coed-y-cymmer

1 See *Architectural Design* January 1959 p 21
2 See *Architectural Design*, December 1964 p. 588
3 See *The Architectural Review* November 1967

17 Housing at Linden Grove, London SE15

1 *Flatlets for old people*, HMSO 1958; *Some aspects of designing for old people*, Design Bulletin no 1 HMSO 1962; *Housing standards and costs: accommodation specially designed for old people*, MoHLG Circular 82/69; *Group flatlets for old people: a sociological study*, Design Bulletin no 2 HMSO 1962

19 Housing and Old People's Home at Burghley Road, London NW5

1 Land Use and Built Form Studies Working Paper 56 *Some elementary models of built form*, Cambridge 1970

21 Housing at The Barbican, City of London

1 Quoted from Barbican, Cement & Concrete Association, 1971
2 Letter to the Lord Mayor of London from the Minister of Housing and Local Government, 28 August 1956
3 Corbusier, Le *Concerning Town Planning* (translated by Clive Entwistle), The Architectural Press Ltd, London 1947
4 *Barbican Redevelopment*, a report prepared on the instructions of the Barbican Committee by Chamberlin, Powell & Bon
5 Brett, Lionel, 'Doubts on the MARS plan for London,' *The Architects' Journal* 9 July 1942.
6 Cotton, Charles Caleb, *Lacon*
7 Milton, John, *Areopagitica*

Acknowledgments

Abbreviations used:

AJ: *The Architects' Journal*   AR: *The Architectural Review*

1	Courtyard Housing at Dundee	AJ	4 March 1964
		AJ	24 March 1967
		AJ	14 January 1970
		AR	November 1967
2	Point Royal Flats, Bracknell	AJ	13 May 1964
3	Housing at Ravenscroft Road, West Ham	AJ	28 October 1964
4	Houses at Frome	AJ	10 March 1965
5	5M Housing at Gloucester Street, Sheffield	AJ	12 May 1965
6	5M Housing at Woodhouse, Sheffield	AJ	12 May 1965
7	Canada Estate, Bermondsey	AJ	5 February 1965
		AJ	6 August 1969
		AR	November 1967
8	Housing at Winstanley Road, Battersea	AJ	30 November 1966
	Appraisal by David Rock	AJ	6 August 1969
		AR	November 1967
9	Housing at St Mary's Redevelopment Area, Oldham	AJ	20 July 1967
		AJ	10 January 1968
		AJ	9 July 1969
		AR	November 1967
10	Housing at Laindon, Basildon	AJ	27 September 1967
		AJ	16 February 1972
11	Housing at Reporton Road, London SW6	AJ	24 July 1968
12	Co-ownership Housing at Barnton, Edinburgh	AJ	25 November 1970
	Appraisal by Pat Bagot		
13	Co-ownership Housing at Barons Down, Lewes	AJ	19 February 1969
		AJ	8 May 1968
		AJ	21 August 1968
14	Housing at Windsor	AJ	22 July 1970
	Appraisal by G D Wilson		
15	Welsh Village Housing at Cefn-coed-y-cymmer	AJ	25 March 1970
	Appraisal by Roger Thomson		
16	Housing Estate at The Lanes, Rotherham	AJ	21 April 1971
	Appraisal by Jack Lynn		
17	Housing at Linden Grove, London SE15	AJ	3 November 1971
	Appraisal by Judi Brett	AR	November 1971
18	Housing Estate at The Brow, Runcorn	AJ	14 October 1970
	Appraisal by Keith Ingham and Frank Williams		
19	Housing and Old People's Home at Burghley Road,	AJ	26 January 1972
	London NW5	AR	November 1967
	Appraisal by Richard MacCormac		
20	Housing at Lillington Street, Westminster	AJ	1 October 1969
	Appraisal (Stage 3) by Sam Lambert	AJ	12 January 1972
		AR	November 1967
21	Housing at The Barbican, City of London	AR	August 1973
	Appraisal by Sherban Cantacuzino		

Photographic Credits

Abbreviations: f.   — frontispiece
                p.   — photographer
                c.   — copyright
                AP   —The Architectural Press Ltd.
                WJT W.J. Toomey

Introduction (by page number)
c. AP, p. WJT 6 top left, 8 top right, bottom left; p. Kenneth Browne 10 top, 10 bottom;
p. Sidney W. Newbery 15 top
p. Peter Pitt 6 top right
p. Henk Snoek 6 bottom
c. Press Association 11 top right
c. Greaves Organisation, W. Bromwich, p. Sidney Darby 13 top left
c. Department of the Environment p. Keith Gibson 13 top right
c. Wates Ltd. 14 all
c. Essex County Council 17
c. Greater London Council 18

Chapter 1 (by illustration number)
c. AP, p. A.L. Hunter f., 1–5, 7–11; p. Viking Dundee 6
c. Architecture Research Unit, Edinburgh University 12–21

Chapter 2
c. AP, p. WJT, 1–4, 10–13
c. Arup Associates p. Colin Westwood 5–8, 14

Chapter 3
c. AP, p. 1–7, 9–11
c. Department of the Environment 8

Chapter 4
c. Whicheloe & Macfarlane, p. D. Balmer, f., 7–8; p. John Macfarlane 1–6

Chapter 5
c. AP, p. WJT 1–12

Chapter 6
c. AP, p. WJT 1–5

Chapter 7
c. AP, p. WJT f., 1–8
c. Greater London Council 9

Chapter 8
c. AP, p. WJT 1, 2, 4, 6, 7, 9–12, 14–19, 22
c. George, Trew & Dunn, p. Henk Snoek f., 3, 5, 8, 13, 20, 21

Chapter 9
c. AP, p. WJT 1–3, 5, 6, 8–11, 13, 15, 17, 18, 20, 23, 25–28, 30, 31, 39; p. Sam Lambert 4, 7, 12, 14, 16, 19, 21, 22, 24, 33–38, 40, 41

Chapter 11
c. AP, p. WJT f., 1–14

Chapter 12
c. AP, p. WJT f., 2, 4–12, 16
c. Roland Wedgwood Associates 13, p. John Dewar 15, 17
p. A.L. Hunter 3
c.p. Planair, Edinburgh 1

Chapter 13
c. AP, p. WJT f., 2, 4, 8–10
c. Phippen, Randall Partners 1, 5–7
p. Henk Snoek 3

Chapter 14
c. AP, p. WJT 3, 4, 7–11, 13, 17, 19, p. Michael Reid 14–16, 18
c. Matthews, Ryan, Simpson, p. Henk Snoek f., 5, 6, 12, D. Carnworth 2
c.p. Aerofioms 1

Chapter 15
c. AP, p. WJT 1–20

Chapter 16
c. AP, p. D.M. Wrightson f., 1–18

Chapter 17
c. AP, p. R. Davies f., 1, 2, 4–11, 14–27, 19–23; p. S. Goldsmith 13, 18; p. Judi Bratt 12, p.c. Harlow Citizen 3

Chapter 18
c. AP, p. Tony Ray-Jones 5–7, 10, 12; p. S. Goldsmith 4, 9
c. p. Keith Ingham 8, 11
c. Runcorn Development Corporation; p. John Mills 13–15

Chapter 19
c. AP, p. R Davies 1, 4, 5, 11–16; p. S. Goldsmith 2, 8–10, 18–19
c. p. Sam Lambert 1, 3, 6, 7, 17

Chapter 20
c. A.P. Galwey 1
c. p. Brecht-Einzig Ltd. 2, 3
c. p. Sam Lambert 4–11

Chapter 21
c. AP, p. Sam Lambert 26–28, 30
c. Chamberlin Powell & Son 5, 8, 9, 13, 18
p. c. Brecht-Einzig Ltd. 21–25, 29